D0079133

THE SCOTTISH POLITICAL SYSTEM

The Scottish Political System

JAMES G. KELLAS

CAMBRIDGE UNIVERSITY PRESS

CAMBRIDGE

LONDON · NEW YORK · MELBOURNE

Published by the Syndics of the Cambridge University Press
The Pitt Building, Trumpington Street, Cambridge CB2 1RP
Bentley House, 200 Euston Road, London NW1 2DB
32 East 57th Street, New York, NY 10022, USA
296 Beaconsfield Parade, Middle Park, Melbourne 3206, Australia

© Cambridge University Press 1973, 1975

First published 1973
Second edition 1975

Library of Congress Cataloguing in Publication Data

Kellas, James G.
    The Scottish political system.
    Bibliography: p. 242.
    Includes index.
    1.   Scotland – Politics and government – 20th century. I. Title.
JN1213 1975.K44   320.4′411   75–2733
ISBN 0 521 20864 5 hard covers
ISBN 0 521 09972 2 paperback
(First edition ISBN 0 521 08669 8 hard covers
              ISBN 0 521 09780 0 paperback)

Printed in Great Britain by
Western Printing Services Ltd
Bristol

Contents

JN
1213
1975
K44
1975

Illustrations and tables

Abbreviations

BBC	British Broadcasting Corporation
CBI	Confederation of British Industry
CNAA	Council for National Academic Awards
DEA	Department of Economic Affairs
DES	Department of Education and Science
E.E.C.	European Economic Community
EIS	Educational Institute of Scotland
GCE	General Certificate of Education
GTC	General Teaching Council
IBA	Independent Broadcasting Authority
IDC	Industrial Development Certificate
ITV	Independent Television
NCB	National Coal Board
NOP	National Opinion Polls
ORC	Opinion Research Centre
RDD	Regional Development Division
SCE	Scottish Certificate of Education
SDG	Scottish Development Group
SED	Scottish Education Department
SEPB	Scottish Economic Planning Board
SEPD	Scottish Economic Planning Department
SIDO	Scottish Industrial Development Office
STUC	Scottish Trades Union Congress
STV	Scottish Television
TUC	Trades Union Congress
UGC	University Grants Committee
U.N.	United Nations

Geo-political glossary

In this book, an attempt is made to use geo-political terms in as precise a manner as the language allows. Although this may at first appear to be pedantic, it is in fact essential to the nature of the argument, which depends on distinctions being made between the different parts of the United Kingdom.

United Kingdom (U.K.)	United Kingdom of Great Britain and Northern Ireland (the British state)
Britain	short version of the above
Great Britain (G.B.)	England, Wales and Scotland (i.e. the U.K. excluding Northern Ireland)
England Wales Scotland	component nations of the above

One unresolved problem of terminology is the adjective 'British'. This can be derived from 'United Kingdom' or from 'Great Britain', although the territories involved are dissimilar. If it is important to make the distinction, the text does so.

Some authorities (e.g. the *Shorter Oxford Dictionary*) do not distinguish between Britain and Great Britain (excluding Northern Ireland from both), but this is not in accord with normal or official usage. In *Britain: An Official Handbook 1972*, Britain (the U.K.) is distinguished from Great Britain (England, Wales, and Scotland).

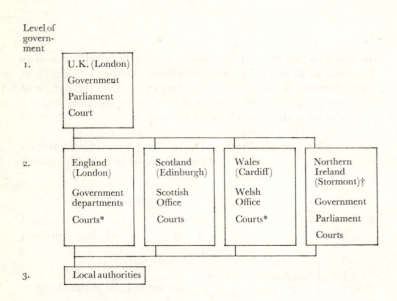

Level of
govern-
ment

1.

U.K. (London)

Government

Parliament

Court

2.

England (London)	Scotland (Edinburgh)	Wales (Cardiff)	Northern Ireland (Stormont)†
Government departments	Scottish Office	Welsh Office	Government
Courts*	Courts	Courts*	Parliament
			Courts

3.

Local authorities

*The courts of England and Wales form part of one judicial system. Strictly
the only U.K. court is the House of Lords (Law Lords).
†The political system of Northern Ireland has changed several times
since 1972.

The territorial governments of the U.K.

Preface

I should like to record my thanks to the many people who have
helped me during the writing of this book. In particular, to my
wife, who undertook the laborious task of compiling a card-index
of Scottish Office administrators.

Interviews granted to me by politicians and civil servants were,
of course, invaluable, as was advice from colleagues, particularly
Professors W. J. M. Mackenzie and A. M. Potter. I must also
thank Charlotte Logan for coping so well with the typing and
editing.

J.G.K.

Glasgow
September 1972

Since the first edition, important changes have taken place in the
Scottish political system. The new local government reforms have
taken effect; the Commission on the Constitution has reported,
and all parties are now pledged to the setting up of a Scottish
Parliament and Government; the Scottish National Party reached
30% of the Scottish vote in the general election of October 1974;
major developments have taken place in the Scottish Office. This
has meant a considerable revision of the text, as well as up-dating.
The inherent strength of the Scottish political system has been
manifested since 1972, and it is probable that a completely new
system will emerge in the latter part of the decade. It will, however, be built on the foundations of the old.

J.G.K.

Glasgow
March 1975

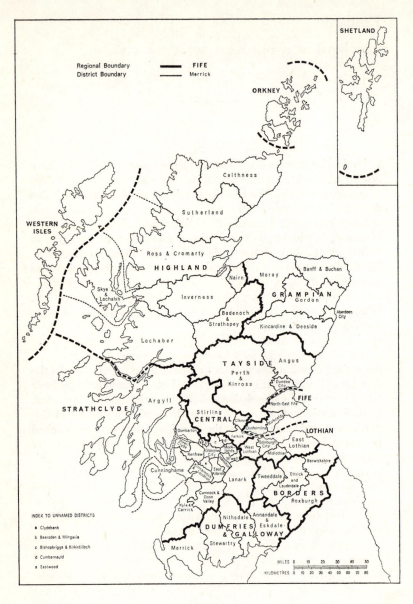

Regional Boundary ─── **FIFE**
District Boundary ─── Merrick

SHETLAND

ORKNEY

WESTERN ISLES

Caithness

Sutherland

Ross & Cromarty

HIGHLAND

Nairn   Moray   Banff & Buchan

GRAMPIAN
Gordon

Skye & Lochalsh

Inverness

Badenoch & Strathspey

Kincardine & Deeside

Aberdeen City

Lochaber

TAYSIDE

Angus

Perth & Kinross

Dundee City

Argyll

STRATHCLYDE

North-East Fife

FIFE

Stirling

CENTRAL

Clkms

Dunfermline   Kirkcaldy

LOTHIAN

Dumbarton

Falkirk

East Lothian

Monk-lands

Edinburgh City

West Lothian

Midlothian

Glasgow City

Renfrew

Berwickshire

Cunninghame

East Kilbride

Lanark

Tweeddale

Ettrick and Lauderdale

BORDERS

Roxburgh

Cumnock & Doon Valley

Kyle & Carrick

Annandale & Eskdale

Nithsdale

DUMFRIES & GALLOWAY

Merrick

Stewartry

INDEX TO UNNAMED DISTRICTS

a Clydebank
b Bearsden & Milngavie
c Bishopbriggs & Kirkintilloch
d Cumbernauld
e Eastwood

MILES 0   10   20   30   40   50
KILOMETRES 0 10 20 30 40 50 60 70 80

Map of the local government boundaries.

I

Scotland as a political system

Political scientists are beginning to realise that the British political system fits rather uneasily into the conventional categories by which it is usually described (see, for example, Rose 3). The concepts of unitary state, nation-state, political homogeneity and sovereignty of parliament, for example, are now being re-examined to see whether they are in fact applicable to Britain. Firstly, the unitary character of the British state is restricted by the existence of various forms of devolution or decentralisation which exist above the level of local government. The most extended of these was the government of Northern Ireland, which from 1920 to 1972 included a separately elected parliament at Stormont, an executive responsible to it, a local government structure and a system of courts. In this period, Northern Ireland was governed partly from Stormont and partly from London, the division of powers being laid down in the Government of Ireland Act of 1920 and subsequent statutes. This was a sort of federal relationship between the government of the U.K. and that of Northern Ireland, and the Ireland Act of 1949 stated that Northern Ireland would not cease to be part of the U.K. without the consent of the Northern Ireland Parliament. In 1972 and 1974, however, the Stormont system was suspended by the British Government, and replaced by 'direct rule', pending the establishment of a new constitution.

Wales is also treated as a distinct area in British central government. The development of various administrative bodies exclusive to Wales led in 1964 to the establishment of the Welsh Office, with a Secretary of State for Wales in the British Cabinet. In the House of Commons, a Welsh Grand Committee has existed since 1960, to discuss Welsh affairs, and legislation relating exclusively to Wales is occasionally passed by Parliament. There is no Welsh legal system, however, and the identity of Wales rests more on language, education and religion than on political institutions. Although it has increased vastly in scope since 1964 (e.g. gaining health and education in 1969 and 1970), the Welsh Office has not the range of functions possessed by the Scottish Office, and the Welsh Grand Committee is not as important as the Scottish

I

committees of the House of Commons, since it cannot discuss Bills or Estimates.

Scotland comes somewhere between Wales and Northern Ireland in political status. While possessing neither a government nor a parliament of its own, it has a strong constitutional identity and a large number of political and social institutions. The Act of Union of 1707, which is the 'fundamental law' joining Scotland with England, laid down that Scotland would retain for all time certain key institutions such as the Scottish legal system, the Presbyterian Church of Scotland (the Established Church), the Scottish educational system, and the 'royal burghs' (local authorities). These became the transmitters of Scottish national identity from one generation to the next.

Political institutions in Scotland were not encouraged. Scottish M.P.s were to be an integral part of the House of Commons, and Scottish peers could elect representatives to the House of Lords. There was initially a Secretary of State for Scotland in the government, but this was dropped in 1746, leaving the chief Scottish law officer, the Lord Advocate, as the principal 'spokesman' for Scotland in the executive. In the nineteenth century, the development of Scottish administrative boards and rising national feeling led to the demand for the creation of a Scottish Office headed by a Secretary for Scotland. In 1885, this Office was established, and the Scottish Secretary soon gained a permanent place in the Cabinet. His department grew in size and range of functions, so that today it is the equivalent in Scotland of several Whitehall departments. Its estimates amounted to £1,188m. in 1971–2, which compared with £280m. for the Home Office and £521m. for the Department of Education and Science (including expenditure on all Great Britain universities and research councils).[1] There is also a large number of Scottish agencies of government loosely related to the Scottish Office, or to Whitehall departments. And there is a separate structure of local authorities, in part derived from the historic 'royal burghs'. A Royal Commission on Local Government in Scotland reported in 1969, and a reformed structure has been introduced to meet the special needs of Scotland.

In the legislative branch, the Union of the Parliaments did not mean the unification of the laws of Scotland and England. As long as there was a separate legal system in Scotland, there was a need for separate legislation for Scotland. The Act of Union attempted to divide the spheres of 'British' and Scottish law, broadly along the lines of public and private law. In the former, Parliament would legislate for the whole of Britain, while the latter, Scotland could have its own arrangements. This division has never been strictly adhered to in practice, and the 1707 settlement did not provide for 'judicial review' of legislation, which could determine which sphere, Scottish or British, an Act properly belonged to. Nor was there any supreme court which could undertake such a task (the nearest was the judicial committee of the House of Lords). Even more remiss was the absence of any machinery for revising the Act of Union, other than by an ordinary Act of Parliament. Nevertheless, the doctrine of the 'sovereignty of Parliament' has been challenged in Scotland by some Scots lawyers, who regard the terms of the Union as more than ordinary legislation to be lightly repealed.[2] Moreover, it is claimed that the Scottish Parliament did not possess the 'sovereignty' attributed to its English counterpart, and so could not transmit this quality to the Parliament of the United Kingdom.[3] These arguments are largely academic, and the relationship between Scotland and England depends more on mutual accommodation and working the Act of Union in a proper spirit.

The process of passing laws separately for Scotland became troublesome, both for the Scottish M.P.s and their English colleagues. Scottish Bills took up the time of the House of Commons, yet only the Scots were really interested in them. By the 1880s, parliamentary time was becoming a valuable commodity, and Scottish Bills were getting squeezed out. It was therefore decided to set up a special committee, the Scottish Grand Committee, to relieve the House of this burden. This dates from 1894, and today there are several Scottish committees of the House, dealing with the various stages of Scottish legislation. There are usually between five and ten purely Scottish Bills passed during each parliamentary session.

The legal system of Scotland is one of the strongest clues to the existence of the Scottish political system. The people of Scotland are subject to many laws which are exclusive to Scotland. They have a system of law courts which are, with one exception, different from, and independent of, the law courts of the rest of Britain. The exception is that the final court of appeal in civil cases is the House of Lords, in its judicial capacity. All other cases, whether under Scots Law or law applying to the whole of Britain, must be decided in Scottish courts. Legal procedures in these courts differ from those in English courts. This gives the Scottish legal system more independence than the legal systems of federal states. In the United States, for example, federal (national) courts are found in all states, and federal law applies throughout the nation. State law and state court decisions are subject to federal judicial review under certain circumstances (e.g. conflict with the Constitution or laws of the United States), in civil and in criminal law. Both federal and state courts have jurisdiction over the population, while in Scotland there is essentially one set of courts, the Scottish courts.

The Scottish legal system is represented in the government by the Lord Advocate and the Solicitor-General for Scotland. But the Lord Advocate is not quite the equivalent of the Lord Chancellor in England and Wales. While the Lord Chancellor heads the English judiciary, in Scotland that position is held by the Lord President of the Court of Session (the supreme Scottish court). The Scottish legal profession is recruited separately from that of England, through the Scottish universities, the Law Society of Scotland and the Faculty of Advocates, and has its own qualifications and traditions.

Scotland then has its distinctive institutions, in the executive, legislative and judicial branches of government. It has also a whole host of party organisations, pressure groups, and advisory bodies as satellites to the institutional structure. These have somehow to be fitted into the concept of the British political system, which encompasses them. It might be possible to call Scotland a 'sub-system' of the British system, but this would be vague and ambiguous. It could, for example, be said that any territorial local authority was a sub-system of the central authority. Since Scotland is not a local authority in British terms, then it would have to be a 'super-sub-system' of the territorial type. The contention here is that the concept of system is more appropriate, since it does justice to the scale and nature of the phenomena which are found in Scottish politics.

A political system is not solely defined by political institutions and organisations, and can be supported by other criteria. Here the description of Britain as a 'nation-state' comes into question. If Britain were truly a nation-state, then it might be difficult to establish the existence of strong political systems within it, such as the Scottish. The U.S.A. is a nation-state, however, and yet contains fifty separate states which are political systems. But Britain is a special form of nation-state, just as it is a special type of unitary state. The criteria for nationhood are never easy to determine, and vary from nation to nation. But they ought to satisfy two broad requirements: that the members of the nation think of themselves primarily as such, and not primarily as members of another nation; and that the nation should have some objective characteristics of its own, such as language, 'complementary habits and facilities of communication',[4] religion, territory, previous statehood, a history of common action, and so on.

The first requirement is well fulfilled in the case of Scotland, and for Wales and Northern Ireland too. In these areas of Britain people today think of themselves primarily as Scots, Welsh or Irish, not British.[5] It is also likely that most Englishmen regard themselves as such and not as Britishers (see p. 234, n. 2). This national consciousness in Britain, which does not correspond to

4

British national consciousness, is a fact which has rarely been taken into account in works on British politics. Of course, it came to the surface during the late 1960s with the rise of political nationalism in Scotland, Wales and Northern Ireland (the last a quite separate variety). But in reality it was always there. The absence of attitude surveys on the subject before the period of political nationalism makes it difficult to document with any degree of precision, but all the other evidence points to such national consciousness having existed over a long period. To take one indicator, the teaching of history in Scottish schools lays stress on the nation-building process in Scotland and the historic warfare with England. Scottish school-children frequently play games of the 'Scots versus the English' type. While this national identification is much less emphasised in secondary education, the early experiences are important in shaping nationalist feeling.

Can we then say that Scots do not feel British at all? If their subjective identification with Scotland were translated into politics, they would apparently be Scottish nationalist and disdain co-operation with the 'English' political parties. That they do not (usually) shows that subjective nationality can be a weak indicator for voting behaviour. But it can be called upon, in certain circumstances, to give a nationalist form to such behaviour. Most of the time, however, the political nationalism lies dormant, and the 'British' pattern of political behaviour prevails. Scots feel British as well as Scottish, and so they should, since Scotland is an integral part of the U.K., a situation accepted by the vast majority of Scots. But their consciousness of 'Britishness' is much less clear than their consciousness of 'Scottishness'. Geographical separation, a separate educational system, and the other 'objective' criteria of nationhood account for this, and reinforce the institutional basis of the Scottish political system.

What is the extent and significance of the other 'objective' criteria of the separateness of Scotland? The differences in political institutions have already been summarised, and it should be emphasised that social institutions such as those of religion and education are as important in determining the nation as the politico-legal ones.[6] In religion for example, Scotland's characteristics are markedly different from elsewhere. Presbyterianism is dominant, with the Church of Scotland the principal and Established Church. Its regular communicants amount to around two-fifths of the adult population. Its influence on the political culture of Scotland has always been strong, for its emphasis on democratic organisation and individualism, coupled with puritanism, have encouraged the application of these principles to government. Scots have shown greater enthusiasm for democratic institutions and equality of opportunity than the English, and they have been less inclined to relax old moral standards in favour of 'permissiveness'.

The Roman Catholic Church shares much of this morality and is proportionately stronger than in England and Wales. (16% of the Scottish population are baptised Catholics, compared to 8% in England and Wales.) It is particularly concentrated in the Glasgow region, as a result of Irish immigration, where it amounts to about one quarter of the population.

In general, religion plays a greater part in Scottish life than it does in English life, since there is a higher proportion of church membership and attendance. The churches are involved in politics in a different way, with the Church of Scotland General Assembly claiming to be a 'Scottish Parliament', and the Roman Catholic schools built and maintained entirely by the state, thus constituting part of the public provision of education. There is also some evidence that religion and voting behaviour are more closely connected in Scotland than in England (Budge and Urwin, pp. 60–3, and Bochel and Denver[7]).

The educational system of Scotland is of course closely involved in socialisation, and we have seen that it has a direct bearing on national consciousness. Its influence permeates Scottish society, and the public sector is stronger than the public sector of education in England. In higher education there is a greater proportion of the Scottish population at university than in England, and the schools and universities are organised (on the whole) along different lines. Scottish educational principles stress equality of opportunity, a liberal education over a wide range of subjects, and a somewhat didactic pedagogy. These approaches have left their mark on the Scots and the structure of Scottish society, for good or ill. As far as politics is concerned, it may be pointed out that the resilience of the educational system in Scotland makes the administrative boundary between Scotland and England a strong one in this field. Scottish schools are the responsibility of the Scottish Education Department, not the Department of Education and Science. Scottish universities are principally subject to the (British) University Grants Committee and so to the British Education Minister, but student grants are provided by the Scottish Education Department, and take account of the differences in course length and content in Scotland. These differences mark most Scottish universities off from their counterparts in England, and help to identify the Scottish nation, or at least its more educated stratum.

A more pervasive influence than the universities on the people is mass communication. Most of the theorists of 'British political homogeneity' point to the power of London-based communications media as evidence that Britain is one nation politically. It is said that the great majority everywhere read London newspapers or consume London broadcasts. But the evidence in Scotland is clearly at variance with regard to the press, and ambiguous about broadcasting. No 'Fleet Street'-published newspaper is read by more than 6% of Scottish adults on week-days and 23% on Sundays.[8] The *Scottish Daily Express* (43%) can be classified as 'Fleet Street' with major qualifications, since about two-thirds of its contents on average is devoted to Scottish material. Some of this material is of a political nature. The other popular papers in Scotland (*Daily Record* (48%), *Sunday Post* (77%), and *Sunday Mail* (52%)), are distinctly Scottish in content. So are the 'quality' papers, the *Scotsman* (5%) and *Glasgow Herald* (6%), which in Scotland partially replace the *Daily Telegraph* (2%), *The Times* (1%), and the *Guardian* (1%). No English region (and not even Wales or Northern Ireland) varies so much in readership from the British average, and this is reinforced by the fact that total daily newspaper readership is greater in Scotland than elsewhere in Britain.

In broadcasting, the BBC recognises the existence of the 'national regions' of Scotland, Wales and Northern Ireland. Scotland and Wales have National Broadcasting Councils which are supposed to control the policy and content of their regions' broadcasts, while Northern Ireland has an Advisory Council whose chairman is a member of the BBC's Board of Governors. English regions are less strongly organised, and with the advent of local radio the BBC's English radio regions were abolished in 1970. The BBC's Scottish radio service was retained, however, and the National Broadcasting Council for Scotland 'felt strongly that Scotland, as a nation, must continue to enjoy a national output'.[9] This output amounts to around 10 hours a week on television and 40 hours on radio. While this is a small share of total output, Scottish programmes are often politically relevant and deal with Scottish political issues.

ITV broadcasting is shared between Scottish Television (Central Scotland), Grampian Television (North-east) and Border Television (English and Scottish borders). STV's own programmes amount to about 10 hours per week, Grampian's 6 hours, and Border's 4 hours. In the case of Border, very few programmes are specifically Scottish in content, for they rely on creating a 'Border community'. This, and the division of Scotland into three for the production of programmes goes against a strong Scottish identity in ITV broadcasting. Instead, there is a regional flavour, more marked than in the BBC, which considers itself Scottish-national. STV, however, since it covers 80% of the Scottish population, regards itself as 'Scottish' rather than regional. Independent local radio is provided by Radio Clyde (Glasgow) and Radio Forth (Edinburgh), with about 135 hours a week on each station.

The mass media in Scotland have to strike a balance between a Scottish- and a British/American-derived output. It seems that the consumers of newspapers in Scotland are more favourable to a Scottish content than is the broadcasting public. But this is partly because it is easier, for economic and professional reasons, to make newspapers than to make broadcasts. Scots are often highly critical of the quality of Scottish broadcasting, while cheerfully accepting lower standards in some of their popular press. At the same time, they support two quality newspapers and a wide range of weeklies and other journals.

Scottish sport is strongly nationalist. There is a separate Scottish Football Association and Scottish Football League, and football loyalties in Scotland are entirely to Scottish teams. Football 'internationals', involving a Scottish team against, for example, England, Wales or a European team, arouse fierce partisanship. Other sports are also organised on a Scottish rather than British basis, and the combined effect of these arrangements is to reinforce national consciousness. It also affects the composition of newspapers and broadcasting in Scotland, for these must pay great attention to reporting Scottish matches.

It is possible to seek for other 'objective' criteria of Scottish nationhood, in the mass of social and economic statistics relating to Scotland. Here some caution should be exercised. In the first place, such statistics are inherently rather weak indicators of nationhood, since it is possible for different nations to be similar in socio-economic structure and yet remain distinct culturally and in their desire for self-government. Countries such as Norway and Sweden, or many of the developing countries in Africa, are similar in socio-economic terms, yet possess strong national characteristics which differentiate them. In the context of the United Kingdom, the profile of Scotland is closer to England in many respects than it is to any 'foreign' country, or indeed to Wales or Northern Ireland. And some regions in England (e.g. the northern) deviate more from the U.K. than does Scotland.

Secondly, only some of the statistics are relevant to politics (but which ones is not very clear). Considerable differences exist in the eating and drinking habits of Scots, as compared with Englishmen. For example, Scots consume more starch and less vitamin C than any region of the U.K.,[10] and (of course) drink more whisky and less beer. The latter fact leads to a high level of alcoholism, and a correspondingly strong temperance or anti-drink movement. 'Local option' (the right of local communities to control liquor licensing) survives in Scotland in 'veto polls', and some areas (especially around Glasgow and in the Highlands) have very few licensed premises. The licensing hours are different in Scotland, with pubs closing earlier than in England. Drink issues

Table 1   U.K. population (1971 Census)

	Population (millions)	% of U.K.	Land area (% of U.K.)	Density per sq. mile (persons)
U.K.	55·3	100	100	594
Scotland	5·2	9·4	32·0	175
England	45·8	82·9	53·8	915
Wales	2·7	4·9	8·6	341
Northern Ireland	1·5	2·8	5·6	292

Table 2   Scottish population (1971 Census)

	Population (thousands)	% of Scotland	Land area (% of Scotland)	Density (persons per sq. mile)
Scotland	5,224	100	100	175
Urban population	3,951	76	1·5	8,939
Landward population	1,273	24	98·5	43

For populations of local government regions, island authorities and city districts, see Table 23, p. 150.

dominated Scottish politics in the late nineteenth and early twentieth centuries, but are much less important today.

Scotland is well served with demographic and other vital statistics. It is listed separately in the U.N. Demographic Year Book as a sub-division of the U.K., along with Wales and Northern Ireland. It also comes into the U.N. Statistical Year Book in the population, housing, education, health and motor transport tables. No other sub-divisions of sovereign unitary states are thus listed, and very few constituent states of federations. One reason for this is that Scotland produces its own Census, and operates an Economics and Statistics Unit, so that such information is readily available. It is thus possible to compare Scotland directly with the other countries of the world, and more extensively, with other parts of the U.K.

The indicators selected here include most of the key ones for comparative purposes, and for the understanding of Scottish politics in its own terms. There is, firstly, the population (size, distribution, and density). The U.K. and Scottish profiles are shown in tables 1 and 2.

Scotland has about one-tenth of the population of the U.K., yet it covers one-third of the land area. The density of population is therefore much smaller than the U.K. average, although within Scotland this varies considerably from the heavily populated central belt to the northern and southern divisions, which have very few people indeed. The contrasts in density are in fact much greater within Scotland than within England, which makes a uniform structure of local government very difficult to devise. According to the area, authorities will be very large territorially or very great in population if they are to be viable. Another striking difference with England is the absence of large towns. Scotland has only four cities with over 100,000 in population, and three of these are in the central Lowlands. Although 76% of Scotland's population is urban, the typical burgh (town) is small, and there is one conurbation, that of Central Clydeside (1,733,000, or one-third of the total population).

Emigration has always been heavy, and net migration rose in 1965–6 to 47,000, more than the natural increase. Since then it has subsided, and in 1973–4 there was a net gain of 7,800, presumably because of increased employment in oil and oil-related industries. While England and Wales gained 311,000 people through migration from 1961 to 1966 Scotland lost 199,000. Scots are less inclined to move far within Scotland than they are to move out of Scotland altogether, and this can be considered a 'safety-valve' or a potential source of national frustration.

Immigration to Scotland has not greatly altered the ethnic composition of the country in recent years. Apart from the population of Irish origin (about a sixth of the whole, and concentrated in the west central division), there are no large minorities. Those born in England and Wales are about 5% of the population, while coloured immigrants form a much smaller group than in England.

The 'Scottish minority' of Gaelic speakers (1½%) is important for its influence on Highland education and broadcasting, but it does not compare in strength with the Welsh speakers in Wales (27%). Scottish nationhood cannot be strictly defined on linguistic grounds, for nearly all Scots speak only English. They speak it with a Scottish accent, however, and many use a large number of 'Scots' (dialect) words in everyday speech. There is thus a division in speech between Scotland and England, which sets up something of a communication barrier. Some writers have sought to increase this separation by adopting an artificial Scots dialect, 'Lallans', but unlike linguistic nationalists in other countries, they have made very little impression on Scottish life. When set alongside the general pattern of communications and transactions of various kinds in Scotland, the linguistic situation confirms the nationhood of Scotland: in Karl Deutsch's words, 'Membership in a people essentially consists in wide complementarity of social communication. It consists in the ability to communicate more effectively, and over a wider range of subjects, with members of one large group than with outsiders.'[11] This

Table 3 *Employees in employment, mid 1970*

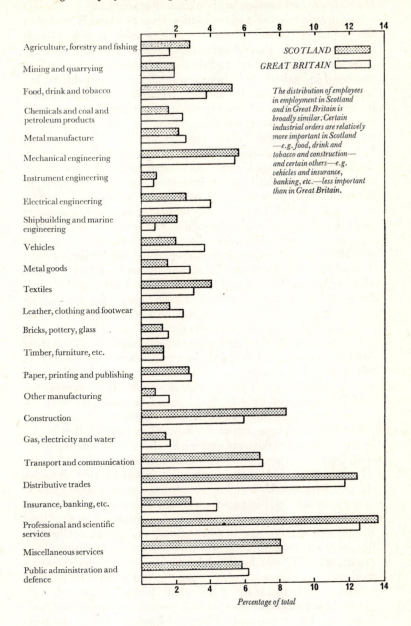

The distribution of employees in employment in Scotland and in Great Britain is broadly similar. Certain industrial orders are relatively more important in Scotland —e.g. food, drink and tobacco and construction— and certain others —e.g. vehicles and insurance, banking, etc.—less important than in Great Britain.

Percentage of total

seems true of the Scottish nation, even when the division between Highlanders and Lowlanders is taken into account.

The drastic migration of population from Scotland is related to the economic structure of the country (see table 3). While this is broadly similar to that of Britain as a whole, it is more heavily dependent on agriculture and declining industries. The number employed in agriculture is, however, small compared with Wales, and much smaller than in Northern Ireland. Scottish agriculture is somewhat different from agriculture elsewhere, having special interests in hill farming, crofting and stock-raising. It is administered by the Scottish Office, not the Ministry of Agriculture, Fisheries and Food, and Scottish farmers have their own union, the National Farmers Union of Scotland. Politically, agriculture and fishing are much more important in Scotland than in England. Twenty-one of the 71 constituencies in Scotland can be called agricultural (i.e. with more than 15% of the male employment in agriculture), while the total in England is 80 out of 516.[12] Agricultural issues thus affect the parties in Scotland to a considerable extent. Crofting is separately regulated by the Crofters Acts and the Crofters Commission, and fishing is protected by the Herring Industry Board and the White Fish Authority. Although these are U.K. bodies, they work in close liaison with the Scottish Office, the former being financed by the Vote of the Department of Agriculture and Fisheries for Scotland.

Categories other than agriculture which vary by 0·5% or more from the figures for Great Britain are: (higher) food, drink and tobacco, textiles, construction, distributive trades and professional and scientific services; (lower) chemicals, electrical engineering, vehicles, other metal goods, clothing and footwear, other manufacturing and insurance and banking services.

The most serious aspect of the Scottish economy is the decline in the level of employment, especially in the older industries of coal, iron and steel, shipbuilding and textiles. This has fallen sharply in the last decade, and the influx of new industry (largely from the U.S. and England) has not been able to compensate for the resulting unemployment. Unemployment in Scotland in recent years has run at 50% to 80% higher than the Great Britain average, and the number of males employed declined by 65,000 from 1964 to 1969 (*Scottish Economic Bulletin*, No. 1 (1971), 5). GDP per head is about 7% lower, though manual workers now earn nearly the average for the U.K. (non-manual, 5% lower). The cost of living is generally higher in Scotland.

On these counts then, the Scottish economy differs substantially from that of the south and midlands of England, though not from the north of England. Politically, Scottish economic problems are of the utmost importance, and much of Scottish politics is devoted to the problem of righting the imbalance of the Scottish economy through regional economic policy which will provide financial incentives to new industry. This involves action by the British government departments, the Scottish Office, Scottish pressure groups, local authorities, and industry itself. It also involves the three Scottish banks (with their own note-issue) and the Scottish Stock Exchange, which together form an autonomous group of financial institutions.

A big change, economically and politically, since 1972 has been the rising importance of North Sea oil for Scotland. With revenues anticipated to yield over £3,000m. per annum by 1980, and the creation of some 30,000 new jobs, oil has transformed the Scottish economy and the Scottish political system. It has shifted the focus of attention of the British Government to Scotland, and it holds out hope for a revival in the fortunes of the Scottish economy. There is, however, danger of an imbalance between the prosperous east of Scotland, nearest the oil developments, and the declining west, which does not benefit so directly. Moreover, since most of the economic gains in the long run will be in the form of revenues rather than employment, Scotland would benefit only insofar as the U.K. government is prepared to channel revenues back to Scotland, or to give a Scottish parliament some share of them. Thus the new oil wealth does not necessarily guarantee economic or political power to Scotland, though it has certainly stimulated demands that such power be established.[13]

Related to the economic structure is the social class structure of the population. As might be expected, this too is roughly the same as for Britain as a whole, but it is rather more weighted to the working class.

Subjective class assessment from social surveys supports the 'objective' class position. In a 1964 survey of Great Britain and a 1968 survey of Northern Ireland, 60% in Scotland assigned themselves to the working class, compared with 50% in England, 54% in Wales and 31% in Northern Ireland. For the middle class, the figures were Scotland 33%, England 42%, Wales 39% and Northern Ireland 47% (Rose 3, p. 18). Social class and voting behaviour are correlated in different ways in the various nations and regions of the U.K., with Scottish working-class voters more favourable to the Labour Party than working-class voters in most of England. Wales is much more working-class/Labour than Scotland, and so is north-east England and Yorkshire (Butler and Stokes, pp. 140–4; Rose 2, p. 14). Trade union affiliation is connected with this pattern of behaviour, for Wales and Scotland are more strongly unionised than England (Rose 3, pp. 18–19).

An important social and economic difference between Scotland

Table 4   (a) *Socio-economic group of economically active males*
          (proportions per 1,000)

	Great Britain	England and Wales	Wales	Scotland
Employers and managers (large)	38	39	28	34
Employers and managers	60	62	49	47
Professional, self-employed	7	7	7	8
Professional, employees	38	39	28	30
Intermediate non-manual	45	45	40	39
Junior non-manual	126	127	99	119
Personal service	10	10	7	11
Foremen and supervisors (manual)	36	36	37	35
Skilled manual	315	314	310	330
Semi-skilled manual	149	149	179	150
Unskilled manual	83	81	96	104
Own account (other than professional)	34	36	35	20
Farmers (employers and managers)	8	7	10	14
Farmers (own account)	9	9	32	10
Agricultural workers	21	19	21	35
Armed forces	15	15	12	12
Indefinite	5	6	9	4

Source: Sample Census 1966. *Great Britain Economic Activity Tables*, Part III, table 31. HMSO, London 1969.

(b) *Social class (all adults)*

		Great Britain %	England %	Wales %	Scotland %
I	Professional, etc. occupations	3·1	3·2	2·6	2·5
II	Intermediate	15·1	15·1	16·6	14·1
III	Skilled occupations	47·9	48·2	44·1	47·3
IV	Partly-skilled occupations	23·0	22·8	24·2	24·2
V	Unskilled occupations	8·3	8·1	9·3	9·9
	Not classified	2·6	2·6	3·1	1·9

Source: Ibid. derived from table 30.

and the rest of the U.K. is housing tenure. About half the population of Scotland rents its housing from a local authority, whereas in England and Wales the proportion is a quarter. Such 'council' housing in Scotland is much more heavily subsidised by government grants and local rates than its counterpart elsewhere. Rents are correspondingly lower. Scotland generally has bad housing conditions, although in the council sector the standard amenities are provided. General 'amenity' does not go much beyond this, however, and some council estates are notoriously run down.

The origins of the Scottish housing situation must be traced well back in Scottish history. A tenement type of house was common in Scottish towns in early modern times, and seems to have been copied from continental (especially French) practice. The feudal system of land tenure encouraged such development, as did shortage of land. But the nineteenth-century industrial revolution, and the large-scale Irish immigration to Glasgow, provided the dreadful legacy of urban slums which are only now being eradicated. Rural slums, such as the Highland 'black houses', are also a thing of the past, but Scotland's housing stock is still well below the average in England for overcrowding, and outside the council-house sector, amenities are deficient. Housing is a major political issue in Scotland, and no political party can afford to offend the large number of 'council-house' voters. Most local politics is dominated by the need to placate either council tenants or owner-occupiers (depending on the social composition of the community), and Scottish housing is given specially favoured treatment within British housing policy.

The picture which can be built up of Scottish society from such indicators is not nearly as sharply defined as the picture derived from Scottish institutions. In terms of crude social and economic indicators, Scotland is perhaps not greatly different from the rest of the U.K., nor indeed from England alone. It is certainly not as 'deviant' as Northern Ireland in economic structure, where unemployment and a lower standard of living interact with religion, politics and nationalism to reinforce the institutional separation. Scotland's economic problems differ from those of England in degree rather than kind, and the trend is towards assimilation in industrial structure, earnings and level of employment. Such assimilation requires government action which will discriminate in Scotland's favour, in economic development and house-building, and political pressures are readily mobilised in Scotland to this end. There is usually a response in London to these demands, largely because the Scottish political machinery is so strong and active. This activity depends on the very existence of the Scottish political system, which acts as a means of communication with the larger British system, as well as affording a communications and decision-making network within Scotland itself in those areas of politics where 'British' considerations are not so involved.

The concept of a 'political system' as applied to Scotland must take account of these two 'activity areas' (the Scottish and the British), and it is obvious that the 'boundaries' of the system are different in each case. Where the Scottish system acts as a communications 'input' to the larger British system its boundaries are most clearly related to the function of communication. Thus in the 'British' sphere of taxation, monetary policy, principles of regional economic development and departmental appropriations, the Scottish political system serves to make known the demands and needs of the Scottish people. As a communications medium the system is sophisticated, institutionalised, and powerful. It is not a 'pressure group', but rather an 'arena' of politics which takes the form of a nation and its organised groups.[14] Within that arena, there are many voices, interests, and opinions, but they show their common origins and concerns, which derive from the characteristics of the Scottish political system.

The decisions in the British sphere are of course taken within the British system, which is itself the principal arena of politics. Just as it is possible to be 'Scottish' and 'British' at the same time, so it is possible for Scotland to participate in the Scottish and British arenas simultaneously. Some Scots become political 'brokers' or go-betweens linking the two arenas. Such men are the ministers and administrators of the Scottish Office, the Scottish M.P.s and the leaders of the Scottish sections of British pressure groups. Their function is to communicate the demands of each arena to the other, and to arrive at a settlement.

In the other activity area of the Scottish political system (i.e. Scotland itself) the boundary is sharper and covers more than the function of communication (though that is included). It ranges from the boundary set by the Scottish legal system to the administrative functions of the Scottish Office. All these activities act *solely* on the population of Scotland, and in the sphere of criminal law the *judicial process* is contained entirely within the system. So in effect is the function of law reform, though it is formally within the British system (i.e. it must pass through Parliament). The distinction between the *effective* and *formal* boundaries of the Scottish system must thus be made, and there is no constitutional way of doing so. The Act of Union of 1707 is of little help, for reasons already stated. What has to be discovered is the range of activity which is effectively Scottish, despite the formal necessity for legislation or executive decision at the British level. This range gives us a sliding scale of boundaries rather than one boundary, but all in this sector should be clearly Scottish rather than British. For example, the activities of the Scottish Office, the *decision-making* in Scottish law reform, Scottish education, housing and local government, are predominantly within the Scottish system (some are almost wholly within it). As for the *outputs* of the system, these act as a defining boundary between Scotland and the rest of the U.K.: those in Scotland are the system's subjects, those elsewhere are not.

There are elements both of clarity and obscurity in this concept. But the case of Scotland cannot be fitted neatly into any of the existing categories of political science. If it fits the concept of 'political system', that may well be because that concept is flexible enough to contain any relatively independent political structure or set of political elements which move together in interaction. David Easton identified the essential activity of the political system as 'the authoritative allocation of values' in a society,[15] but he said that such systems can vary in size from 'the smallest bushman band to the most complex industrial society'.[16] Karl Deutsch defines a political system as 'a collection of recognizable units, which are characterized by cohesion and covariance', and he identifies ten system levels in politics, from the individual to the U.N.[17] Another approach is that of Talcott Parsons, who sees the political system as a 'sub-system' of an all-embracing social system.[18] This stresses the 'functional' character of the system, as opposed to the organisational definitions of Easton and Deutsch. All systems theorists are concerned about the feasibility of drawing a boundary round a system, and about the need to establish the interdependence (rather than random contact) of the elements composing it. Finally, most are interested in the processes by which a system is maintained or altered, and seek to discover the functions which must be performed if a system is to survive.

Taking these points in turn, we find that Scotland has a political system composed of many institutions and organisations, which are 'characterized by cohesion and covariance' (i.e. they act and move together). It can be seen (in Parsons' terms) as a sub-system of Scottish society, or (in Deutsch's terms) as a lower level of system than the British. Easton's condition that the system should authoritatively allocate values, is clearly met by the different content of Scots Law, religion, education and much else in Scottish life. That this content derives primarily from the 'political system' may be argued. It is, however, maintained by Scottish legislation, administration, etc., which are political in character.

The only problem is that of defining the boundary: it is not clear in all cases whether it is the *British* system which is allocating Scottish (i.e. applying only to Scotland) values, or the Scottish.

Nor is it clear how important *Scottish* (as opposed to British) values are in Scotland. The Scottish system is both dependent and independent within the British system, and the latter emerges as a less homogeneous entity as a result, since it is modified by the existence of the Scottish and other systems within it. Moreover, the way in which the systems are maintained is given a new perspective by the altered view of their constituent elements and functions. The British system can only be maintained by accommodation with the national systems within it. Thus nationality and national interest become important props of the 'multi-national United Kingdom'. At the same time, such centrifugal forces can only go so far if the system is to survive.

As a corollary, the Scottish system also seeks to maintain itself. The vested Scottish interests are numerous and powerful. They include the institutions of church, law, education and government. These hope to preserve Scotland, and through it themselves. But it is not so obvious that Scots outside these groups wish whole-heartedly to maintain or strengthen the system. The forces for change pull in opposite directions: a considerable body of Scottish opinion would like further autonomy in decision-making, but an equal tendency is towards assimilation with England, or with general 'British' standards. Many M.P.s for Scottish constituencies see themselves as members of a British party first and as Scottish M.P.s second (though they usually take an interest only in Scottish matters). So too do members of British trade unions, whether affiliated to the Labour Party or not.

Scots in general maintain the system by their national consciousness, but the intensity of such feeling is modified by British aspirations of 'equality-all-round'. Political man in Scotland stands on two legs, one Scottish and one British, and both are needed if he is to remain upright. His cousins in England, Wales and Northern Ireland are also two-legged in this sense, although they may prefer to walk on one leg, dragging the other behind them. Walking or limping, British political man is usually a good traveller, and it is to his journeys within Scotland that we now turn.

2

The constitutional inheritance

Scotland and England came together as a political unity in 1707, as a result of the Act of Union passed by the Parliaments of the two countries. After that date, the separate Parliaments of Scotland and England were abolished and were replaced by the Parliament of the United Kingdom of Great Britain. Since 1603, the Crowns of Scotland and England had been united, but while this gave England and Scotland the same king, it did not merge these kingdoms nor give them a joint Privy Council, joint state officials, or a joint Parliament. Each country retained its own institutions, and the arrangement was essentially a 'dual monarchy', illustrated by the title 'James VI of Scotland and I of England'.

The Union of 1707 has been subjected to much historical analysis, and legal discussion. Only part of this discourse has definite relevance to the study of the political system today. For example, the question of how the 'Treaty' was negotiated and passed, involving such matters as bribery and secret diplomacy, is of little importance in explaining its position today.

But the fact that it was not (overtly) imposed on Scotland gives Scotland a *locus standi* in the United Kingdom, unmatched by Wales or Ireland. Scotland was apparently guaranteed certain institutions and rights in 1707 as a result of a freely negotiated bargain. This was (and is) psychologically important to Scots, who have never considered themselves annexed by England, although some think they were tricked into signing away rights which could have been retained.

The principal provisions in the Act are union of the Scottish and English parliaments, the guarantee of freedom of trade within the U.K. and its possessions, and the perpetual safeguards given to the Presbyterian Established Church, to the Scottish legal system and courts, and to the universities. Thus the three bulwarks of Scottish culture (church, law and education) are recognised as indestructible (in theory).

Just as important is the absence in the Act of any 'federal' features. There is to be no 'blocking mechanism' in the U.K. Parliament, whereby Scotland could exercise a veto. Scottish

19

M.P.s are to be an integral part of the House of Commons, and Scottish peers similarly in the House of Lords. Initially, a quota was given to Scotland in each House (45 and 16 respectively), but Acts of Parliament have subsequently altered the proportions. Today there are 71 M.P.s and as many Scots as have been created peers (around 100).

Another feature which denotes the lack of federalism is the absence of any special law court to interpret the Constitution. In the U.S., and in some other federal countries, this is the function of the Supreme Court. In Britain, on the other hand, no court (Scottish or English) has ruled an Act of Parliament unconstitutional, and it is generally accepted that Parliament is 'sovereign' and can by ordinary legislation 'amend the Constitution'.

The contradiction posed between a simple 'sovereignty of Parliament' theory and the terms of the Act of Union has on occasion caused some anxiety. It does seem odd that something guaranteed 'for all time' should nevertheless be subject to amendment by Parliament. It is, however, a convention of the Constitution that some laws are more 'fundamental' than others, and cannot lightly be changed. Such a law is the Act of Union, and an attempt to alter its principal provisions would be the subject of constitutional and political controversy, even now.[1]

Nevertheless, changes have been made over the years, and many of these have gone unnoticed. For example, university professors in Scotland need no longer subscribe to the Westminster Confession of Faith, and the clause forbidding special inducements to trade in any part of the United Kingdom has been repeatedly breached. It is possible to distinguish these 'altered' parts of the Act from the more 'unalterable' part, such as those relating to the principal law courts and Presbyterianism. Even here, by a process of consent of the relevant parties within the British parliamentary system, legislation has brought changes. Examples are the Acts altering the establishment of Court of Session judges, and the Church of Scotland Acts, 1921 and 1925. The latter make up the basic constitution of the Church of Scotland today.

The doctrine, propounded by the English constitutionalist A. V. Dicey,[2] and others, that in Britain sovereignty cannot be divided, has been challenged in the recent past by some Scottish lawyers. Lord Cooper, in the case of *MacCormick and Another v. The Lord Advocate, 1953*, maintained that the principle of the unlimited sovereignty of Parliament 'is a distinctively English principle which has no counterpart in Scottish constitutional law'.[3] He was commenting on the (unsuccessful) attempt by the Scottish Nationalist J. M. MacCormick to have the title 'Elizabeth II' made illegal in Scotland. MacCormick considered that since there had never been a 'First' Elizabeth in the U.K., there could not now be a 'Second'. He tried to show that the proclamation of the latter title was contrary to the Act of Union, but in this he failed. Nevertheless, he elicited from some of the Scottish judges various assertions about Scottish constitutional law which have remained tantalisingly enigmatic to this day. If Parliament cannot alter the Act of Union, who can? The original parties are no more, for this was an 'incorporating union'. If the U.K. Parliament inherits some of the features of the old Scottish Parliament, as was suggested, how are they to be recognised, let alone made the basis of action?

From time to time, other Scottish lawyers have followed some of Cooper's thoughts. Professor T. B. Smith has called for judicial review of Acts of Parliament,[4] and Lord Kilbrandon has hinted that the Act of Union might present difficulties in law for Scotland's entry into the Common Market.[5] The mainstream of legal thought in Scotland, however, does not regard these as practical issues. Acts of Parliament have never been successfully challenged in Scottish courts, nor are they likely to be. Moreover, Scotland has no *de iure* status in international law, though its separate legal system will have to be taken into account in the legal institutions of E.E.C. Since it is derived from Roman Law, it is more

Table 5   (a) *The law court structure in Scotland*

Civil	Criminal
House of Lords	Court of Criminal Appeal
Court of Session	High Court of Justiciary
Sheriff Court	Sheriff Court
	District Court

(b) *The judicial and legal-administrative establishment*

Judges		Government law officers and principal officials	
Court of Session and High Court of Justiciary	(20)	Lord Advocate	
		Solicitor-General for Scotland	
Sheriffs-principal	(6)	Crown Agent	
Sheriffs	(63)	Procurators-fiscal	(43)

Note: The head of the judiciary in Scotland is the Lord President of the Court of Session, and not the Lord Advocate, who is the chief law officer of the Crown. This is unlike the position in England, where the Lord Chancellor fulfils both functions. The Law Society of Scotland recommended to the Commission on the Constitution that Scotland should have the equivalent of the Lord Chancellor's Office (*Memorandum of Evidence of the Law Society of Scotland* (1970), p. 6).

akin to the laws of the European countries than is that of England. This may give it a useful function as a bridge between the English and Roman systems.

The significance of Scots Law for the present operations of the Scottish political system is very great. To lawyers, it represents the touchstone of Scottish nationality, without which Scotland would cease to be a nation. Churchmen and educationists make similar claims for their institutions. In a sense, the law has priority. It lays down the rights of the others, and the courts must uphold them. The Scottish courts form an autonomous group within Britain, the principal exception being that in civil cases an appeal can be taken to the House of Lords, where only two of the five Lords of Appeal are Scottish judges. In nearly all cases, and in all criminal cases, the Scottish courts decide the law. This applies to law relating to Britain as well as to Scotland.

The highest courts in Scotland are the Court of Session (civil cases) and the High Court of Justiciary (criminal cases). The same judges officiate in both these courts, and the total number is twenty at present. Appointments to the Scottish bench are often given to the principal government law officers as a political reward. Eight of the eighteen judges in 1970 were in this category, the remaining being former sheriffs or advocates, including four deans of the faculty of Advocates. This led to some criticism, especially as the Lord Advocate is in a position to elevate himself to the bench. In 1970, the heads of the Scottish judiciary, the Lord President of the Court of Session, and the Lord Justice Clerk, illustrated the link between politics and the law in Scotland.

> Lord President of the Court of Session – Lord Clyde.
>> Conservative M.P. for Edinburgh North, 1950–5.
>> Lord Advocate, 1951–4.
>> Lord President, 1955.
> Lord Justice Clerk – Lord Grant.
>> Conservative M.P. for Glasgow Woodside, 1955–62.
>> Solicitor General for Scotland, 1955–60.
>> Lord Advocate, 1960–2.
>> Lord Justice Clerk, 1962.

> Note: In March 1972, Lord Emslie succeeded Lord Clyde, and Lord Wheatley succeeded Lord Grant as Lord Justice Clerk in December 1972.

On the bench, Scottish judges see themselves very much as public figures. They man important government committees, and pronounce on topical questions. In 1968, one judge, Lord Avonside, accepted an invitation to be a member of the Scottish Conservative Party's Constitutional Committee, which was examining Edward Heath's proposal for a Scottish Convention.

Pressure from the Labour government, however, forced him to withdraw, under protest. His wife became National Governor of the BBC in Scotland. In 1970 a Scottish judge, Lord Wheatley, became a life peer, and was soon active as legislator in the House of Lords in Scottish legal matters, as well as an interpreter of the law on the bench. Lord Kilbrandon is another important public figure.

The principal territorial courts of Scotland are the Sheriff Courts, and they cover a wide jurisdiction in both civil and criminal cases. There is also the Scottish Land Court, for cases arising under agricultural law.

In Scottish courts, procedure is different from that in England. Public prosecutions, under the direction of procurators-fiscal, are the rule, and replace police and private prosecutions. This system has been commended to England by the lawyers organisation, Justice.[6] Majority and 'not proven' verdicts are also used, and a modified version of the former was introduced in England in 1967.

Local courts in the districts can have elected councillors as magistrates, which bring politics in at a lower level. Called 'bailies' under the old system, they are now re-styled 'Justices of the Peace'. Former Justices of the Peace are also appointed to these positions.

The personnel of the Scottish legal profession is quite distinct from that in England. Scottish solicitors, advocates (barristers) and judges are nearly always Scots, and have received at least part of their legal education in Scotland. Very few Scots lawyers are qualified to practise in England, and few become M.P.s because of the loss of earnings, which cannot be made up by legal work in London. This separation of the legal professions of Scotland and England is similar to that in school-teaching, and greater than that in public administration. Scots lawyers are thus strongly interested in maintaining the autonomy of Scotland in matters which concern them, and some of these matters impinge on politics.

The difference between the substance of Scots Law and English Law is obviously relevant to the political system. In the first place, separate laws are often passed in Parliament for Scotland, and this has led to the establishment of special Scottish committees of the House of Commons. At the same time, clauses relating only to Scotland are often tacked on to British legislation. Between five and ten purely Scottish Bills are passed each session, while over seventy Acts which apply to Scotland are passed in the same period.

The decision to legislate separately for Scotland is most likely to be taken in matters relating to law reform, education, local government and (to a lesser degree) agriculture. In the last, important provisions relating to Scotland are also found in British statutes. Most revenue, social security and economic legislation is British. While these make up the bulk of policy-making, the existence of separate Scottish legislation is important in strengthening the autonomy of Scottish politics. No region of England requires separate laws, and Wales rarely does. Scots lawyers complain that the differences between Scots and English Law are not adequately respected in the Scottish adaptation clauses in British Bills. They would like to see much more Scottish legislation. But the pressure on the Scottish committees would probably be too great for this.

Separate Scottish legislation affects the Scottish M.P.s in the House of Commons, and all government departments and local authorities in Scotland. Each must relate its activities to the existence of the separate legal system, and become part of the Scottish 'system'. Although a process of assimilation between the legal systems is taking place, enough differences remain to perpetuate this division at the political and administrative level.

The legal differences are more noticeable in private and property law than in public, commercial and constitutional law. The existence of Scottish constitutional law, though asserted by Scots lawyers, does not seem to be much in evidence in practice, and the distinction between it and English constitutional law is not easy to draw.[7] The Church of Scotland, as the Established Church, is undoubtedly unique in its freedom from state control. Scottish courts have sometimes taken a stronger line in cases involving administrative discretion than have courts in England. But these differences have grown less important in recent years, and the powers of government departments and administrative tribunals are essentially the same in both countries.

Civil liberties (e.g. the freedom from arbitrary arrest, freedom of speech and assembly) are similar throughout Britain, even although in Scotland they derive from Scots Law. But Scottish 'permissive' legislation (relating to divorce, homosexuality, licensing and Sunday entertainments) has not been passed.

The relationship between the Scottish legal and political systems is perhaps the strongest single reason for the autonomy of the latter within the British state. Separate laws engender separate politics and administration. A whole host of vested interests is thereby established which cannot be easily assimilated with those in England. Thus while the laws of Scotland and England grow daily closer together in substance, the lawyers who operate them (including clerks of local authorities and others with a Scottish legal training employed by public bodies and business firms) remain as separated as before. So too, to a lesser extent, do the administrators and politicians, since they have to deal with the laws and the lawyers. To the administrators and politicians we now turn our attention.

3

The Secretary of State for Scotland and the Scottish Office

The Secretary of State for Scotland has been called 'Scotland's Prime Minister'. He is Scotland's representative in the Cabinet (although other Scots or Scottish M.P.s can be members – Sir Alec Douglas-Home has been Prime Minister and Foreign Secretary while a Scottish M.P.). The Scottish Secretary's department is the Scottish Office, with its headquarters in St Andrew's House, Edinburgh. There is also a small office in Whitehall at Dover House, which serves as a centre for liaison with Whitehall departments, and as a base for the conduct of parliamentary business.

The ministerial 'team' at the Scottish Office usually consists of the Secretary of State, a Minister of State, and three Under-Secretaries of State. The junior ministers are given 'subject briefs'. At the beginning of 1975, there were two Ministers of State and three Under-Secretaries. If the Scottish Secretary is Scotland's Prime Minister, these men then comprise his 'Cabinet'.

But is he really a Prime Minister in any meaningful sense? The title has been fondly used by Scottish Secretaries in the past, but no doubt with a heavy dose of wishful thinking. It might perhaps be an attempt to compensate for the rather minor status of the office in the Cabinet, where, for example, key committees sometimes do not include the Scottish Secretary. Seen from Downing Street, there is only *one* Prime Minister – the man in No. 10.

Seen from Edinburgh, the view changes somewhat. With an official residence in Bute House, and a large establishment at St Andrew's House and elsewhere in Scotland, the Secretary of State personifies 'Scottish government'. It is partly a proconsular role: if he 'speaks for Scotland' in London, he also 'speaks for London' in Scotland. He is not the chosen leader of the majority party in Scotland, but the Scottish spokesman of the majority party in Westminster. It sometimes happens that the two majorities do not coincide, so that Scotland is ruled by ministers whose party has a minority of the Scottish seats. In 1970, Gordon Campbell, a Conservative, became Scottish Secretary, although his party won only 23 of the 71 House of Commons seats in Scotland, and received only 38% of the votes. Such a situation could not arise if the Scottish Office were responsible to an elected Scottish parliament, but it does occur under the existing system, where governments are formed from British majorities. It will also happen that a general election result can force England to accept a government for which it did not provide a majority, yet which had a majority in Scotland (for example, the Labour government elected in 1964). In these ways, the U.K. political system displays its primacy over the 'Scottish', 'English', and other systems within it.

This does not destroy the subsidiary systems, and they do not disappear through such quirks of fate. Just as Her Majesty's Opposition remains 'loyal' in defeat, and participates in the legislative process, so too the mechanisms of the territorial systems in the U.K. keep turning despite the possible incongruities of the representative situations in these areas. A Conservative Secretary of State for Scotland in a Labour Scotland must still 'speak for Scotland' in the Cabinet and in the House of Commons. His 'legitimacy' is accepted by the major parties, for they agree to operate on the basis of the unity of Parliament. A Conservative Secretary tries to shape Conservative policies for Scottish consumption, and thereby becomes an integral part of the Scottish political system, as the target of its pressures.

Not the sole target, however. 'Scotland's Prime Minister' has not enough *power* to justify that. If he really did govern Scotland, the position would be clear, and all demands could be channelled to St Andrew's House. But Scotland is subject to the British Cabinet, of which the Scottish Secretary is just a member. 'Collective responsibility' is the cardinal principle on which 'British Cabinet Government' is based, and so policies for Scotland (whether exclusive to it or not) are all in theory devised by the Cabinet. Scots are well aware that ultimate executive power resides there.

Yet the Cabinet has little time for Scotland as such. Scottish Secretaries may not object to this situation, for it means that they can avoid a lot of awkward questioning from their colleagues about Scottish administration. If policies for Scotland are to be different from elsewhere this may require some justification, especially if more money than in other places is to be spent there for the same services. To a Scottish Secretary these arguments are usually better kept at a lower level, in inter-departmental committees of civil servants, or in direct dealings with other ministers. So much of Scottish policy-making lies hidden from view, even from the Cabinet.

Why does the Scottish Office exist at all, and what does it do? In the organisation of British central administration, government departments usually operate on a functional, rather than a territorial basis, a principle generally accepted in Britain from the Haldane Report on the machinery of government (1918, Cd.

9230) to the White Paper on *The Reorganisation of Central Government* (October 1970, Cmnd. 4506). Thus education, trade and industry, agriculture, and so on, are administered by separate departments. The exceptions to this are the Scottish and Welsh Offices (Northern Ireland, of course, has its own departments but their position is different, since they were, and may be again, responsible to a separate Parliament at Stormont). While the Welsh Office under a Secretary of State for Wales is a comparative newcomer (1964), the Scottish Office dates from 1885.

Yet long before these departments were created, there were in Scotland and Wales administrative bodies whose jurisdiction was both functional and territorial. In the case of Scotland (to which we restrict our attention), such bodies or officials were found immediately after the Union of 1707 in the shape of the Secretary of State for Scotland and the Lord Advocate. The former minister was entrusted generally with the government of Scotland, while the latter was (and is) the chief government law officer in Scotland. In 1746 the Scottish Secretaryship was abolished, and the Lord Advocate assumed the responsibility for government business in Scotland. Thus the key position of Scots Law in preserving Scotland's identity in the government was emphasised.

During the nineteenth century, the functions of government increased, especially at the local level. Poor law relief, public health, road-building and education became the responsibilities of bodies which were specialised local government authorities. At the same time, the main local authorities (i.e. certain burghs, and after 1889, the counties) became active in various forms of 'improvement' such as water supply, drainage, hospitals and town planning. Of course, much of this was inspired by central government policy, though local authorities themselves sought to increase their powers by Private Bills (one of the most famous being Glasgow's Act to bring water from Loch Katrine in 1859). The seat of administration was essentially local in Victorian times, and central government control was intermittent and seemed a long way off.

Yet some control was needed. Governments could not wash their hands entirely of local government, for clearly certain standards had to be maintained, since grants were being expended. There thus arose supervisory boards, such as the Board of Supervision for Poor Relief (1845–94) and the Scotch Education Department (from 1872). Their job was to superintend the activities of the parochial boards and school boards respectively. What is interesting about this development, from the point of view of the origins of the Scottish Office, is that where 'intermediate' authorities were established in Scotland, between local and central government, they took a Scottish form. Thus by 1885, there were several Scottish administrative bodies, whose main task was the superintendence of local government functions, and who were finally (though vaguely) the responsibility of the Home Secretary. This minister had, since 1828, been formally put 'in charge of Scotland', but since he usually knew very little about Scottish affairs, the Lord Advocate was still regarded as the voice of Scotland in the government, and took the lead in Scottish debates. The legal system of Scotland ensured his survival, while the Scottish local government structure led to the creation of the Scottish boards.[1] In this way, both legacies from the Act of Union paved the way for the Scottish Office.

These were practical considerations. Scotland could not be governed efficiently from London, as long as Scots Law and 'the burghs' survived. And London did not really mind their survival (though in the case of the law something of a war of attrition took place through House of Lords decisions and the development of 'British' law). But the system of boards had its faults: it was difficult to see who was responsible for them, in the absence of a Cabinet minister who knew Scotland, and they were staffed by amateurs, not professional civil servants. They increased government patronage, something which Scotland knew well and perhaps loved, but which offended against the liberal and democratic tendencies of the later Victorian age.

Scottish M.P.s were particularly restless, and in 1869 they sent a memorial to Gladstone requesting the appointment of a Scottish Secretary with responsibility for the boards. They disliked the power assumed by a lawyer, the Lord Advocate, over the general affairs of Scotland and felt that Scottish Bills were being neglected for lack of a proper government sponsor. This was particularly clear in the case of educational reform, which would have come much earlier than in 1872, if the Scottish M.P.s had had their way.

Such considerations (still of a practical nature) linked up with, or stimulated, the growth of Scottish nationalism. Partly inspired by the example of the Irish Home Rulers of the time, but also 'native' in origin, nationalism found support among many Scottish M.P.s, members of the Scottish aristocracy (Rosebery, Argyll and Fife), the Convention of Royal Burghs, and a large section of Scottish public opinion. By 1884, Gladstone found the combination of arguments in favour of setting up the Scottish Office, with a Scottish Scottish Secretary, irresistible, and a Bill was introduced in 1884 to this effect.

From its rather modest beginnings (ironically, it was the Conservatives who actually provided the first Scottish Secretary in 1885), the Scottish Office has grown continuously in size and scope, until today it covers the functions of several Whitehall departments. This was by no means obvious at the start, and the Home Office jealously guarded its rights to interfere in Scotland. The Lord Advocate, too, was on the defensive, and resented any implication that he was subject to the Scottish Secretary (Hanham 2). In fact, the transfer of functions to the Scottish Office was at the expense of these ministers as well as the Privy Council, the Treasury and the Local Government Board for England. Principal functions transferred were poor law, public health, Fishery Board, General Register House, police, prisons, roads and bridges, parliamentary divisions (from the Home Office); Board of Manufacturers (from the Treasury); Public Works Local Commissioners (from the Local Government Board for England).

The Scottish boards came under the Secretary's authority, but somewhat indirectly, since they still retained their statutory duties. Scottish education, for example, was still administered by the Scotch Education Department, a committee of the Privy Council, although the Scottish Secretary was now made the minister answerable to Parliament on the subject. The problem of the executive functions of the Scottish Office was not finally settled until 1939, when the remaining boards were absorbed within the Scottish Office, and the Scottish Secretary made directly responsible for them. The Secretary for Scotland was not a member of the Cabinet between 1885 and 1892, but after 1892 his place there became assured. In 1926, he was dignified with the title of Secretary of State, although his salary remained £3,000 lower than other Secretaries of State. In 1937, the Ministers of the Crown Act gave all Cabinet ministers £5,000 a year and in 1974 their ministerial salary was £13,000.

Table 6   *Chronology of the Scottish Office*

1746	Office of Secretary of State for Scotland lapses; Lord Advocate thereafter chief Scottish minister.
1828	Home Secretary made formally responsible for Scottish affairs, but Lord Advocate in practice responsible.
1845	Board of Supervision for Poor Relief established (to 1894); thereafter Local Government Board for Scotland (to 1919).
1849	Fishery Board (established 1808) restricts operation to Scotland.
1857	General Board of Commissioners in Lunacy (to 1913); thereafter, General Board of Control (to 1962).
1872	Scotch Education Department (committee of Privy Council); 1918 renamed Scottish Education Department.
1877	Prisons Commission (to 1928).
1885	SCOTTISH OFFICE established, taking most Home Office functions, and education. Scottish Secretary responsible to Parliament for Scottish boards.
1886	Crofters Commission (to 1911, and from 1955).

1892	Secretary for Scotland in the Cabinet.
1897	Congested Districts Board (to 1911). Responsible for Highland resettlement.
1911	Scottish Insurance Commissioners (to 1919). National Insurance.
1912	Scottish Board of Agriculture (to 1928).
1913	Highlands and Islands Medical Services Board (to 1919).
1919	Scottish Board of Health (to 1928), absorbs Insurance Commissioners, Highland Medical Board, and Local Government Board for Scotland. Parliamentary Under-Secretary for Health for Scotland created.
1926	Elevation of Secretary for Scotland to rank of a Principal Secretary of State. Parliamentary Under-Secretary for Health for Scotland becomes Parliamentary Under-Secretary of State for Scotland.
1929	Creation of Departments of Agriculture for Scotland, Health for Scotland and Prisons Department, replacing boards (1912, 1919 above) and Commission (1877, above).
1937	Gilmour Committee Report on Scottish Administration (Cmnd. 5563) recommends Edinburgh-based Scottish Office, and tighter control of Scottish administration by Scottish Secretary.
1939	Opening of St Andrew's House, Edinburgh, and vesting of powers of Scottish Office (now four departments of Agriculture, Education, Health and Home) directly in Secretary of State.
1939–75	Piecemeal transfer of functions to and from the Scottish Office, and successive Scottish Office departmental reorganisations. Main additions: electricity, roads, some transport; increased activity in economic planning, agriculture, health, social work, Highland development, aspects of oil and industrial development. Main loss: social security (National Insurance).

Present departments: Agriculture and Fisheries, Development, Home and Health, Education, Economic Planning.

Two additional Under-Secretaries of State (1940, 1951); Minister of State (1951); Second Minister of State replaced one of the Under-Secretaries (1969–70), returns with three Under-Secretaries (1974–   ).

This is not the place for a detailed history of the development of the Scottish Office (for this, see especially Hanham 2; and in Wolfe, pp. 51–70; and Milne), since we are more concerned with the situation which exists today, and which may exist in the future. But the general features of that history are of great importance in understanding Scottish politics.

There is first of all the question of the development of the range of functions exercised by the Scottish Office. It is normally assumed that such functions are determined by the degree to which Scotland differs from the rest of the country. For example, where Scots Law, local government or education are involved, then it is appropriate to place these under the Scottish Office. But where there is no distinctly Scottish characteristic about a government function, it should be performed by a Great Britain (or United Kingdom, if Northern Ireland is also covered) department. This approach is sensible and convincing until one reflects that perhaps all administration in Scotland has to deal with 'distinctly Scottish characteristics', since these arise out of the separateness of Scottish society itself. In the words of the former Permanent Under-Secretary of State at the Scottish Office, Sir Douglas Haddow, in answer to Lord Crowther, then chairman of the Commission on the Constitution, 'This is of course the basic case for Scottish administration, that our decisions in Scotland are taken in full knowledge of all the surrounding Scottish circumstances – history, tradition, law, everything.' (Kilbrandon 4, p. 12.)

If this is so, then perhaps all government functions in Scotland should come under the Scottish Office. Yet one could argue that such knowledge is not the prerogative of the Scottish Office, and that British departments operating in Scotland are able to adapt their administration, where necessary, to Scottish needs, without incurring the expense and complication involved in setting up a separate department. In fact, Scottish administration is based on both these approaches, and the result is a compromise between London-based and Edinburgh-based government, whose relative merits are extremely difficult to establish.

How does the existing division of powers implement the case for Scottish administration? (See table 7.) The largest category of Scottish Office functions derives from the need for the central government to supervise the activities of local authorities. Over the past hundred years, local government has come more closely under the wing of the central government, and some local functions have been transferred entirely to the centre. But while for the most of Britain 'the centre' means London, in this respect it usually means Edinburgh. Thus the strengthening of the centre at the expense of local government in Scotland strengthened the 'middle tier' (the Scottish Office), not Whitehall. The middle tier is part of central government, but it is much more closely related to, and in touch with, local government than the London-based departments. In this way, the accession of power at the centre in Scotland has not affected local government so severely, since the distance between local and central government and the scale of the supervisory department is not as great as in England.

The Scottish Office functions which derive from local government include education, health, housing, road construction and social work. Apart from roads, these are essentially supervisory of local or health authorities, and the supervision is close and

Table 7 *The functions of central government in Scotland, 1975*

British Departments

Treasury
  Taxation, interest rates
  Departmental appropriations
  Linked body: Department of National Savings
Board of Inland Revenue
Customs and Excise
  Collection of import duties and V.A.T.
Department of Trade
  Regulation of imports and exports
  Regulation of companies and insurance
  Marine inspection and accidents
  Linked bodies: Civil Aviation Authority (Highland airports), British Airports Authority (Scottish Airports), British Airways Board (Scottish Airways), Northern Lighthouse Board
Department of Industry
  Direction and support of industry (from July 1975 selective regional assistance was transferred to the Scottish Office)
  Relations with shipbuilding, engineering, vehicles, and aerospace industries
  Posts and Telecommunications (including technological aspects of BBC and IBA. The non-technological side comes under the Home Office with Scottish Office participation)
  Linked bodies: National Enterprise Board, British Steel Corporation, Scottish Postal Board, Scottish Telecommunications Board

Scottish Departments

Scottish Office
  Department of Agriculture and Fisheries for Scotland
    Land settlement, estate management, regulation of crofting
    Agricultural education, advisory service and research (three colleges)
    Administration of U.K. and E.E.C. price support and fisheries policies
    Royal Botanic Garden, Edinburgh
    Linked bodies: Crofters Commission, Red Deer Commission, Herring Industry Board, White Fish Authority (Scottish Committee)
  Scottish Development Department
    Local government (including grants)
    Town and country planning
    Housing and building control
    Roads and local transport planning
    North Sea oil infrastructure
    Ancient monuments and historic buildings
    Linked bodies: Scottish Special Housing Association, Countryside Commission for Scotland, Historic Buildings Council for Scotland
  Scottish Economic Planning Department
    Industrial and economic development (Regional Development Division, Economics and Statistics Unit)
    North Sea Oil (North Sea Oil Support Group)
    Selective regional assistance to industry and factory building

Table 7 (contd.)

Department of Energy
Energy production
Linked bodies: Offshore Supplies Office for Scotland, British National Oil Corporation (Glasgow), British Gas Corporation (Scottish Gas), National Coal Board (two Scottish Areas), Atomic Energy Authority (Chapelcross, Dounreay).
Department of Prices and Consumer Protection
Department of Employment
Industrial relations, industrial training and employment offices. Regional employment premium
Department of the Environment
Transport (rail and Stranraer–Larne shipping)
Ports, docks, waterways, freight
Public buildings and works
Linked bodies: British Rail, National Freight Corporation, etc.
Department of Health and Social Security
National insurance, family allowances and other cash benefits
Department of Education and Science
Universities and higher research
Linked bodies: University Grants Committee and Research Councils (Agricultural, Medical, Natural Environment, Social Science, Science)
Ministry of Defence
Linked bodies: Service establishments and Meteorological Office
Ministry of Agriculture, Fisheries and Food
Animal health

New Towns
Electricity (two boards)
Highland and rural development
Passenger road and sea transport and tourism
Linked bodies: Scottish Development Agency and Scottish Industrial Estates Corporation, Oil Development Council for Scotland, Highlands and Islands Development Board, New Town Development Corporations, Small Industries Council, Scottish Transport Group, Scottish Tourist Board
Scottish Education Department
Control and development of schools and colleges (not universities). Includes research, teacher training, student grants
Public libraries
Youth and Community Services
Recreation and the Arts
Social Work Services Group (child care, probation, welfare and mental health)
Linked bodies: Royal Fine Art Commission for Scotland, Royal Scottish Museum, National Galleries of Scotland, National Library of Scotland, National Museum of Antiquities of Scotland, Scottish Sports Council, etc.
Scottish Home and Health Department
Law and order (police, fire, civil defence, civil and criminal law, prisons, Royal Prerogative of Mercy)
Representation of the people
Regulation of liquor licensing, betting, entertainment
National Health Service ('Scottish Health Service')

Table 7 (*contd.*)

Emergency food supply and sponsorship of food-processing industries

Home Office
  Aliens, immigration
  Explosives
  Vivisection, cruelty to animals
Foreign and Commonwealth Office
  Passports
Civil Service Department
  Recruitment and conditions of civil service

(including school health, health education and public health), Linked bodies: health boards, Common Services Agency, and Scottish Health Service Planning Council

Other linked bodies: Scottish Record Office (Keeper of the Records of Scotland), Department of Registers for Scotland, Registrar General for Scotland, Lord Lyon, Mental Welfare Commission, Lands Tribunal, Scottish Law Commission

Central Services
  Establishment
  Solicitor
  Finance
  Scottish Information Office
  Computer and statistical services
  Devolution
Scottish Courts Administration (partly responsible to Lord Advocate)

Lord Advocate's Department
  Chief Scottish Law Officer of the Crown (public prosecutions, legal appointments, drafting of Bills, courts)
  Linked body: Scottish Law Commission
Crown Office (criminal prosecutions)
Crown Estate Commissioners
Forestry Commission (H.Q. in Edinburgh; under Scottish Secretary in Scotland)
Scottish Economic Council (before 1970 called the Scottish Economic Planning Council)

Civil service Inter-Departmental committees (including members of British and Scottish departments)
Scottish Economic Planning Board (chaired by Scottish Office)
North Sea Oil Task Force (chaired by Scottish Office)

decisive. A function directly transferred to the Scottish Office from local government is health, while others have come to the Scottish Office from local government after having been exercised for a time by British departments (roads, transport other than rail, and electricity in the south of Scotland).

In the field of social security, unemployment benefits moved from local government to a British authority (the Unemployment Assistance Board) in 1934, and health and pensions insurance was transferred from the Scottish Office to the Ministry of National Insurance in 1945. The remainder of public assistance was transferred from local authorities to the National Assistance Board in 1948, which was an enlarged version of the Unemployment Assistance Board. When the National Health Service was set up in 1948 this was given to the Scottish Office, so that the administration of the welfare state was completely split between Scottish and British departments. This did, however, mean a net gain in activity to the Scottish Office, for its health functions expanded greatly.

The pre-1885 Scottish functions such as law, education and registration remained part of Scottish administration, and the Scottish Secretary is still in varying degrees responsible for them. He shares responsibility for the legal system of Scotland with the Lord Advocate, and with the Registrar General for Scotland (a civil servant on the establishment of the Scottish Office) for the organisation of the Census of Scotland and other demographic statistics. Scottish schools, further education, education, art, and technical colleges are the responsibility of local authorities, or of governing bodies and the Scottish Education Department, but Scottish universities deal through the University Grants Committee and research councils with the Department of Education and Science. There are thus two education ministers for Scotland.

These functions are inherited from the legacy of the past independence of Scotland; many of them (law, education, local government) were mentioned specifically in the Union settlement of 1707. But there has been a vast increase in the functions of the Scottish Office, in directions not contemplated in the Union. They result from the increasing government intervention throughout Britain in economic and social affairs. Governments do far more today to regulate the economy and to provide social security than they did when the Scottish Office was set up in 1885, and it has been decided that some of this activity should be organised separately in Scotland. In agriculture, the Crofters Act of 1886 established a separate administrative structure for the seven 'crofting counties' (Orkney, Shetland, Caithness, Sutherland, Ross and Cromarty, Inverness and Argyll), and this is preserved today, with the addition since 1965 of the Highlands and Islands

Development Board. The Board's function is 'to prepare, concert, promote, assist and undertake measures for the economic and social development of the Highlands and Islands' (SCSA 3, p. 2). The rest of Scottish agriculture is also partly governed by special legislation. The Scottish Board of Agriculture was formed in 1912, and its descendant is the Department of Agriculture and Fisheries for Scotland (established 1960). The agricultural policies during and after the Second World War unified British agriculture to some extent. There is no separate Scottish farm price review, and products receive the same level of support in Scotland as elsewhere. Yet the tradition that Scottish agriculture has its own problems persists, and agriculture and fisheries are important functions of the Scottish Office.

The non-agricultural sector of the Scottish economy must also concern the Scottish Secretary, although here he is more conscious of the interests and powers of his colleagues in the Cabinet. He has probably not shared proportionately in the great increase in the economic decision-making power exercised by the Treasury and the other large economic departments in London. Yet he must try to shape the Scottish economy as best he can. What he cannot do by persuasion of other ministers he attempts to do himself: he has functions of road-building, transport, electricity and housing – the 'infrastructure' of economic development, and he can try to attract industry to Scotland by promotion campaigns. In the 1960s, the Scottish Office pioneered the concept of regional economic planning, producing its own plans and administrative machinery to implement them (see pp. 186–96). More and more economic functions came its way, but the main powers (over taxation, fiscal policy and distribution of industry) did not. Regional economic planning meant planning *for* the regions by the centre, not by the regions themselves, and so the dominance of the U.K. political and economic systems was maintained. Opinion was divided anyway as to whether you could plan the Scottish economy from Scotland itself, and it was generally accepted that only certain economic functions were proper to Scottish administration. The practical result of this is that co-ordination with other departments is a problem, for the Scottish Office has only limited authority over the executions of its economic plans. Since 1973, the division of responsibility on North Sea oil development between the Scottish Office and the Department of Energy has become the most sensitive and confusing part of Scottish administration. In 1975, the establishment of the Scottish Development Agency in the Scottish Office to promote industrial development did nothing to solve the question of who was responsible for the Scottish economy, though it was a significant increase in the executive functions of St Andrew's House. Selective regional assistance now came under the Scottish Office, which represented about one quarter of all regional assistance in Scotland. So too did some public participation in industry, though the major policy decisions on regional policy and nationalisation remained with Whitehall, and the National Enterprise Board (1975) was to operate throughout the United Kingdom. Once more, this seemed a recipe for confusion and over-lapping jurisdictions.

Along with the increase in functions, the Scottish Office has greatly increased its complement of civil servants. The centre of gravity in the Scottish Office shifted to Edinburgh after the Report on Scottish Administration of the Gilmour Committee in 1937 (Cmd. 5563). This recommended bringing together the Scottish Office staff under one roof in Edinburgh, and vesting all Scottish functions directly in the Secretary of State for Scotland. This was done in 1939, when St Andrew's House opened its doors, and under the Reorganisation of Offices (Scotland) Act 1939, the functions of the four administrative departments of the Scottish Office (Home, Health, Education and Agriculture) came under the Scottish Secretary. Today, the five departments are Home and Health, Development, Education, Agriculture and Fisheries and Economic Planning (see table 7).

In the late 1960s and early 1970s, largely because of the rise of nationalism, but also because regional administration was being increasingly studied in Britain, the Scottish Office was subjected to close scrutiny. The Labour government in June 1966 set up the Royal Commission on Local Government in Scotland (the Wheatley Commission), in December 1968 the Commission on the Constitution (the Crowther (now called Kilbrandon), Commission), and in November 1969 the House of Commons Select Committee on Scottish Affairs, and these bodies received evidence from ministers and civil servants of the Scottish Office. Unofficial inquiries into Scottish government by the political parties in Scotland took place from 1967 to 1970, and the Conservative Party in Scotland surprised many observers by proposing in May 1968 that an elected Scottish convention should be instituted to deal with Scottish Bills and to discuss Scottish affairs. Outside Scotland, the evidence to the Crowther Commission, especially in Wales, frequently referred to the Scottish Office as a model for regional administration, and some attempt was made to understand it in England.

What did this critical examination discover, and what proposals have been made to improve Scottish administration? In the first place, it was soon seen that the degree of decentralisation to Scotland, however great it might appear to be, has little effect on the consciousness of mass public opinion in Scotland. Scots know very little of it, and what they know they probably regard as a subsidiary part of British government having few independent powers of its own. Scottish Secretaries are not thought of as powerful politicians, though they might be seen to be hard-working administrators. The major British politicians are just as well known in Scotland, if not more so, than the Secretary of State, as a result of the focussing of the news media (especially TV) on them.

Of course, this kind of generalisation does not bite very deep. Any Scot who has an interest in politics, especially if he is active in local government, trade unionism or in other interest groups, soon makes himself aware of what St Andrew's House can, or cannot, do. But there are areas of confusion. The division of functions between Edinburgh and London is often unclear, and 'Scotland's Minister', though charged with the oversight of all Scottish affairs, and not merely those functions vested directly in him, can be a poor substitute for the appropriate London minister when action is required. British Rail, the former Upper Clyde Shipbuilders, the British Steel Corporation, and the National Coal Board are perhaps more vital to Scotland's economy than any responsibility of the Scottish Office, and pressure from Scotland must be exerted in London if the appropriate ministers are to be directly reached.

To the Scottish Secretary this can represent the greatest frustration of the job. Tiring as the administration of multifarious functions may be to a minister, it is much worse to bear the brunt of criticism for actions taken by other ministers with which he may not agree. Unemployment, emigration, and industrial closures dominate the Scottish economy, but there is very little that the Scottish Secretary can do within his own department to check them. He can use his influence with other departments, notably the Treasury, but he must compete with other ministers for a favourable decision. Even in areas of administration less dependent on purely financial considerations, such as law, education and the structure of local government, the need to conform with a pattern established by the corresponding ministries in England is strongly felt. Scotland cannot diverge too far from the norms of the rest of the country if the general desire for equality before the law, social justice, and mobility of labour is to be satisfied.

After the Kilbrandon Commission reported in October 1973 (Kilbrandon 5), more radical proposals to change the governmental structure achieved widespread acceptance (see below, ch. 7, pp. 133–42). Devolution, involving a greater or lesser degree of economic power for a Scottish Parliament and Government, clearly overtook the milder reform schemes of the past as 'practical politics'.

What sort of man becomes Scottish Secretary, and how does he promote the interests of his department? Since 1885, when the office was created anew, there have been 33 Secretaries or Secretaries of State for Scotland. The office is virtually the prerogative of a Scot, although an Englishman, Sir George Trevelyan, held it in 1886, and from 1892 to 1895. Another was Ernest Brown (1940–1). In the early years, it was common to appoint a peer to the job, and on the whole Scottish Secretaries have not been noted 'House of Commons men'. This has probably diminished their prestige within their parties, and it results partly from the practical difficulty of making a mark in the Commons in Scottish debates, which are of little interest to English M.P.s. In addition, Scottish committee work and the need to spend a fair amount of time in Edinburgh during parliamentary sessions reduces the number of opportunities for effective parliamentary performance. These considerations work against the prestige of the Scottish Secretary, and make it difficult for him to establish popularity on a wide front.

When Labour went into Opposition in 1970, William Ross, who had been Scottish Secretary in the Labour governments from 1964 to 1970, did not at first secure a place on the Parliamentary Committee of the Labour Party ('the Shadow Cabinet'). This body includes 12 members elected by the Parliamentary Labour Party (the Labour M.P.s), and gives an indication of the popularity of the party leaders. Ross narrowly missed being elected, and was subsequently co-opted to the Committee when Douglas Houghton resigned on becoming chairman of the Parliamentary Labour Party. In a sense he did well to beat other ex-Cabinet ministers such as Michael Stewart, Cledwyn Hughes, Roy Mason, George Thomas (his Welsh counterpart), and Peter Shore, but he did not get as many votes as George Thomson, M.P. for Dundee East, who, as Chancellor of the Duchy of Lancaster, had been in charge of the negotiations for Britain's attempted entry into the European Economic Community.

Previous Labour Scottish Secretaries were mostly not prominent in the party, though some of them proved effective ministers. It may be surmised that the job was treated by them as a sort of fiefdom, rather than as a stepping-stone to other (higher?) things. At any rate, none of them did move on to other departments, and for Labour ministers especially it has been something of a dead end. William Ross stayed in the Cabinet from 1964 to 1970 (a record for that period equalled only by Harold Wilson, the Prime Minister, and Denis Healey, the Secretary of State for Defence), from which we may deduce that he was on good terms with Wilson and that he was given plenty of time to master the intricacies of his office. He returned in February 1974 to the same post.

Scottish Office duties are of course considerable, and an extended stay in the office may be almost essential if a Scottish Secretary is to become more than the tool of his civil servants. At the same time, such prolonged tenures do not make for flexible and dynamic policies, and the practice has tended to stultify Scottish administration.[2]

Conservative Scottish Secretaries have been rather more mobile. A. J. Balfour (1886–7) became Prime Minister (1902–5). Sir John Gilmour (1924–9) became Minister of Agriculture and Fisheries (1931–2), Home Secretary (1932–5) and Minister for Shipping (1939–40). Walter Elliot (1936–8) was Minister of Agriculture and Fisheries (1932–6) and Minister of Health (1938–1940). John S. Maclay (Viscount Muirshiel) (1957–62) was Minister of Transport and Civil Aviation (1951–2) and Minister of State in the Colonial Office (1956–7) before coming to the Scottish Office. Michael Noble (1962–4) became President of the Board of Trade in 1970, which office became Minister for Trade soon afterwards.

It is probably true to say that the Conservative Scottish Secretaries have carried as much weight within the Cabinet as the Labour ones, despite the fact that Conservative M.P.s are relatively few on the ground in Scotland (at least since 1959). This may be because there are 'hidden Scots' in many Tory Cabinets: men like Iain Macleod, who always signed his nationality 'Scottish' in hotel registers. Harold Macmillan (Prime Minister, 1957–63) was also proud of his Scottish ancestry, as of course is Sir Alec Douglas-Home (previously 14th Earl of Home). Winston Churchill, though no Scot, gave his support to Scottish Secretaries such as Thomas Johnston (1941–5) and James Stuart (later Viscount Findhorn) (1951–7). With such allies, Scottish Secretaries in Conservative or Coalition Cabinets have carried disproportionate weight, and there has also been the political desire to 'do something for Scotland' in order to make up electoral lost ground there.

Labour Secretaries have faced a rather different situation. Their party's solid support in Scotland in recent years has sometimes led to complacency or intransigence, especially on the nationalist question. The advent of a Labour government usually heralds a revival of nationalism in Scotland (as in the late 1940s and mid-1960s), and Labour Cabinets have been notably unsympathetic to its demands. Clement Attlee did not understand the force of Scottish national sentiment, nor did many of his colleagues such as Aneurin Bevan and Herbert Morrison. Their mission was to secure a uniform system of social justice for Britain, not to break that system into different parts.

The same goes for Harold Wilson, although by the 1960s

regional economic planning was much more the accepted wisdom, modifying the centralist thought of the party. At this time William Ross, the Scottish Secretary, stood opposed to the current wave of nationalism, and resisted any further decentralisation to the Scottish Office. Yet he resolutely campaigned for economic discrimination in Scotland's favour, and strengthened the machinery of the Scottish Office in economic planning. Other Labour ministers, such as Richard Crossman, and quite a few Labour activists in Scotland, Wales and even England, were more sympathetic towards devolution than Ross, who at that same time saw the Scottish National Party as his chief antagonist and a serious threat to the position of the Labour Party in Scotland. Ross prevailed on his Scottish henchmen and Wilson not to budge one inch in opposing nationalism, but at the same time to dampen its fires by remedial economic action. While he apparently succeeded here, if one can judge by the result of the 1970 election, the recurrence of nationalism was inevitable, since many of the problems it uncovered remain unsolved. Thus it was that after the second SNP upsurge in 1974, Ross and the Scottish Labour Executive were forced to concede that a Scottish assembly should be established.

Junior Ministers (Labour as well as Conservative) in the Scottish Office differ from the position of the Secretary of State in that many do move to or from other departments. Table 8 shows the shifts that took place between 1945 and 1970. On the other hand, eleven junior ministers in the Scottish Office from 1945 to 1970 did not serve outside that department.

When one examines the educational background of Scottish Office ministers, one finds an almost complete contrast between the Labour and Conservative office-holders. Of the 14 Labour ministers between 1945 and 1970, 12 attended a Scottish day school, 6 a Scottish university, 2 English day schools and 1 an English university. Of the 20 Conservative ministers, 12 attended English public schools, 9 English universities, and only 3 attended Scottish day schools and 3 Scottish universities. Four attended Scottish public schools, and one (Lady Tweedsmuir) was educated abroad. The comparison should not only be between the parties, however. The Scottish Office ministers in Labour governments are distinctly more state-educated than Labour ministers in other departments, especially since 1964. The dominance of Oxford and Cambridge in the Labour leadership in the 1950s and 1960s reflected the central position of these institutions in the higher education of England and Wales, but their pull has always been much less in Scotland. The state school system is also more pervasive there. Thus the Scottish Labour leaders do not share the educational background of their colleagues in the south.

The Conservative leadership, on the other hand, is far more homogeneous, since the Scottish upper class often prefers an English or Anglicised upper-class education. The Scottish Office under the Conservatives is usually run by Anglicised Scots, who are of course untypical of the mass of Conservatives in Scotland. It

Table 8 *Movement of junior ministers between the Scottish Office and other government departments, 1945–70*

	Scottish Office	Other departments
George Buchanan	Under-Secretary, 1945–7	Minister of Pensions, 1947–8
Thomas Fraser	Under-Secretary, 1945–51	Minister of Transport, 1964–5
Margaret Herbison	Under-Secretary, 1950–1	Minister of Pensions and National Insurance, 1964–6 Minister of Social Security, 1966–7
Earl of Home (Sir Alec Douglas-Home)	Minister of State, 1951–5	Secretary of State for Commonwealth Relations, 1955–1960 Lord President, 1957–60 Foreign Secretary, 1960–3 Prime Minister, 1963–4 Foreign Secretary, 1970–
T. G. D. Galbraith	Under-Secretary, 1959–62	Whip, 1950–7 Civil Lord of the Admiralty, 1957–9 Ministry of Transport, Parliamentary Secretary, 1963–4
Niall Macpherson (Lord Drumalbyn)	Under-Secretary, 1955–60	Board of Trade, Parliamentary Secretary, 1960–2 Minister of Pensions and National Insurance, 1962–3 Board of Trade, Minister of State, 1963–4 Minister without Portfolio, 1970–
Lord John Hope	Under-Secretary, 1957–9	Commonwealth Relations Office, Under-Secretary, 1956–7 Minister of Works, 1959–62
R. Brooman-White	Under-Secretary, 1960–3	Whip, 1957–60
J. A. Stodart	Under-Secretary, 1963–4	Agriculture, Fisheries and Food, Parliamentary Secretary, 1970–
Gordon Campbell	Under-Secretary, 1963–4	Whip, 1962–3

	Scottish Office	Other departments
Judith Hart	Under-Secretary, 1964–6	Commonwealth Relations Office, Minister of State, 1966–7 Minister of Social Security, 1967–8 Paymaster General, 1968–9 Minister of Overseas Development, 1969–70
Bruce Millan	Under-Secretary, 1966–70	Defence, Under-Secretary for Air Force, 1964–6

often happens that a Scottish Secretary has been educated entirely in England, yet finds himself in charge of the Scottish educational system. Labour Scottish Secretaries, by contrast, have invariably been educated at Scottish day schools and universities.

These facts have several implications for the power of the Scottish ministers. In the case of the Labour Party, their Scottish M.P.s and ministers display such a distinctively Scottish character that they are in danger of being isolated from the rest of the party in the Commons and in the government. They are seen at Westminster as Scottish specialists, and their ministerial immobility reflects this. Perhaps sensing the danger of this, many adamantly refuse to sanction more devolution which would cut them off further from the floor of the House or advancement within British government. The Scottish Conservatives, being socially integrated with the rest of the party, and quite mobile as ministers, feel more confident to experiment with devolution, as the Scottish convention proposal shows. This is despite the fact that the Conservatives would rarely command a majority in such a body. Within the Cabinet, the Labour Secretary commands respect for the solid Labour constituency he represents. The Conservative Secretary makes up for his lack of grass-roots support by the very good social contacts which he usually has with the Prime Minister and other leaders of his party.

In Scotland, the party distinction has a slightly different effect. Labour Secretaries know their Scotland very well, but like the Scottish 'dominie' (school master), they want their pupils to keep their distance. They tend to think that they 'know what is best for Scotland' and to resent criticism. Conservative Secretaries are less sure of their ground, and find social communication more of a problem. But their contacts with business are good, and they soon learn the economic and political facts of Scottish life. They are flexible, and although Anglicised, show a surprising pride in many things Scottish. Most of the increase in the powers of the Scottish Office has come under Conservative governments. Examples are the additional functions of electricity (1954), roads (1956), and economic planning (1962), and the appointment of a Minister of State in 1951. The move to St Andrew's House in 1939 was accomplished under a Conservative Secretary of State for Scotland, D. J. Colville.

Just how the Secretary of State for Scotland goes about his task of 'getting the goods for Scotland' must remain something of a mystery, in view of the secrecy of Cabinet proceedings and administration generally in Britain. Occasionally the publication of memoirs throws some light on the situation, as does the evidence given to official bodies such as the Select Committee on Scottish Affairs and the Commission on the Constitution. But one of the hall-marks of the present system of Scottish (or indeed British) government is that the public rarely gets to know all the factors which determine the decisions which are taken. It cannot tell what the Scottish Secretary has done within the privacy of the Cabinet, nor how Scottish Office civil servants have argued the Scottish case in Whitehall. The official consensus is that this system pays Scotland, since it prevents wider political pressures (presumably from England) raising objections to a favoured treatment for Scotland. A contrary view stresses that an open system of negotiation, in which a Scottish government bargained with a British government in London for resources, would produce much better results for Scotland.

Analogies with other countries are mostly inconclusive. In federal systems for example, notably the United States, there is much competition between the states for federal aid, and much of the bargaining takes place openly in Congress. It is difficult for the poorer states to maintain an equality of services with the richer, since there is usually a requirement that federal assistance must be matched by a contribution from the states. Poor states cannot afford this matching element as easily as richer states. This inequality is fast disappearing in the United States, however, as federal subsidies grow, and more centralised federal systems, such as the German Federal Republic and Australia, combine autonomous units of government with a financial system which subsidises the poor ones at the expense of the rich. Although more open than in Britain, the negotiations for such subsidies are less 'political' than they are in the United States. The Northern Ireland arrangement provided an equality of services with the rest of the U.K. through an elaborate, and secret, negotiating machinery between the two governments. In recent years, however, the Stormont system has collapsed under the strain of civil disturbances.

These examples from countries relatively close to Great Britain in political culture, yet diverse in constitution, give little guidance to understanding the Scottish case. It is impossible to show that Scotland would be better off financially if a separate Scottish government negotiated with a British one in London. Federal systems, especially decentralised ones, seem to place obstacles in the way of the poorer states (and Scotland is somewhat poorer than England) gaining at the expense of the rich. On the other hand, political pressure, if organised in a state legislature, government agency, party machine, or interest group, is more effective than if no such organisations existed. The existence of the Scottish Office, and other Scottish political and industrial organisations, gives Scotland a political advantage not possessed by any region of England. Perhaps a separate Scottish government and legislature would increase that advantage, not diminish it. It would certainly allow for a greater range of variation in policy-making between Scotland and England, since the necessity for Cabinet approval for purely Scottish matters would disappear.

How much does Cabinet approval for these matters bear on the situation under the present system? Here it is necessary to return to the old question, what is Scottish and what is British? The Cabinet spend very little time on purely Scottish affairs, but this does not mean that what it does decide will not affect Scotland equally with the rest of the country. A decision to raise taxes for example, or to extend the range of social services, will apply to the whole of the U.K. In education, the raising of the school-leaving age, or a policy of comprehensive schools, will apply to the separate educational systems of England, Wales and Scotland. Proposals to reform industrial relations, to negotiate for entry into the E.E.C., or to change the structure of the National Health Service (to mention some of the most important policy decisions of recent years) affect the whole country. Even such peculiarly Scottish arrangements as the structure of local government and Highland crofting depend on decisions taken on local government and agriculture generally in Britain.

All this means that the Scottish Secretary must play a full part in Cabinet discussions, and indeed be more widely briefed than the majority of his colleagues, whose departmental responsibilities are narrower. Decisions taken by English ministers may have immediate repercussions in Scotland – usually because Scots demand parity with England. Examples of this can be found in the level of wage increases for teachers (negotiated separately for Scottish and English teachers, but made 'comparable' by demand), the amount of road-building and the level of subsidy to public transport.

To be thus watchful in the Cabinet imposes a tremendous strain on a Scottish Secretary, and there is a danger that he will be known there entirely for his interjections 'But remember, Scotland is different' or 'Of course Scotland will need as much, or rather more' to everyone else's proposal. A sort of 'log-rolling' can develop in which the Scottish Secretary backs up the Minister for Agriculture or Education or Transport, in the knowledge that increased expenditure for these departments will not penalise but help him in securing more for Scotland. He thus has many potential allies in the Cabinet, who will not resent Scotland getting perhaps more than its share of housing subsidies, schools, and roads in return for support for their policies.

Not all such decisions will be taken at meetings of the full Cabinet. Many important policy decisions are taken by Cabinet committees and merely ratified by the Cabinet. Membership on such committees is a test of whether a minister rates highly in the Cabinet as a key decision-maker, and here some Scottish Secretaries have had a low score. William Ross (1964–70; 1974–) was not a permanent member of the Economic Policy Committee[3] or of the 'Inner Cabinet',[4] despite its importance for Scotland, and most Scottish Secretaries are absent from the Foreign Policy Committee. Their attendance there may be thought to be unnecessary, since Scotland is not specifically involved, yet such subjects as fiscal policy and foreign trade (including policy towards E.E.C.) affect Scotland intimately, and the Scottish viewpoint may be lost in the Secretary's absence. The Minister of State, or an official of the department, may be present however. In the Conservative government formed in 1970, the representation of the Scottish Office in Cabinet committees dealing with economic matters passed from the Minister of State to the Parliamentary Under-Secretary of State for Development. This meant that the Scottish Office was represented by a more junior minister than other departments.[5]

Michael Noble (1962–4) was able to sit on whichever Cabinet committee he chose, but he could not be on everything, and in practice some decisions of significance to Scotland were almost settled in committee without his knowledge. In these cases, objections could be raised in the Cabinet itself, as was done over the siting of the Post Office Savings Bank, which Noble got transferred at the last minute from Newcastle to Glasgow.

Occasionally a dispute takes place in the Cabinet between the Scottish Secretary and other ministers, the tenor of which is reported (rightly or wrongly) in the press. Such was the alleged struggle between William Ross and Barbara Castle over the Transport Bill of 1967. Ross was anxious to increase the power of the Scottish Office over transport by establishing a Scottish Transport Group covering passenger road transport and ships. This was resisted by the Ministry of Transport and the Transport

Holding Company. He also battled against the clauses in the Bill which penalised long-distance private hauliers, since the alternative of rail haulage was not available in large areas of Scotland. He won his Transport Group, but achieved only minor concessions on the road haulage levy (cf. *Glasgow Herald*, 21 December 1967). Later, concessions were made in regulations under the Act.

Most cases involving the Scottish Secretary in a Cabinet fight have concerned government decisions on industrial matters. The siting of the steel strip-mill at Ravenscraig (Lanarkshire) in 1958 was a classic case of this kind. It was only after vigorous argument in the Cabinet and elsewhere that the unlikely decision was taken to divide the strip-mill between Scotland and Wales. More recent examples of such bargaining are found in the discussions relating to the siting of the Dounreay fast breeder reactor (1966), the Invergordon aluminium smelter (1968), aid to Upper Clyde Shipbuilders (1968–9), and its successor Govan Shipbuilders (1971), and the siting of the British Steel Corporation's new major steel plant (1971–2). In these disputes, the whole weight of the 'Scottish lobby' comes behind the Scottish Secretary in his efforts, and he must hope to win the support of the Prime Minister and the Chancellor of the Exchequer if he is to succeed. Although the Scottish Office is not the department primarily responsible for such decisions, its interests are so involved that it must take an active part in influencing them. So too, since 1964, must the Welsh Office, leaving the British department the duty of 'remembering England', which it no doubt does as a matter of course.

The spread of functions in the Scottish Office means that the Scottish Secretary is less specialised than many of his Cabinet colleagues. To them, subjects like education or agriculture or industry are the main interest, and they use most of their energies in promoting their department's point of view. There is a danger that a Scottish Secretary will neglect an area within his responsibilities that he is not personally attracted to, or knowledgeable of. Conservative Secretaries, for reasons already mentioned, seem unlikely to be greatly concerned with the details of the Scottish educational system. And few Secretaries are grounded in Scots Law, although part of their responsibility lies in this field (the same can be said of Home Secretaries and English Law). Some delegation of responsibility to the junior ministers in the Scottish Office is essential and the four junior ministers specialise in different areas of administration. Since 1970, the Under-Secretaries have been given specific titles (e.g. Parliamentary Under-Secretaries of State for Development, for Home Affairs and Agriculture, for Health and Education). They are usually put in charge of legislation in these areas during the committee stage, and they develop close relations with the appropriate departments of the Scottish Office. Ministers of State at the Scottish Office are not designated further, and one is often a member of the House of Lords. Ministers of State are, however, informally charged with special responsibilities, such as the reorganisation of local government, or regional and Highland development, which are thought to be particularly important at the time. In the closing months (October 1969 to June 1970) of the Labour government, there were two Ministers of State, one of whom was in the House of Lords, and only two Under-Secretaries. In 1974, there were two Ministers of State and three Under-Secretaries.

The junior ministers do not detract in any way from the constitutional responsibility of the Secretary for all the affairs of the Scottish Office, and he is answerable for them to the House of Commons at question time. In practice, however, junior ministers take some of these question times. Scottish Office oral questions are answered in rotation with questions to other ministers, and Scottish question times are not as frequent as the range of the Secretary's responsibilities might demand. Until session 1970–1 the Scottish Secretary answered questions orally once in five weeks, but in 1970–1 this became once in three weeks. Scottish M.P.s sometimes complain that their opportunities to ask questions are limited by these infrequent appearances, and they contrast their position with that of English M.P.s, whose questions can be directed at a greater number of ministers. But ample use is made of the opportunity to obtain written answers, which are unrestricted by the timetable of the House.

A demand is heard that the number of ministers at the Scottish Office should be increased, with a division of the Secretary's responsibilities between more than one minister. This has always been resisted on the grounds that it is essential that the Scottish Secretary be a member of the Cabinet, and if two or more ministers were responsible for the Scottish Office only one could be a member. Thus the heavy administrative responsibility of the office is the price paid for a seat at the Cabinet table.

The Lord Advocate is also a responsible minister, and is the chief law officer of the government in Scotland. Yet he was outside the House completely from October 1962 to June 1970, and although now a member, most questions to him have been ruled out of order by the Speaker as falling outside his responsibilities and within the responsibilities of the Secretary of State. The confusion arises from the fact that the administration of justice, and law and order, have been brought more closely under the Scottish Secretary's control in recent years. The reform of the sheriff courts (1971) strengthens his position in this respect, for the Scottish Office now has its own Sheriff Courts Administration. The Lord Advocate retains much of the day-to-day administrative power over the courts, including the effective power to nominate judges and sheriffs (Kilbrandon 4, p. 48).

But since he is also the chief public prosecutor (a key position under Scots criminal law) it is considered inequitable to assign to him the constitutional responsibility for the courts as well. If the Lord Advocate were to transfer his prosecuting function to the Solicitor-General for Scotland, he could become a Scottish Minister for Justice in the manner of the Lord Chancellor in England and Wales. This would relieve the Secretary of State of some of his legal burden, and clarify the Lord Advocate's position as the chief law officer of the Crown in Scotland. The written evidence of the Lord Advocate's department to the Constitutional Commission in 1969 stressed that the Lord Advocate is independent of the Secretary of State as a minister and retains all the powers which he possessed before 1885 (Kilbrandon 2, pp. 65–6). But the practice, and public understanding, of the office has been rather different, and some modification of the situation is desirable in the interests of responsible government. In December 1972, ministerial responsibility over most judicial matters was transferred to the Lord Advocate.

Reforming the structure?

The Scottish Office has not been subject to the frequent and fundamental reorganisations of government departments which have taken place in Whitehall during the 1960s. The London departments have been subject to a frenzy of desk-shifting, alteration of name-plates and erasure of letter-heads, which must have left many civil servants exhausted and cynical.

The stability of the Scottish Office rests largely on the solid foundations of nationalist vested interest and the flexibility accorded to the Secretary of State for Scotland in matters of departmental organisation. National sentiment has made it very difficult for any functions to be removed from the Scottish Office once they are granted. And any additional functions can be grafted on to the existing structure with ease, since the range of functions already operating within the Scottish Office is so great. It is difficult to think of any function which could not conceivably become part of the Scottish Office, especially as the Secretary of State is informally held to be responsible for all government in Scotland (Gilmour, pp. 25, 65; Kilbrandon 2, p. 4). This would, of course, require the agreement of other ministers. Such agreement is not required for a reorganisation within the Scottish Office, however. In 1962, the Scottish Development Department was created by taking some of the functions from the Scottish Home Department and the Department of Health for Scotland and giving them to the new department. What was left of the two original departments then became the Scottish Home and Health Department. In 1973, a similar re-arrangement produced the Scottish Economic Planning Department.

The history of the Scottish Office would seem to point to two main influences in its development. One is nationalism, which demands that more administration be conducted in Scotland. The other is the pressure from within the administration to decentralise functions to Scotland, on grounds of convenience and efficiency. It is of course possible for the latter to be a disguise for the former, especially as the civil servants of the Scottish Office are themselves the important administrative pressure for decentralisation. In their case, nationalism may be confused with the vested interest which any administrative organisation has in furthering its own power. The wider nationalism helps to strengthen their position in relation to Whitehall, but it weakens it in Scotland. Scottish Nationalists attack the Scottish Office as the stooge of London government, and see an increase in its powers as a sham. Many other Scots distrust its complexity and secrecy, and would prefer a more open form of Scottish government. But a large residue are probably indifferent to how the machinery of government is shaped – they are concerned only with the results of policies. The Kilbrandon Report revealed that more than half of the respondents questioned in a survey in Scotland had not heard of the Scottish Office, and the remaining respondents were largely ignorant of its responsibilities (Kilbrandon 5, par. 379).

One could argue that the range of functions exercised by the Scottish Office is both too great and too small. Too great in that it means that one man, the Scottish Secretary, is made constitutionally responsible for subjects as varied as law and order, education, agriculture and economic development. Even under the new super-ministries in Whitehall, such diversity is not reached. The Scottish Secretary must, of necessity, leave a great deal of policy formulation to his civil servants or to his junior ministers, who could suffer from a lack of strong direction. The machine is so big that it threatens to become the master.

But in another sense it is not big enough. There are curious gaps in the Scottish Office's powers, where it shares the responsibility for a function with another department. The principal divisions of authority occur in (1) education, (2) energy, (3) transport, (4) economic development, and (5) health and social security.

Finally, it should be remembered that devolution involves a fundamental restructuring of the system to include a Scottish legislative, as well as an administrative, branch.

(1) *Education.* Universities and research councils belong loosely with the Department of Education and Science (DES), while

schools and the rest of higher education belong with the Scottish Education Department. But the Scottish Secretary has responsibilities for the four ancient universities (St Andrews, Glasgow, Aberdeen and Edinburgh) under the Universities (Scotland) Acts, and through his patronage of Principals and Regius Chairs. Student grants are administered by the Scottish Education Department, though their amount is determined by the Secretary of State for Education and Science (see Mrs Thatcher's announcement on grants for students in Scottish universities in May 1971, *Glasgow Herald*, 22 May 1971). The Scottish Department also plans for the development of all higher education in Scotland (cf. *Student Numbers in Higher Education in Scotland*, Memorandum by Scottish Education Department, HMSO, Edinburgh 1970).

The recent enquiries have looked at the position and have not recommended any change. It is argued for the *status quo* that since the universities are only loosely under ministerial control in Britain, and are subject to an intermediate body, the University Grants Committee (UGC), the position of the Scottish universities is one of greater independence that might at first appear from their relationship with the DES. The alternative of a Scottish University Grants Committee is claimed to be unsatisfactory in that its academic members would be unable to detach themselves sufficiently from the pressures of their own universities, something they can do in the UGC, since its 14 academic members represent 43 universities. The Scottish universities, it is argued, are part of the larger British system of university education (a fifth of the students are English), and therefore British administration is appropriate. There is a fear, even in Scotland, that the Scottish universities might become too parochial or politicised under Scottish control (Kilbrandon 4, pp. 101–10; W. H. Walsh in Wolfe, pp. 120–2, *Scotsman*, 5 March 1975).

On the other side, it is said that since the Scottish educational system is made up of inter-related parts it should all be brought under Scottish administration. The distinct pattern of Scottish schooling leads on to both sectors of higher education (university and non-university), for the Scottish SCE examinations, which differ from the English GCE in range of subjects and standard, are the basic entrance requirements. The rapid development of the non-university sector of higher education, which is subject to the Scottish Office, has increased the case for an integrated administrative structure, especially as some colleges of education are awarding degrees in collaboration with the universities.

But the demand for change is muted, with the universities largely satisfied with the present structure (but see R. E. Bell in Wolfe, pp. 108–19). The Scottish Office is represented on the UGC by the Secretary of the Scottish Education Department (a civil servant), and on the Council for National Academic Awards (CNAA) by an H.M. Inspector. These bodies have not obviously affected the considerable diversity between Scotland and England in types of degree and diploma.

As for the schools sector, the close control by the Scottish Education Department (SED) seems to meet with general approval. It is at any rate one of the most autonomous parts of Scottish administration, for the English Ministry exerts almost no influence in Scotland at this level (cf. ch. 11). Thus any impetus for reform of Scottish educational administration seems likely to come from the institutions of higher education other than the universities, for they feel that the Scottish Office, by increasing its control over the universities, could integrate higher education and avoid the 'binary' structure adopted in England. This structure has so far not been followed in Scotland, where 'polytechnics' on the English model have not been established. There are three types of higher education institutions in Scotland: (1) universities, under the UGC, DES, and SED, (2) central institutions (colleges of art, domestic science, music and technical colleges) and colleges of education under the SED, and (3) colleges of further education, and technical (etc.) colleges, under local authorities. In England, the system is binary, for there are no 'central institutions'. The independence of such institutions from local authorities in Scotland is especially noteworthy, given the tensions which have arisen on account of that connection in England.

(2) *Energy*.   The post-1945 nationalisation of coal and gas placed these industries under a British ministry (Fuel and Power). Some decentralisation exists, however, through the two Scottish areas of the National Coal Board and the Scottish Gas Board (which acts in conjunction with the Gas Council). Atomic energy (other than some nuclear-powered electricity generating stations) is developed by the Atomic Energy Authority. All these now come under the Department of Industry.

Electricity, on the other hand, is totally under the Scottish Office (through two boards). This did not take place without a struggle. Thomas Johnston, the Secretary of State during most of the Second World War, secured for his department the North of Scotland Hydro-Electric Board (created in 1943), and the South of Scotland Electricity Board was transferred to the Scottish Office from the British Electricity Authority in 1954, as a sympathetic gesture towards the devolutionist sentiments of the time (cf. the *Report of the Royal Commission on Scottish Affairs, 1954*, Cmd. 9212, 'Balfour Commission').

There are obvious problems in the above arrangements. While the gas and electricity boards are autonomous in respect of pricing policies (Scottish prices are relatively high for gas but low for electricity), the price of coal is fixed for the whole country by the National Coal Board (NCB), and this also affects gas and electricity. The electricity industry is expected to sustain coal-mining by purchases of coal for power stations, although it is more expensive to do so than to use oil, thus leading to higher electricity prices. If all were under the same department, co-ordination might be easier. On the other hand, the development of natural gas from the North Sea, with a pipeline from source to consumer, supports a British administration and will lead to further centralisation through the Gas Council as supplier.

North Sea oil is much less clear in its implications for administration in Scotland. As the discoveries were made in the waters off the Scottish coast, the Scottish Office was immediately involved. It had, for example, to give final planning permission for on-shore support bases, including construction sites, harbours and refineries. It was also the department to supervise local government in providing 'infrastructure' (housing, roads, water, etc.).

After some hesitation, the Conservative government in 1973 appointed Lord Polwarth as Minister of State in the Scottish Office with special responsibility for oil. He was also to chair an advisory body, the Oil Development Council for Scotland. The new Scottish Economic Planning Department soon busied itself with the question of on-shore oil developments, and the Scottish Secretary had to sanction these, often after lengthy public inquiries.

But the Department of Energy had no intention of relinquishing its hold on oil, and the Offshore Supplies Office (though moved to Glasgow) was part of its responsibilities. There is thus the dilemma of divided departmental control over oil developments, with all the added political implications which flow from this in a period of heightened nationalism. Both the Labour and Conservative parties have pledged themselves to use oil revenues to benefit Scottish industry, but the rate and conditions of oil exploitation seem to be firmly within the remit of Whitehall (though under strong pressure from Edinburgh).

(3) *Transport.* Transport in Scotland is a politically sensitive area of administration, and has distinct problems of its own. Large distances on land have to be covered by public transport over uneconomic routes, especially in the Highlands. There is the additional problem of sea and air routes to Orkney, Shetland and the west-coast islands, which emphasises further the special features of Scotland's geography. Related to the provision of transport is the building of roads, railways, harbours and airports.

The case for an integrated transport policy has been argued

for many years, and in the case of Scotland, it might appear to be imperative. Yet it is not easily obtained by the administrative structure. The Scottish Office has only recently entered the field, and it is by no means in control of transport policy for Scotland. It has been building roads and bridges since 1956, as a result of a recommendation of the Balfour Commission. Harbours, however, are not a Scottish Office responsibility, and are subject to the National Ports Council and the Department of the Environment. Airports are now built and maintained either by the British Airports Authority (Scottish Airports), or by the Civil Aviation Authority (the Highland airports). BAA and CAA come under the Department of Industry.

The provision of transport itself is similarly split between different authorities. Railways belong to British Rail, and thus to the Department of the Environment (ex-Ministry of Transport). State air services are provided by British Airways, which have a separate unit, Scottish Airways (established 1971), to run their domestic Scottish flights. These are all linked to the Department of Industry, in so far as ministerial responsibility is involved. Passenger road transport and sea transport (except Stranraer–Larne) were transferred from the Ministry of Transport to the Scottish Office by the Transport Act of 1968. The actual operating unit is the Scottish Transport Group, appointed by the Scottish Secretary. Freight transport does not come under the Scottish Office, but under the National Freight Corporation and the Department of the Environment.

All this amounts once more to a confusion of functional and geographic administration. The function of transport is split between various authorities, and so is the operating area of these authorities. Much criticism has been levied at the system. The Scottish Council (Development and Industry) called for a Scottish Ports Authority at the end of 1969, and others have attacked the exclusion of the Stranraer–Larne shipping route from the Scottish Transport Group, especially since it is the only profitable public shipping line operating in Scotland. The closure of railway lines by a British Minister, although such lines often play a large part in the economic and social life of rural areas of Scotland, may be considered unsatisfactory. For example, the economic development of the Borders and the Highlands depends largely on the provision of good rail communications, and the closure of the Edinburgh–Hawick–Carlisle line in 1969 contributed to the failure of the Borders Plan, which the Scottish Office was promoting at the time. Similarly, the Dingwall–Kyle of Lochalsh closure was proposed in 1970 by British Rail at a time when no satisfactory road alternative was available.

The then Ministry of Transport told the Select Committee on

Scottish Affairs that the division of responsibility for the various transport media was 'on the face of it not sensible' (SCSA 1, p. 35), but they considered that a transfer of railways to the Scottish Office would cause formidable administrative difficulties, notably in respect for investment in rolling-stock and inter-regional services and track. They did agree that there was maybe a case for making the Scottish Secretary responsible for payments of grants for unremunerative passenger services in Scotland. The Committee also thought this could be done, especially as local authorities might soon be asked to subsidise uneconomic services. The decision on whether to close a line or a service would then be taken in Scotland, and the subsidy found there. (Michael Noble, when Scottish Secretary (1962–4), had the power (subject to Cabinet approval) to delay rail closures in Scotland which he did not approve of.) But they concluded that on balance it was better for British Rail to deal with one government department rather than two since 'if British Rail are compelled to negotiate with different departments on what is basically the same problem, and if different criteria are to be used by different departments, it is unlikely that either British Rail or the users or the taxpayers will be satisfied with the fairness of the result' (SCSA 1, p. 38). So no change. These remarks, incidentally, do not square up with the practice of Scottish administration in other fields, and it is open to question whether British Rail does face 'basically the same problem' in Scotland as elsewhere.

Similarly, with air, ships and freight the Committee stood by the *status quo*. While deprecating the fact that only the airlines themselves had to look at the needs of the community for air services, they suggested that the Scottish Economic Planning Board and the Department of Trade and Industry could fulfil this function (although the airlines are not represented on the former). Despite the obvious ministerial struggles during the passage of the Transport Act 1968, and the difficulty of reconciling Scottish with English needs, no change was suggested on ships or freight. Behind much of the conventional wisdom on transport administration lies the assumption that transport between Scotland and England or Northern Ireland must come under a British authority (hence the solution for rail, long-distance freight, Stranraer–Larne, and the air services from Glasgow and Edinburgh to London and abroad). This must be balanced against the need to plan for an integrated transport policy to account for Scotland's special needs. It seems quite probable that despite the caution of the Select Committee's 1970 Report, future practice will increasingly emphasise a purely Scottish administration for most of the rail, road, and air services now under British authorities.

(4) *Economic development.* For many years, the Secretary of State has been charged informally with the oversight of the Scottish economy. Scottish ministers speak in parliamentary debates on the Scottish aspects of British economic legislation, although they are not constitutionally responsible for the work of other departments (except in the sense of the 'collective responsibility' of all ministers for government actions). Most matters of economic policy fall to non-Scottish departments, yet since 1962 the Scottish Office has entered the field of economic planning. It did so without actually increasing its executive functions. Economic plans (*Central Scotland*, 1963, Cmnd. 2188; *The Scottish Economy, 1965 to 1970*, 1966, Cmnd. 2864) have been produced and economic planning agencies (the Regional Development Division of the Scottish Office, 1964; the Scottish Economic Planning Board and Council, 1965; the Highlands and Islands Development Board, 1965; Economics and Statistics Unit, 1970; Scottish Economic Planning Department, 1973; Scottish Development Agency, 1975) formed. In this way, it has generally taken a much more active interest in the economic life of Scotland. An assessment of the policy-making process in this field will be found in chapter 11.

Here the functional distribution will be briefly assessed. Most of the enquiries into Scottish administration have been exercised on this topic, but until 1973–4 very few material alterations were suggested. Taxation has nearly always been considered the prerogative of the Treasury, but regional allowances and investment grants (e.g. the regional employment premium from 1967 to manufacturing industries in development areas) are now standard practice. It is stressed that these are not given to Scotland as such, but to development areas throughout Britain. Moreover, the provision of a 'Scottish Budget', although realised in 1969, is fraught with complications and was not attempted again. Such a budget is, however, necessary when devolution is introduced, and would relate either to Scottish Office expenditure only or to all public expenditure in Scotland. Under the Labour government's proposals in 1974, the former seems likely. The sources of revenue in the Scottish Budget are also open to argument. Few proposals suggest major tax powers for a Scottish Parliament, and the usual solution is to give minor tax powers with most revenue coming from a block grant voted by the United Kingdom Parliament. Nevertheless, this represents quite a marked shift from the conservatism of earlier enquiries, which rejected any notion of a separate Scottish Budget (see the Balfour Commission *Report*, 1954; the Toothill Committee *Report on the Scottish Economy*, 1961; and the Select Committee Report on Scottish Affairs *Report*, 1970). It is more in line with the Scottish Liberal Party's evidence to the Kilbrandon Commission (*Scottish Self-Government*, 1970), and the views of John Mackintosh (Mackintosh 1, pp. 204–7).

The administrative problems of economic development have also become more controversial of late, and opinion has swung away from retaining the monopoly of Whitehall in this respect. Under the old system, the 'Board of Trade' functions relating to the distribution and support of industry (now in the Department of Industry) placed economic development largely outside Scottish administration. This was justified on the grounds that industry could not be steered to Scotland from England if the steering ministry were not British. Firms are diverted to Scotland and other development areas not only by the 'carrot' of grants and other allowances but by the 'stick' of being denied an industrial development certificate (IDC) in the prosperous south. A purely Scottish department could not wield the stick against English firms, and an English department would have no inclination to support a Scottish development area outside its jurisdiction. Since Scottish industrial development depends largely on economic policy in England, G.B. Departments of Trade and Industry are considered logical. The same is held to be true of the organisation of the large industries such as steel, shipbuilding and aerospace engineering. In each case, a British strategy is required, and Scotland must not be seen as having its own steel, etc., industry.

Pressure during 1971 from the Scottish Office and the Scottish Council (Development and Industry), as well as from other Scottish industrial organisations, convinced the government that some changes were needed in the administration of industrial incentives. A Scottish Industrial Development Office (SIDO) was set up in March 1972, with a director appointed from the private sector. Although it was within the Department of Trade and Industry, and not within the Scottish Office, the SIDO had powers to select firms for industrial grants, and to administer these grants in Scotland, without reference back to Whitehall. Moreover, it was in close liaison with the Scottish Office, through the Scottish Economic Planning Board (of which its director was a member), the Scottish Economic Planning Department and a new advisory Scottish Industrial Development Board. Similar arrangements were made for Wales, and for the English regions (*Industrial and Regional Development*, Cmnd. 4942, HMSO, March 1972).

The thinking behind this development was largely inspired by the Scottish Office, and by Scottish industrialists such as the late Hugh Stenhouse (who chaired Govan Shipbuilders, the successors of Upper Clyde Shipbuilders, for a few months). Their proposals went to the Cabinet, and were endorsed at the end of 1971 (*Glasgow Herald*, 24 March 1972). Although the devolved industrial offices were reproduced in Wales and the English regions, the superior resources of the Scottish Office in the government machinery once more gave Scotland the edge over the rest of the country. Perhaps one indication of this was the massive subsidy given to Govan Shipbuilders in March 1972.

A major change in thinking about administration in Scottish economic development came in 1974, when the Labour government announced the setting up of a Scottish Development Agency in the Scottish Office. This agency aids the regeneration of Scottish industry, and will supplement in Scotland the functions of the National Enterprise Board (which has powers to extend state ownership). Selective regional assistance also comes under the Scottish Office from 1975. This marks an important acquisition of economic administrative powers for the Scottish Office, and anticipated economic powers for a devolved Scottish government, although sections of Labour opinion wanted to keep such powers apart from the Scottish devolution structure, and under the Secretary of State for Scotland, who would remain a member of the U.K. Government.

(5) *Health and social security*. The creation of the Department of Health and Social Security in October 1968 brought about a new anomaly in British administration. This department combined the Ministry of Health and the Ministry of Social Security, so that in England the National Health Service and social services (comprising both personal care and cash benefits) now came together under one Minister. In Wales and Scotland, however, the National Health Service and personal care services were left under the administration of the Welsh and Scottish Offices, with the Department of Health and Social Security operating there in its cash benefits capacity only. Thus England enjoys a unified administration of health and social security, while Wales and Scotland do not.

The reasons for giving the National Health Service to the Scottish Office in 1948 related to the existing tradition of health administration in the Department of Health for Scotland, the distinct local government structure from which many health services were inherited, the greater predominance of the teaching hospitals in the hospital system, and the problems of sparsely populated areas. National Insurance, on the other hand, was transferred to the Ministry of National Insurance from the Department of Health for Scotland in 1945, on the grounds that since cash benefits were uniform throughout the country, they should be administered uniformly. War and disablement pensions remained with the Ministry of Pensions, where they had been since 1916, until in 1953 these ministers were combined to form the Ministry of Pensions and National Insurance.

In 1968 the government felt that it was desirable to integrate health and social security administration, and the Department of Health and Social Security was formed to achieve this in England. As for Scotland, two alternatives for change were open. Either the Ministry of Social Security could lose its functions in Scotland to the Scottish Office, or the Scottish Office could lose its health and personal social services functions to the Department of Health and Social Security. In the event, no change occurred, largely because of London based administrative vested interest in the case of the first alternative, and because of Scottish nationalism and Scottish Office administrative vested interest in the case of the second.

The result is another 'odd arrangement', in the words of the Secretary of the Scottish Home and Health Department (Kilbrandon 4, p. 43). While the system does not purport to give a 'different kind of service with a different objective in Scotland than in England and Wales' (loc. cit.), Scotland does come off better in terms of the ratio of G.P.s to patients, and of staffed hospital beds and health expenditure to the population than England and Wales. Much of this is due to the uneven distribution of the population and the different historical tradition (medicine is exceptionally well provided for in the universities, with about one quarter of all British medical graduates coming from Scotland). Some of the result can also be accredited to the Scottish Office, for successfully maintaining the differential.

On the social security side, the principle of equality of benefit may also work to Scotland's advantage. Despite the lower income level in Scotland, benefits are the same in London, Glasgow or Stornoway (the unemployment rate in the last-named often reaches 30%). Earnings-related benefits and other personal payments have modified this situation, but there seems to be as great (or as little) a case for putting benefits under Scottish administration as having health there. A Scottish administration would mean that Scottish variations could be taken into account, and liaison made easier with the local authority social work departments, whose activities are co-ordinated by the Social Work Services Group of the Scottish Education Department. The integration of the health service (comprising hospitals, G.P.s and local authority health services) in area health boards was engineered by the Scottish Office, and it would be desirable to take account of social services, both cash and personal, somewhere in the scheme. On the other hand, some would argue that a uniform standard in both health and social security is best achieved by one department operating over the whole of the United Kingdom. This is another area of Scottish administration in which the arguments have yet to be resolved, but where further decentralisation seems likely.

Conclusion

Scotland is governed by three levels of government: London, Edinburgh and the local authority. It differs from England in having a strong middle tier, representing the central government decentralised to a region. The Scottish Office is more than a device of government, however, since its origins are historic as well as administrative, and the region comprises a nation. The previous statehood of Scotland and the provisions of the Union of 1707 are its heredity, and national consciousness provides its life-force. The Secretary of State for Scotland represents Scotland in the British government but he occupies a difficult position, in that his freedom of action is circumscribed by the need for collective policy-making by the British Cabinet. This inevitably means that he often merely administers British policies in Scotland. The major British departments usually carry more weight than the Scottish Office in such deliberations, and if a conflict arises 'Scotland's interests' may have to be sacrificed to a greater British interest.

But if it is suggested that the Scottish Secretary's wishes should always prevail, this would negate Cabinet government and the collective responsibility of the British government for all its policies. It is also impossible, in the present system, to use the argument that the political representation of Scotland can on its own determine the policies for Scotland. A Labour Scotland must accept a Conservative administration.

The record of Scottish administration is surprisingly good, despite its built-in disadvantages. Scottish Secretaries have not ranked among the foremost politicians of the land, partly because they impose on themselves a self-denying ordinance in taking Scotland for their parish instead of the greater parliamentary and executive arenas, and partly because the work-load is so crippling, reducing them often to political shadows. It is also true that Scottish M.P.s have not provided a fertile field of recruitment to high office, for reasons to be discussed later.

The division of functions between the Scottish Office and G.B. departments, while defensible, is in many places illogical. Defining what is predominantly 'British' and what is predominantly 'Scottish' has led to notable impasses and anomalies. Short of independence for Scotland, there will always be this problem, but devolution should improve the structure and extend the area of Scottish decision-making. Scottish government should serve two purposes: to run those things which must be done differently in Scotland (e.g. law, education, housing and industrial development), and to co-ordinate government activity on all fronts to take account of Scottish needs (e.g. economic planning). This already happens in some measure, and the signs are that Scotland will strengthen its grip on both fronts in the future.

4

The public service in Scotland

The full extent of the public service in Scotland, and indeed in the United Kingdom as a whole, is extremely difficult to determine with accuracy. It can be held to include not only the civil servants in government departments as popularly understood, but a vast array of industrial civil servants, such as naval dockyard workers, employees of public corporations like the Post Office, British Rail, the National Coal Board and the British Steel Corporation, and the staff of the National Health Service. Numerous other bodies are in close relationship with the central public service and are publicly financed, such as the research institutes and councils, which employ many university graduates, and distinctively Scottish bodies like the Crofters Commission and the Scottish Tourist Board. Members of the armed forces and the staff of defence establishments must also be taken into account, from the rocket-testers on the Isle of Barra to the crews of submarines in the Gare Loch.

Local government provides another large sector of public employment, and encompasses not only the administrators of the local authorities, but also other employees such as schoolteachers, housebuilders, bus drivers and conductors. Further removed are nominally private bodies such as the universities, Govan Shipbuilders, and the Scottish Council (Development and Industry), which rely heavily on public funds.

Taken together, these bodies are very important in the pattern of Scottish employment, and it may be that the public sector is disproportionately strong in Scotland. Many of the heavy industries, such as coal, steel and shipbuilding, which are particularly important in the Scottish economy (see table 3, p. 11), have been nationalised or are heavily subsidised by the state. The construction industry, transport, education and medicine are also important in Scotland, and are largely dependent on public employment for funds.

If Scotland is thus heavily committed to the public sector, it is relevant to ask what implications this has for the Scottish political system. Does it reinforce the autonomy of that system within that of the U.K., or does it weaken it by setting up more numerous ties with London and overall British policy-making?

It is clear that only a small sphere of the employment in the public sector is taken up by purely 'Scottish' bodies. Most of the large employers such as the public corporations and nationalised industries, are London-based, in terms of the location of their headquarters. And if one restricts one's attention to the civil service (non-industrial civil servants), the picture of London dominance is further maintained.

In table 9(a), the category 'other Scottish departments' consists of departments, agencies and legal services whose headquarters are in Scotland. The principal ones are the Sheriff Clerk's Service (357), the Registers of Scotland (267), the Procurator Fiscal Service (266) and the General Register Office (Scotland) (243). In table 9(c), the category 'all Scottish departments' refers to all departments whose functions are confined to Scotland, and is thus a combination of the Scottish Office and 'other Scottish departments'.

Within Scotland, civil servants are distributed between the principal groups in the following proportions: Scottish Office, 14·5%; all Scottish departments, 16·9%; G.B./U.K. departments, 83·1%. Most of the industrial staff in the Ministry of Defence in Scotland are employed in naval establishments such as Rosyth dockyard and Faslane submarine base.

Table 9   (a) *Non-industrial staff of civil service departments employed in Scotland, July 1970*

Department	No. of staff (rounded off)	
Scottish Office		
Agriculture and Fisheries for Scotland	2,900 ⎫	
Scottish Development	1,000 ⎪	
Scottish Education	900 ⎬	8,300
Scottish Home and Health (incl. prisons)	3,500 ⎭	
Other Scottish departments	1,910	
Customs and Excise	2,000	
Defence	7,300	
Employment and Productivity (now Employment)	3,700	
Health and Social Security	5,900	
Inland Revenue	5,100	
National Savings	2,700	
Public Buildings and Works (now Environment)	1,700	
Technology (now Trade and Industry)	1,200	
Trade (now Trade and Industry)	1,500	
Other departments	1,590	
All departments	42,900	

(b) *Industrial staff of civil service departments employed in Scotland, July 1970*

Department	No. of staff
Scottish Office	
Agriculture and Fisheries for Scotland	511 ⎫
Scottish Development	24 ⎬ 980
Scottish Home and Health	445 ⎭
Scottish Record Office	23
Board of Trade	258
Defence	15,913
Public Buildings and Works	2,997
Technology	490
Other departments	544
All departments	21,205

(c) *Proportions of U.K. home civil servants employed in (i) all departments in Scotland, (ii) all Scottish departments (i.e. excluding G.B., U.K.), and (iii) the Scottish Office, July 1970*

		No. of staff	% of comparable U.K. category
(i)	All departments in Scotland	64,105	9·1
	Non-industrial	42,900	8·6
	Industrial	21,205	10·3
(ii)	All Scottish departments	10,882	1·5
	Non-industrial	9,879	1·9
	Industrial	1,003	0·5
(iii)	Scottish Office	9,280	1·3
	Non-industrial	8,300	1·7
	Industrial	980	0·5

(Figures supplied by the Civil Service Department. Those for January 1970 are published in *Civil Service Statistics 1970*, HMSO, 1971.)

The fact that the Scottish departments are outnumbered by the non-Scottish in the ratio of five to one is not a good guide to the relative importance of the Scottish and non-Scottish parts of the civil service, nor can it be assumed that the non-Scottish bodies do in practice look more to London than to Edinburgh for guidance. In the first place, the position of the Scottish Office in the public service is pre-eminent on account of the range of functions it possesses and the responsibility of the Secretary of State for Scotland as overseer of all the affairs of Scotland. In some way, all departments are answerable to him for what they do in Scotland, and his voice in the Cabinet is heard on their activities as well as the voices of their respective ministers.

Secondly, the status of the Scottish Office civil servants is markedly higher than those of the other departments in Scotland. In 1970 there were about 160 members of the administrative class in the Scottish Office. This represented about 6% of the total of the former administrative class. Within the Scottish Office, the distribution was evenly shared among the constituent departments. Other departments in Scotland could muster only half-a-dozen between them (usually Scottish Controllers at Assistant Secretary rank). This is important, since the administrative class has traditionally represented that part of the civil service nearest to Ministers in the formulation and administration of policies. Although the administrative class was abolished in January 1971, the new classifications will not alter the superiority of the Scottish Office in this respect. The same is true of its strength in the establishment of professional and scientific civil servants, who, together with the senior members of the new administration group, constitute the higher civil service.

The Scottish Office's co-ordinating role, and its high status, lead it to dominate the public service in Scotland. This is partly because formal consultation is required between it and the Great Britain departments, whose Scottish controllers must deal with St Andrew's House, and not Whitehall, on many subjects. Their counterparts in the English regions find such negotiations being carried on by the men at the London headquarters. This process of consultation, with its focus on Edinburgh, tends to give the Scottish Office the lead, and to bring the G.B. departments into 'Scottish' ways, which they would not follow in England. For example, the Department of Health and Social Security in Scotland is strongly influenced by the powers of the Scottish Office and the local authorities in social work, by the existence of Scots Law in their legal activities, and by the STUC and trade unions in their industrial injuries administration. Wherever local government or legal matters are involved in the work of a G.B. department, the Scottish Office as supervising and grant-giving department is also concerned.

The non-Scottish departments are of course not necessarily non-Scottish in personnel. In fact, the overwhelming majority (about 90%) are Scots, and have been recruited in Scotland. There is, however, a greater tendency for the top jobs in these departments to be held by Englishmen, or by Scots who have worked in England, than is the case in the Scottish Office. (Only one of the six Scottish Controllers of British departments in 1970 was a Scot who had worked continuously in Scotland.) This may not be important, for most soon become Scots by adoption, partly as a result of pressure from other elements in the Scottish political system, and partly because they tend to play a Scottish role within their departments. In the words of the Regional Officer of the Ministry of Technology, giving evidence to the Select Committee on Scottish Affairs in 1969, 'I split myself into two persons, one the Ministry of Technology person nationally, the other the Ministry of Technology regional person, when I look at firms in Scotland' (SCSA, 2, p. 241).

Other British departments, such as the Ministry of Defence, tend to have a large number of non-Scottish personnel, although it should be remembered that Scottish regiments do much to stimulate a sort of Scottish nationalism (e.g. the campaign to 'Save the Argylls', 1968–70). On the fringe of the public service, the research councils are more non-Scottish than the Scottish universities, and Scotland has 10 of the 79 Medical Research Council research units (1971). These and other similar bodies give Scotland an international status and outlook, which is almost totally detached from the Scottish political system.

When one turns to the Scottish Office, the full 'Scottish' character of the public service in Scotland becomes evident. Its members are an integral part of the Home Civil Service of Great Britain, since that Service is governed by the conditions laid down by the Civil Service Department. The Civil Service Commissioners conduct the entrance examinations for the recruitment of 'established' (permanent and pensionable) staff in all departments, including the Scottish Office. Applicants from Scotland for the higher posts equivalent to those in the old administrative class go to London to be interviewed for a place in one of the departments. Strictly speaking, there is no freedom for an applicant to choose the department which he wishes to join, although he is asked to state his preferences. Some Scots will choose a British department as a first preference, while some English applicants may choose the Scottish Office.

These preferences are not published, and one must hazard a guess at their character from the actual placings, which show that the Scottish Office recruits Scots[1] overwhelmingly, but that they represent only half of the total number of Scots who are successful. This is because Scots are relatively successful in the Civil Service examinations (see below), while only two or three posts at assistant principal grade have been filled in the Scottish Office each year. It may therefore be that as many Scots as wish to, go to Edinburgh, while the others go to England or the Diplomatic Service (entry for the latter is by separate tests, however). Under the new system, begun in 1971, recruitment of non-professional graduates is normally to the administration trainee grade (formerly the assistant principal grade), which may lead to appointment as a principal after training. The number of administration trainees recruited to the Scottish Office annually is around 10 (some graduates fresh from university, some graduate and non-graduate civil servants of executive officer or equivalent professional or scientific level). Around two-thirds of these trainees will move out into the mainstream as higher executive officers after 2–3 years, and the remainder will move into the 'fast stream' for another 2–3 years' training before becoming principals.

As an illustration of a typical intake under the old system one may take that of 1968 (derived from the Civil Service Commissioners' Report for that year). This lists the successful candidates' names, the departments they are assigned to, and their education. Extracting the 'Scots', and those entering the Scottish Office, one gets this result:

C. J. A. Chivers (Treasury). Glasgow High School, Glasgow University, 1st Cl. Classics.

Evelyn Dobson (Public Building and Works), Bromley High School, St Andrew's University, 1st Cl. History. (Probably English)

J. M. Currie (Scottish Home and Health), Blairs College, Glasgow University, 2nd Cl. French/American Studies.

Elizabeth Graham (Agriculture and Fisheries for Scotland), Dunfermline High School, Edinburgh University, Cl. II(i) History.

B. V. Philp (Scottish Home and Health) Heriots (Edinburgh), Edinburgh University, Cl. II(i) Economics.

C. A. Munro (Inland Revenue), Watsons (Edinburgh), Edinburgh University, Cl. II(ii) French.

J. S. B. Martin (Scottish Education), Bell-Baxter (Cupar), St Andrew's University, Cl. I Chemistry.

G. Robson (no placing published; now in the Scottish Development Department), St Joseph's (Dumfries), Edinburgh University, Cl. II(i) Politics/History.

B. S. Morris (Treasury), Morgan Academy (Dundee), Dundee University, Cl. II(i) Politics/Psychology.

I. C. Orr (Diplomatic Service), Kirkcaldy High School, St Andrew's University, Cl. I Philosophy.

A. M. Layden (Diplomatic Service), Holy Cross Academy (Edinburgh), Edinburgh University, Cl. II(i) Law/Economics.

W. B. Sinton (Diplomatic Service), Kirkcaldy High School, Edinburgh University, Cl. II(i) French.

P. Morrice (Diplomatic Service – Limited Competition), Gordonstoun, Grade 9 Officer since 1963.

In 1968, then, the Scottish Office recruited 5 Scots, while 6 went to other departments and 4 to the Diplomatic Service. During the 1960s, 6 out of a total of 30 recruits entered the Scottish Office who had been educated totally in England. At the same time 48 recruits with at least part of their education in

Scotland entered other departments, or the Diplomatic (Foreign) Service.

The Estimates Committee of the House of Commons in 1964 analysed the university degrees of the direct-entrant recruits to the administrative class from 1948 to 1963. They discovered that Scottish graduates made up 5·3% of the total entrants, while Oxford and Cambridge provided 81%, London 8% and the other British and Irish universities 4·4%.[2] Although this is by no means proportional to the number of graduates from Scottish universities (who amounted to 15–20% of the U.K. total over the period), it is distinctly better than the contribution of the English and Welsh 'red-brick' universities (40–50% of the total). Scottish graduates at the time did extremely well in the 'Method I' examinations, which were of an academic nature (18·5% of candidates successful), but less well by 'Method II' which was based on interviews and practical tests (5% successful). The success rate for all candidates was 18·7% by Method I, and 9·5% by Method II.[3] Since 1969 Method II has become the only method of direct entry from the universities to the higher civil service.

Table 10   *University background of the administrative class in the Scottish Office, May 1968*

	Oxford/Cambridge		Other universities		Non-graduates		Total
	No.	%	No.	%	No.	%	
DAFS	4	10	16	42	18	48	38
SDD	11	24	24	53	10	22	45
SED	4	14	20	69	5	17	29
SHHD	16	29	25	45	14	25	55
Total	35	21	85	51	47	28	167

Key: DAFS: Department of Agriculture and Fisheries for Scotland
SDD: Scottish Development Department
SED: Scottish Education Department
SHHD: Scottish Home and Health Department

Note: This table includes some posts graded administrative, but held for the time being by executive officers. While it does not distinguish Scottish universities from the others, it may be safely assumed that the former predominate. Between 1949 and 1969, 72 per cent of direct entrants from the universities had Scottish degrees.

Within the Scottish Office, the distribution of university degrees among the higher civil servants can be gleaned from a survey of the administrative class in May 1968. This gave the result shown in table 10.

In the Scottish Office administrative class, 'Oxbridge' graduates amounted to around one-fifth of the total, while in that class throughout the civil service they amount to just under a half. Non-graduates in the Scottish Office were 28%, compared to 24% for the whole class (Fulton 2, pp. 26–7). The difference between the Scottish Office and the other departments reflects the character of the Scottish educational system, for Oxford and Cambridge play only a marginal part in 'creaming off' the best pupils from Scottish schools. 'Oxbridge' graduates may feel reluctant to come to the Scottish Office, though it should be borne in mind that several of those who do come are in fact Scots, so that the total number of Scots in the posts equivalent to the administrative class is probably above four-fifths. In the other posts, a greater number are Scots, and entrance examinations for these, and for executive officers in other departments, are conducted by the Civil Service Commissioners in Scotland. Clerical officers are recruited locally by the Scottish departments themselves. Professional and scientific staff are recruited from all over the U.K. to a greater extent than other civil servants. For example, the Scottish Office's Chief Architect, Chief Planner, and Director of Fisheries Research were non-Scots in 1970.

There seems to have been no problem in filling the administrative posts in the Scottish Office, and as far as can be ascertained, there is no marked difference in quality between Edinburgh and Whitehall in the higher civil service. Certainly there has been no recruitment problem such as faced the Welsh Office in its initial years after 1964, when it was found that Welsh university graduates were reluctant to opt for the Welsh Office (Kilbrandon 3, p. 108).

The early history of the Scottish Office gave little indication that the department would grow to its present size and be attractive to career civil servants. The dominance of the boards and the Lord Advocate's department meant that administrative posts were filled by ministerial patronage or by lawyers, rather than by graduate administrators (Hanham, in Wolfe, pp. 55–6). The total establishment in Scotland, including the boards, cannot have been much above 200 in 1885, and the Scottish Office proper (i.e. the Secretary for Scotland's staff) existed with under a dozen civil servants (Hanham 1, pp. 234–7). The only board run on civil service lines was the Scotch Education Department, with a staff in London of 34 and a team of 40 school inspectors (Hanham 1, p. 237).

The growth of the Scottish Office is strikingly illustrated by its numerical strength at three dates: 1937, 1953 and 1970. The figures are:

1937: 2,400   1953: 5,500   1970: 8,300

These figures do not include the other Scottish departments, total-
ling 1,910 non-industrial civil servants in July 1970.

The increase in the size of Scottish administration must be
accounted an indicator of its now solidly entrenched position
within the structure of British government. Things have changed
greatly from the early days when the Treasury opposed all staff
increases in the Scottish Office on the grounds that there was no
work to do there (Hanham 2, p. 233). At that time the Scottish
Secretary's base in Edinburgh consisted of a few rooms in Parliament House. Today the Scottish agencies are impressively housed
in St Andrew's House, Edinburgh, and in offices throughout Scotland. They make up a distinct bureaucracy.

The careers of the top civil servants provide evidence of this
distinctness from Whitehall, with whom they nevertheless are
linked as members of one service. An analysis of the careers of the
374 administrative class civil servants at the Scottish Office
between 1946 and 1970 shows how few have moved between
Edinburgh and London. Table 11(*a*) gives the translations from
the Scottish Office to Whitehall departments, and table 11(*b*) the
movements from outside to the Scottish Office. As some moved to
London and back to Edinburgh again at a later date, the total
number of movements recorded is greater than the number of civil
servants who moved during their careers.

Table 11 (*a*) shows 25 movements from Edinburgh to Whitehall
during the period 1946 to 1970. To this should be added the occa-

Table 11 (*a*) *Movements of Scottish Office administrative class civil servants to Whitehall departments, 1946–70*

| From | To | | | | | | |
	Home	Educ	Av/ C Av	Trans.	T & C Pig	Health/ DHSS	Agric	Others
DAS/ DAFS								1 (ARC)
DHS	1				2	1		
SDD							1	1 (Treasury)
SED		2	1	1			1	2 (Col Off; COI)
SHD	3		1	1				2 (Customs and Excise; Central Land Board)
SHHD						1	1	1 (CSD)
SO (AUSS)								1 (PBW)

(b) Movements to the Scottish Office of Whitehall administrative class civil servants, 1946–70

From	To DAS/DAFS	DHS	SDD	SED	SHD	SHHD
Agriculture	2					
Air		1				
Board of Trade		1			1	
Cabinet Office				1		
Central Land Board					2	
Colonial Office			1			
Education				1		
Health						1
Housing and Local Government			1			
Inland Revenue	1					
Labour					1	
Pensions		1				
Post Office		1			1	
Public Assistance Board		1				
PBW/Works		1	1			
Treasury					1	1
War Office		1				

Key to table 11

ARC	Agricultural Research Council
Av/CAv	Aviation/Civil Aviation
COI	Central Office of Information
CSD	Civil Service Department
Col Off	Colonial Office
DAS	Department of Agriculture for Scotland (to 1960)
DAFS	Department of Agriculture and Fisheries for Scotland (from 1960)
DHS	Department of Health for Scotland (to 1962)
DHSS	Department of Health and Social Security (from 1968)
Educ	Education
PBW	Public Building and Works
SDD	Scottish Development Department (from 1962)
SED	Scottish Education Department
SHD	Scottish Home Department (to 1962)
SHHD	Scottish Home and Health Department (from 1962)
SO (AUSS)	Scottish Office (Assistant Under-Secretary of State)
T & C Plg	Town and Country Planning
Trans	Transport

Source: Imperial Calendars, HMSO.

sional secondment, for a period of two or three years, of Scottish Office personnel to the Treasury or the Cabinet Office (five cases are recorded). Many of the movements are to high-ranking positions (2 Permanent Under-Secretaries; 1 Deputy Under-Secretary of State; 3 Under-Secretaries and 4 Assistant Secretaries, making 10 out of the 25). Thus a high proportion of these translations come to men well advanced in their careers, and it is unusual for the ordinary Scottish Office principal or even Assistant Secretary to move to Whitehall.

Table 11 (b) shows 23 movements to Edinburgh from Whitehall, and of these 9 were to high positions in the Scottish Office (1 Secretary of the Scottish Education Department, 1 Secretary of the Scottish Development Department, 1 Under-Secretary and 6 Assistant Secretaries).

It must therefore be concluded that movements to and from the Scottish Office affect only a small proportion of the establishment of higher civil servants, and this fact serves to distinguish further the Scottish Office from the rest of the Service. The Fulton Committee on the civil service was worried by the high number and frequency of departmental translations taking place in Whitehall, which it felt was unsettling for administrators and bad for the development of specialist skills in particular areas of administration (Fulton 1, p. 40). These considerations do not apply nearly so strongly to the Scottish Office, where such major translations rarely take place.

What does happen, however, is that higher civil servants frequently move between the different departments of the Scottish Office (table 12). Since these are the equivalent in function to several Whitehall departments, something of the same mobility will appertain as in Whitehall. But the fact that these shifts take place usually within one building (and under one Secretary of State and one Permanent Under-Secretary) makes the change less noticeable. The civil servant can continue to use his specialist knowledge of Scotland in whichever Scottish Office department he serves. Since his clientèle is only five million people, with a fairly small number of local authorities and interest organisations, the principal political and official leaders will be known to him already. This is indeed one of the strengths of the Scottish Office as compared with Whitehall: personal contacts with the localities are good, making for frequent face-to-face contacts between central and local government.

Here, the professional and scientific civil servants play as large a part as the administrative men, and act as a leavening in the Scottish political system. Such Scottish Office officials as the Chief Social Work Adviser, the Chief Medical Officer, the Chief Planning Officer and the Chief Engineer act as links between central

Table 12 *Movements of administrative class civil servants within the Scottish Office, 1946–70*

From	To								
	DAS	DAFS	DHS	SDD	SED	SHD	SHHD	SO	Others
DAS		(21)		2				5	
DAFS				3	1		2	11	1 (Registrar-General for Scotland)
DHS				(26)	2	1	(24)	8	2 (Registrars-General for Scotland)
SDD	1				2		7	17	1 (Scottish Commissioner of the Peace)
SED	3	1		3		1	1	7	
SHD	(9)	1		(9)	4		(25)	14	1 (Scottish Commissioner of the Peace)
SHHD	1			7	9			8	1 (Registrar-General for Scotland)
SO	5	7	5	7	7	15	5		

Key: As for table 11. Figures in brackets represent nominal movements to new departments. SO (Scottish Office) positions as used here are usually private secretaries to ministers, and are held for one or two years only. The Regional Development Division (from 1965) is also included in SO, as are the Permanent and Assistant Under-Secretaries of State.

government and local government, as well as with the organisations outside government altogether. The origins and careers of the 'professionals/scientists' vary in some measure from the 'administrators', although the picture is not very clear. Legal, educational and medical officials tend to be Scottish because of the distinct Scottish institutions involved. Architects, planning officers, social workers and scientists are more likely to be non-Scottish or to have worked for some time outside Scotland. As in the case of the G.B. departments, they soon become absorbed in the Scottish system, but their experience perhaps gives their work a broader outlook than the civil servants who are more rooted in Edinburgh.

The co-option of administrative personnel from outside occupa-

tions is perhaps not so marked in the Scottish Office as in Whitehall, and the Fulton Committee's recommendations (Fulton 1,
p. 43) that this should increase is especially relevant. At the
moment, the bureaucrats remain a separate group in the community, joining the other élite groups of Edinburgh, such as the
lawyers, the churchmen and the academics.

The leaders of the bureaucratic élite in Scotland are the Permanent Under-Secretary of State and the Secretaries of the five
departments within the Scottish Office. Brief biographical profiles
of these men (derived from *Who's Who*) indicate their origins and
careers. In 1972 they were all Scottish and had worked almost
entirely in the Scottish Office. In 1973, however, four of these
positions changed hands, and Englishmen were appointed. This
illustrates the point made earlier that the very senior civil servants
have greater mobility than the others, but it is also something of a
novelty for the Scottish Office, and may have a political purpose
in integrating the Scottish Office with Whitehall during a period
of nationalism and decentralisation of functions.

> Permanent Under-Secretary of State: Sir Nicholas G. Morrison.
>   b. 1918 in England. Educated, Cheltenham College, Cambridge
>   University. War Office, Ministry of Defence and Civil Service
>   Department to 1972. Deputy Under-Secretary of State, Scottish
>   Office, 1972–3. (Has address in England as well as in Scotland.)
> Secretary, Scottish Home and Health Department: R. P. Fraser.
>   b. 1917 in Scotland. Educated, Daniel Stewart's College, Edin-
>   burgh, Edinburgh University and Oxford. Scottish Office,
>   1940–7. Cabinet Office, 1947–50. Scottish Office, 1950–68.
>   Ministry of Agriculture, Fisheries and Food, 1968–71. Recreation:
>   walking.
> Secretary, Department of Agriculture and Fisheries for Scotland:
>   James I. Smith.
>   b. 1924 in Scotland. Educated, Alderman Newton's School,
>   Leicester, and St Andrew's University. Scottish Office since
>   1949. Recreation: golf.
> Secretary, Scottish Development Department: Kenneth Newis.
>   b. 1916 in England. Educated, Manchester Grammar School,
>   Cambridge University. Office of Works, Ministry of Public
>   Building and Works, 1938–70. Scottish Office, 1970–. Recreation:
>   music.
> Secretary, Scottish Education Department: John M. Fearn.
>   b. 1916 in Scotland. Educated, Dundee High School, St Andrew's
>   and Oxford Universities. Indian Civil Service, 1940–7. Scottish
>   Office, 1947–. Recreation: golf.
> Secretary, Scottish Economic Planning Department: Tony Godden.
>   b. 1927 in England. Educated, Barnstaple Grammar School,
>   London School of Economics. Colonial Office, 1951–7. Cabinet
>   Office, 1957–9. Scottish Office, 1961–. Recreations: philately,
>   photography, music.

Recent Permanent Under-Secretaries of State at the Scottish Office have been Scottish, since the English Sir Horace Hamilton (1937–46). They were:

> Sir David Milne (1946–59), b. 1896, Edinburgh; d. 1972. Educated, Daniel Stewart's College, Edinburgh, Edinburgh University. Entered Scottish Office, 1921.
> Sir William Murrie (1959–64), b. 1903, Dundee. Educated, Harris Academy, Dundee, Edinburgh and Oxford Universities. Scottish Office, 1927–44. Cabinet Office, 1944–8. Home Office, 1948–52. Scottish Office, 1952–64.
> Sir David Milne (1946–59), b. 1896, Edinburgh; d. 1972. Educated, George Watson's College, Edinburgh, Edinburgh and Cambridge Universities. Entered Scottish Office, 1935. Recreation: golf.

The organisation of the Scottish Office has federal features, in that the Secretaries of the five administrative departments report directly to the Secretary of State, not to the Permanent Under-Secretary. The Permanent Under-Secretary meets regularly once a week with the Secretaries of the five departments to enable them to reach collective decisions on matters of common interest, but since they are the accounting officers for their departments and have direct access to the Minister, his power is somewhat less than that of the Permanent Under-Secretary of Whitehall departments, who is the sole accounting officer. The Permanent Under-Secretary at the Scottish Office is himself an accounting officer for the Central Services of the Scottish Office, which comprise the Directorate of Establishments (personnel, organisation, management, office and computer services), the co-ordination of finance work and statistical work, the Solicitor's Office, and the Scottish Information Office. He is of course the Secretary of State's senior adviser, and thus Scotland's 'chief bureaucrat'.

The federal organisation is a legacy of the former independence of the Scottish departments and boards, and was preserved in the 1939 reorganisation. It allows for considerable specialisation within the Scottish Office, and to some extent enhances career prospects there by opening up more positions of high responsibility. The minister has more channels of advice open to him than under the 'pyramid' departmental structure with one Permanent Under-Secretary at the top. The advantages of this type of structure were recognised by the Fulton Report, which recommended the establishment of 'accountable' units within departments (Fulton 1, pp. 51–2). Departmental changes in Whitehall since 1970 have in fact moved in this direction.

The nature of the work done in the Scottish Office, and the life-style of the administrators, is in many ways different from that of Whitehall. In the first place, St Andrew's House is 400 miles distant from Parliament, where ministers must of necessity spend much of their time. Scottish higher civil servants find themselves constantly commuting between London and Edinburgh, and many will be posted for a time to Dover House, the Whitehall base of the Scottish Office.

During the passage of a Scottish Bill, or at Scottish question time, there will be some difficulty in briefing ministers, since most of the files have to be kept in Edinburgh. Civil servants must prepare a formal submission to the minister, which is kept separate from the files and which gives the details of the case.[4] This is an added burden, and when unexpected matters are raised during a debate, telephone calls have to be made to and from Edinburgh to provide information. Other departments' files are usually within walking distance of Parliament. The strain imposed by constant travel and the difficulty of communications makes the job a hard one for the Edinburgh civil servant. Yet Edinburgh life has become relatively more attractive in recent years, as the living conditions in London have deteriorated. Long-distance travel to work is not required, and the facilities for recreation are good (many top Scottish Office men list golf or gardening among their hobbies).

Despite the frequent visits to London, there is surprisingly little extended contact between St Andrew's House and Whitehall. The need to 'check out' any policies with opposite numbers in Whitehall does not loom so large as is sometimes assumed (as in Mackintosh 1, p. 131). In education, for example, the organisation and curricula of the schools, teacher-training and the conditions of service of teachers, are determined by the Scottish Education Department, in conjunction with the local education authorities and Scottish educational organisations. There is practically no reference to the Department of Education and Science. Each department conducts its own educational system, and only very large issues such as the school-leaving age and comprehensivation are determined on a British basis (even here Scottish differences persist). Much the same could be said of a large part of health and social work administration, local government and legal matters. Where a matter appears to be 'political', or affects other departments, St Andrew's House will act more cautiously and Ministers and Scottish Office officials will consult their colleagues, but a great deal of what the Scottish Office does is not likely to affect the interests of other departments directly. This allows it a real freedom to go its own way with a different solution from England (for further development of these points, see ch. 11).

Function for function, there are obviously fewer civil servants employed in Scotland than in England. For example, three times as many administrators are involved in the branches relating to teachers in the Department of Education and Science as are employed in the corresponding divisions of the Scottish Education Department. Thus it could be said that one man in Edinburgh covers the ground of three in Whitehall (he has of course only one-tenth of the clientèle). When it comes to research and policy-formulation there will be more specialists in the larger department, but the smaller will have the broader view. On the whole, this tends to favour the larger department taking the initiative, since the Scottish Office man spreads himself too thinly to make a real contribution in any one area. He may look to Whitehall for the latest ideas in his field, though he will not always accept them. This could explain why some educational and social welfare reforms have been adopted in England before they came to Scotland. But other reforms have come more quickly in Scotland (e.g. the Social Work Act of 1968) because the comprehension of the Scottish Office's organisation and viewpoint facilitated reforms, where Whitehall's separate empires and specialists hindered them (see ch. 11).

Administration on the scale of the Scottish Office thus has its share of strength and weakness. It provides, for Scotland, a bureaucracy derived from, and knowledgeable of, its people and their special needs. For the men who staff it, it gives some technical problems not present in Whitehall relating to parliamentary business and liaison with other departments. The type of work they do makes them generalists rather than specialists, although they probably remain within the same department to a much greater extent than do civil servants in Whitehall. This has given the Scottish Office in recent years an overall sense of direction lacking in much of Whitehall, and certainly in any region of England. The chief examples are the development of regional economic planning and of medical and social services. Nevertheless, 'the Scottish bureaucracy' may sacrifice depth and vision to a thin parochialism as a result of its 'isolation' in Edinburgh. Some of Scottish administration lacks the stimulus of continual interchange of ideas with the outside world, but the post-Fulton developments in the training of civil servants may alter this. Civil Service College courses will be taken jointly by civil servants of all departments. There is an Edinburgh centre of the Civil Service College, but it is not confined to Scottish administrators. Indeed, what is surprising is the lack of a course specifically related to the problems of Scottish administration, which is however the province of the Scottish Office Training Unit, and of the courses on public administration at Scottish universities and colleges.

The strength of the Scottish bureaucracy in the Scottish political system lies partly in the relative weakness of the other parts of that system. Without a Scottish parliament, the legislative checks are more remote, for the Scottish Grand Committee, the Scottish Standing Committees, the Select Committee on Scottish Affairs, 1969–70; 1971–72) and Scottish question time provide only an intermittent and largely ineffective threat to the administrators. The vast range of functions in the Scottish Office puts the Ministers at a disadvantage in acquiring expertise, while the other departments in Scotland cannot compete in the status of their administrators, and soon come under the influence of the Scottish Office. Scottish local authorities are financially subservient, and Scottish public opinion is docile (even a nationalist upsurge primarily attacks London government rather than the Edinburgh government which already exists). The only challenge to the Scottish Office comes from Whitehall, where the Treasury arbitrates between, or dictates to, all departments, and where the Civil Service Department controls the civil service. The record here, as judged by favoured treatment for Scotland (cf. ch. 11), and by the growth of the Scottish Office establishment, is that the Scottish bureaucracy can, at the least, hold its own against all comers.

The future, however, is uncertain, for a devolved Scottish government will have its own Scottish civil service. What this means for the Scottish Office is as yet unclear, but it points in the direction of greater distinctness of administration, more Scots in top administrative posts in Scotland, and less 'Whitehall control'.

5
Parliament

The Scottish M.P.s

Since 1950, there have been 71 M.P.s from Scottish constituencies in the House of Commons. This is an over-representation in terms of the ratio of seats to population. In 1885 Scotland had 72 seats, or 12·7% of the Great Britain total (i.e. excluding Ireland); in 1974, it had 11·2% of the G.B. total. But in the meantime, its population proportion had fallen from 12·1% to 9·5%.

In the October 1974 general election, the average electorate per constituency was 51,898 in Scotland, and 64,634 in England. Thirteen Scottish constituencies had electorates of under 40,000 – including four in the Highlands and four in Glasgow. At the same time, 7 were over 65,000. The extreme range was Western Isles (22,477) to Midlothian (89,191). While the redistricting of seats in 1974 ironed out many of the inequalities, the total number of seats in Scotland remained the same. This is the result of a 'gentleman's agreement' made in 1948.[1] Moreover, among the new constituencies there are still the same sparsely populated constituencies of the Highlands, and some very large ones in the central Lowlands. It is politically difficult to merge Highland constituencies because of the immense area that would be involved. The relatively low Scottish average electorate, therefore, continues to conceal some large seats in the heavily populated areas.

Scottish M.P.s are a distinct group in the House of Commons. They have their own Bills to discuss; their own committees to sit on; and their own ministers to question. These activities set them apart from other members, who do not share these duties or interests. Unfortunately for the non-Scottish M.P.s, however, the parliamentary system involves them in purely Scottish affairs, whether they like it or not. Scottish Bills are sometimes taken on the floor of the House; the Scottish Grand Committee has English M.P.s co-opted to it to preserve the party balance; and Scottish question time is in the House as a whole. In these ways, therefore, the workings of the House of Commons display the interaction of the Scottish and British political systems in a concentrated form.

The parliamentary segment of the Scottish political system consists primarily of the Scottish M.P.s (Scottish peers in the House of Lords play a less important role). Of the 71 M.P.s elected in October 1974, 41 were Labour, 16 Conservative, 3 Liberal and 11 Scottish Nationalist. In the whole House there were 319 Labour, 276 Conservative, 13 Liberal, 11 Scottish Nationalist and 16 other M.P.s. Scotland was thus committed to the Labour Party in terms of seats, although the Labour vote was only 36.3%. The Conservatives were much weaker in Scotland than in England, and the SNP was a major force (second in terms of votes).

In 1955, the party distribution among the Scottish M.P.s was more like that of the whole House. There were then 34 Labour, 36 Conservative and 1 Liberal M.P.s, out of a total of 277 Labour, 344 Conservative, 6 Liberal and 3 other M.P.s. Thus from 1955 to 1974 there was a massive swing away from the Conservative Party in Scotland, which was unmatched in any other part of the U.K. (for 1955 to 1970 see Butler and Pinto-Duschinsky, pp. 356–7).

The characteristics of the Scottish M.P.s have accordingly changed. In 1955, there were more non-Scots sitting for Scottish seats. There was also a wider range of occupations. The Tory ranks consisted mainly of ex-army men, landowners and businessmen. But there were also strong politicians such as Walter Elliot, Sir Robert Boothby, James Stuart, and Sir William Anstruther-Gray, chairman of the back-bench 1922 Committee from 1962 to 1964. Labour was nearly all working class or professional, and its 'politicians' included such figures as John Strachey, Hector McNeil, Emrys Hughes, Tom Fraser, Jean Mann and Margaret Herbison.

By 1974, the Scottish representation had become much more indigenous. Scottish seats were being reserved for Scots, and Scottish affairs were more of a specialism in the House. The decline of the Tories in the 1960s, and their retreat to the hard-core rural areas, gave them more of an aristocratic or landed image. Many of their M.P.s had English public school educations, and spoke with 'English' accents. Few were natural politicians.

Labour's expansion did not seem to greatly change the style of its M.P.s. Many were old hands, and had already given service as local councillors. Only one or two were active in debates on British or foreign affairs, and most gave their exclusive attention to Scottish or constituency matters.[2] There was a relative lack of the university-educated and middle-class type of Labour M.P., which had been a feature of the party since 1964. While 54% of the Labour M.P.s elected to Parliament in 1970 had university degrees, only 41% of the Scottish Labour M.P.s had been to a university. The Labour Party in Scotland remained rooted in the working or lower middle class, the trade unions, and local government.

The Liberals, who numbered 5 in 1966, were reduced to 3 from 1970. They were all university-educated and middle class. The SNP's 11 M.P.s in October 1974 were largely professional, and university educated.

Table 13   *Scottish M.P.s, 1955 and 1974 (October)*

	1955 Con	Lab	Lib	1974 (October) Con	Lab	Lib	SNP
No. of M.P.s	36	34	1	16	41	3	11
Average age	54	55	42	43	50	46	39
Non-Scots	4	6		3			
Educated outside Scotland	26	6	1	8	5	1	
University education	21	10	1	7	16	3	10
Former councillor	2	9		5	23		3
Women	1	3		1	1		2
Occupation							
Land/farming	8			3			1
Business	16	6	1	8	5	2	3
Armed services	11						
Professions	6	16	1	3	20	2	5
Scots lawyers	2	1		3	2		2
Unskilled/skilled		16			15		

Note: Some M.P.s are entered twice under occupations, as when a barrister has strong business interests (e.g. Jo Grimond). If one extends the comparison back to 1910, one finds that there were then more non-Scots, more graduates, and more lawyers among the Scottish M.P.s. Dr C. J. Larner of Glasgow University has analysed the characteristics of Scottish M.P.s from 1910, and sees a sharp turn towards parochialism in the choice of M.P.s between 1910 and 1924 a decline in the number attaining ministerial office thereafter (unpublished paper).

One important deficiency in the House of Commons is that of Scots lawyers. There were only 3 in 1955 and 7 in 1974 (lawyers trained in English law are excluded: there were 2 in 1955 and 3 in 1974). When it is considered that there must be two Scottish government law officers, and that much Scottish legislation has to deal with technical matters of Scots Law, it is clear that the House of Commons is starved of the appropriate legal expertise. (English Law was well served by the presence of over 100 M.P. lawyers in 1974.) From 1962 to 1970 the Lord Advocate was not in the House, and since 1960 (with the exception of the four months December 1963 to April 1964) the Solicitor-General for Scotland has not been a member.

The difficulty in obtaining candidates with Scottish legal qualifications comes from the fact that Scottish legal practice cannot be pursued in London. Many lawyers combine attendance in the House with some legal work, but the Scots cannot normally do this. For those who make the sacrifice, however, appointment as a government law officer is almost assured, followed possibly by elevation to the highest positions in the Scottish bench (see ch. 2). There are thus rich rewards for the tiny group of Scottish legal-politicians. It is obvious that a legislative body in Edinburgh would attract far more lawyers as members than does the House of Commons, and would make the principal Scottish legal bodies more accessible during the passage of law reform Bills.[3]

What is the position of Scotland in the work of Parliament? In the session 1968–9, debates on purely Scottish Bills and topics occupied about 50 hours of the time of the House of Commons. This included major debates, lasting several hours, on the Education, Town and Country Planning, and Housing Bills. There was also about 10 hours of parliamentary questions to ministers on Scottish topics, with the Scottish Secretary or other Scottish Office ministers taking about two-thirds of the time. During the session, something like 1,300 written answers and 200 oral answers on Scottish topics were provided by government departments. Over and above this, Scottish M.P.s spoke about Scotland in general debates covering the whole of Britain.

Beyond the floor of the House itself, the Scottish committees of the House of Commons in 50 sittings spent 125 hours in debate. (See table 16. A normal sitting lasts $2\frac{1}{2}$ hours.)

These Scottish activities of the House of Commons represent the Scottish political system in its parliamentary aspect. The boundary of the system can be defined even in Westminster, for Scottish affairs interest mainly the Scottish M.P.s, and Scottish debates and question times have a character of their own. Needless to say, the Scots jealously preserve their right to an audience on the floor of the House for Scottish matters, while they have the added advantage of an exclusive 'club' of their own in the Scottish committees.

The Scottish Committees
These committees are now four in number, though two are not in continuous existence.

(1) *The Scottish Grand Committee.* Established in 1894, it consists of all 71 Scottish M.P.s, with 10 to 15 others added to bring the Committee's party balance into line with that in the House as a whole. Its functions are in three categories: first, Bills. (*a*) It considers Scottish Bills which are referred to it at the second reading debate stage. Such referral is dependent on the Speaker certifying

that such Bills relate exclusively to Scotland, and the motion to refer them to the Scottish Grand Committee must be made by a government minister. Private Members' Bills are thus practically excluded. If 10 M.P.s object, the Bill must stay on the floor of the House. Such a veto has happened only twice in the last 14 years. (*b*) It reports to the House that it has considered such Bills, so that the formal second reading may take place there (and not in the Committee). A vote at this point is extremely unusual, and of doubtful meaning. Only two are recorded in the last decade, and that on 11 November 1969 was allowed to give 'freedom of expression of opinion', not to decide the second reading. (*c*) It can take the report stage of Scottish Bills which have been considered by the Committee at second reading, and the Scottish Standing Committee at committee stage. This is a recent innovation, and so far it has not been used. However, it is now possible for a Scottish Bill to go through all its stages, apart from formal second and third readings, in the Scottish committees (see table 14, p. 83).

Second, Scottish Estimates debates. Selected Scottish Estimates may be debated in the Committee, on up to six days each session. The Votes are grouped together into such categories as 'Crime' or 'Health', and are chosen by the opposition.

Third, Matter day debates. Matters of concern to Scotland may be debated on up to two days each session. The topics are chosen by the government.

(2/3) *The Scottish Standing Committees.* There are now two, the first having been established in 1957, and the second in 1962. These committees take the clause-by-clause examination of Bills, and vote on such clauses and amendments to them (the 'committee' stage). Important Bills go to the first committee, and minor ones to the second. If six or more M.P.s propose an amendment at the second reading stage, there will be a second reading debate on the Bill in the House. This happened in 1961, over the Crofters Bill. The composition of the two committees before November 1971 was:

(i) 30 Scottish M.P.s, nominated by the Committee of Selection in respect of each Bill, with the discretionary addition of up to 20 other M.P.s (who need not be Scottish).

(ii) Between 16 and 50 M.P.s, nominated by the Committee of Selection, of whom not less than 16 must represent Scottish constituencies.

In November 1971, the House voted in favour of reducing the minimum size of the first committee to 16, so that both Scottish Standing Committees are now of the same size. In practice, however, major Scottish Bills will be committed to a Scottish Standing Committee above the minimum size, and the Housing (Financial Provisions) (Scotland) Bill 1971, was dealt with in a committee of 26. This meant that no Liberal or SNP M.P.s got a place, and forced the Parliamentary Under-Secretary for Health and Education at the Scottish Office to attend, in order to maintain the government majority, although he had no direct connection with the Bill.

In selecting the Scottish Standing Committees, regard is paid to the qualifications of the members and the composition of the House. The second committee is not often used, and neither com-

Table 14 *House of Commons Procedure for Scottish Bills*

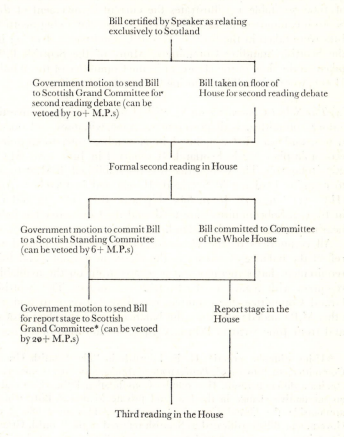

*This procedure is available only for Bills considered previously in the Scottish Grand Committee.

mittee can sit when the Scottish Grand Committee is in session. Tuesdays and Thursdays, from 10.30 a.m. to 1 p.m. are the usual hours for the Scottish committees, but they have met at all hours on some occasions (e.g. the debate on the Education Bill 1970 and the Housing (Financial Provisions) Bill 1971). The procedure for Scottish Bills in the House of Commons is shown in table 14.

The proportion of Scottish Bills going to the Scottish Committees has risen in recent years, especially since the establishment of the Scottish Standing Committees. From 1948 to 1959 less than a third of Scottish Bills went to the Grand Committee for second reading, and a little over two-thirds for the committee stage.[4] In the 1960s, however, the proportions were over half and three-quarters respectively. The record of two sessions in the Parliament of 1966–70 (table 15) illustrates the current involvement of the Scottish committees in legislation. This shows that 12/23 Scottish Bills were taken in the Scottish Grand Committee, and 17/23 in the Scottish Standing Committees. Many of the Scottish Bills taken on the floor of the House, or in the Committee of the Whole House, were minor Bills requiring little or no debate.*

(4) *The Select Committee on Scottish Affairs.* This is an investigatory committee, with power to examine witnesses and documents, and was first appointed in November 1969 to examine economic planning in Scotland. It reported in June 1970 (H.C. 267 (1969–70)). The Committee was re-established in May 1971, to examine land use in Scotland. It reported in October 1972 (H.C. 511 (1971–2)). Its membership was 16 in 1969–70 and 14 in 1971–2. Subcommittees are used, and the Committee has held hearings in London and Scotland.

All committees of the House of Commons are supposed to reflect the balance of parties in the House as a whole, and this requirement has sometimes put a severe strain on the available resources with regard to the Scottish committees. The Scottish Grand Committee, for example, can have between 10 and 15 other M.P.s added to produce this balance, but from 1962 to 1964, and from June 1970 to February 1974, the addition of 15 non-

* Using different criteria, G. E. Edwards in 'The Scottish Grand Committee, 1958 to 1970', *Parliamentary Affairs*, xxv (1972), 307, 314, obtains a different result. He excludes Consolidation Bills, which make no substantive change in the law, and private Members' Bills, which are outside the Grand Committee procedure. This gives 86.4% of Government Bills certificated as Scottish referred to the Scottish Grand Committee between 1958 and 1970. 81% of all Government Scottish Bills (including Consolidation Bills) were committed to a Scottish Standing Committee. 20 out of 23 Scottish Private Members' Bills went there.

Table 15 *Scottish Bills in the House of Commons, sessions 1966–1967 and 1967–8*

BILL	SGC	SSC	HC	CWH
1966–7				
Law Reform (Miscellaneous Provisions) (Scotland)	×	×		
Local Government (Scotland)	×	×		
Housing (Financial Provisions) (Scotland)	×	×		
Water (Scotland)	×	×		
Remuneration of Teachers (Scotland)	×	×		
Countryside (Scotland)	×	×		
Police (Scotland)	×	×		
Licensing (Certificates in Suspense) (Scotland)		×	×	
Deer (Amendment) (Scotland)		×	×	
Legal Aid (Scotland)			×	×
Police (Scotland) (No. 2)			×	×
Housing (Scotland)			×	×
1967–8				
Teachers Superannuation (Scotland)	×	×		
Erskine Bridge Tolls	×	×		
Sewerage (Scotland)	×	×		
Legitimation (Scotland)	×	×		
Law Reform (Miscellaneous Provisions) (Scotland)	×	×		
Sale of Venison (Scotland) (No. 2)		×	×	
Highlands and Islands Industry		×	×	
Social Work (Scotland)		×	×	
New Towns (Scotland)			×	×
Housing (Financial Provisions) (Scotland)			×	×
Prevention of Crime (Scotland)			×	

Key: SGC   Second reading debate in Scottish Grand Committee
SSC   Committee stage in a Scottish Standing Committee
HC   Second reading debate on floor of House
CWH Committee stage in Committee of the Whole House

Scottish Conservatives could not produce a Conservative majority on the committee. This does not matter greatly politically, since no legislative vote takes place there. In 1922, when the committee did vote on the committee stage of Bills, the adverse majority for the government at that time meant that all Scottish Bills had to be kept on the floor of the House.[5]

Today, the smaller Scottish Standing Committees take the committee stage. Until it was reduced in size in November 1971, the first committee gave the Conservative Government considerable problems as regards the maintenance of its majority there.

The Conservatives in Scotland had only 23 M.P.s, and, under the old rules, 16 were required for a majority on the committee. Several Scottish M.P.s were members of the government, and their continual presence on the committee could not be expected. Although the rules allowed for it, no English M.P.s were co-opted on to the committee, and those that are co-opted on to the Scottish Grand Committee are unwilling participants, and find their occasional remarks resented by the Scottish M.P.s.[6]

The total work of the Scottish committees may be further illustrated by the record of a typical session (1968–9). During that session the Scottish Grand Committee considered (a) 5 Bills in relation to their principle (i.e. second reading debate) at 7 sittings; (b) 13 Estimates at 6 sittings; and (c) 1 Matter at 1 sitting. The First Scottish Standing Committee considered 4 Bills at 35 sittings, and the second Scottish Standing Committee 3 Bills at 3 sittings (see table 16).

The Scottish committees are thus very active, and take up a great deal of the time of the Scottish M.P.s. The Scots are among the most hard-working M.P.s in terms of committee attendance, and they sit on other committees as well as the Scottish ones.[7] In part, their zeal is due to the relative isolation they feel in London, making them habitués of the Commons. There they find both company and work of interest. The same might be said of M.P.s from the north of England.

Nevertheless, Scottish M.P.s are sometimes unable to find time to serve on both Scottish and U.K. committees, and the latter may be totally deprived of Scottish representation, even when Bills of some importance to Scotland are going through. Thus, the Education (Milk) Bill 1971, which aroused much opposition from Scottish local authorities, went through a committee which contained no Scottish M.P.s, and so did the Land Commission (Dissolution) Bill 1971. Scottish M.P.s may be members of two committees sitting simultaneously, and they develop a fine art of travelling swiftly between them to record their votes at divisions. Of course, many of these votes are placed in ignorance of the preceding debate.[8]

The content of Scottish committee work is not very momentous. No Bills are introduced in the Grand Committee which are controversial in a party sense, or have implications for England, and local government affairs dominate. Recent controversial Scottish Bills, such as the Deer Bill 1958, the Licensing Bill 1961, the Highlands and Islands Development Bill 1965, the Social Work Bill 1968, the Education Bills of 1969 and 1970, the Housing (Financial Provisions) Bill 1971, and the Offshore Petroleum Development Bill 1974, have been taken on the floor of the House.

Controversy does break out in the Standing Committees, how-

Table 16   *Work of the Scottish committees, session 1968–9*

Subject	Sittings	Members present (excluding chairman)
Scottish Grand Committee		
Electricity Bill	1	51
Agricultural Spring Traps Bill	1	45
Town and Country Planning Bill	2	48, 38
Housing Bill	2	38, 39
Age of Majority Bill	1	45
Estimates	6	44, 46, 42, 34, 44, 42
Matter: Arts and Amenities	1	39
First Scottish Standing Committee		
Agricultural Spring Traps Bill	2	24, 21
Education Bill	14	Between 16 and 29
Town and Country Planning Bill	11	Between 18 and 29
Housing Bill	6	Between 19 and 26
Second Scottish Standing Committee		
Electricity Bill	1	18
National Mod Bill	1	12
Age of Majority Bill	1	12

Source: Standing Committees. Return for Session 1968–9, H.C. 9 (1969–70).

ever. Numerous sittings took place on the Social Work Bill 1968, the Conveyancing Bill 1970 and the Education Bill 1970. The last took three months and 75 hours of debate at the committee stage owing to a prolonged filibuster by the Labour group. This led to sittings during the night, and demonstrated the Conservative government's inability or unwillingness to clamp down on debate by closure or guillotine. Such procedures would have required a vote of 100 M.P.s, more than the total for the Scottish seats.

This is the crux of the problem for the Scottish political system within Parliament. The Scottish committees give the Scottish M.P.s the right to discuss Scottish legislation and affairs, but not to overturn the wishes of the government. If the majority of Scottish M.P.s are of a different party from the government, the result is a sparring-match which can grind the parliamentary machinery almost to a halt. Yet neither party wishes to dismantle the system, and so does not go too far. Labour will not support the profitable (for them) expedient of giving real power to the Scottish M.P.s or to a Scottish legislature; the Conservatives will not over-rule the Scottish majority too much since they are now committed to devolution through a Scottish Convention. That body would take over the Scottish committee work, and be manned by directly elected Scottish members. There would then be a potential clash between two legislative bodies, one in Westminster and one in Edinburgh.

While some debates in the Scottish committees appear interminable, others might be considered brief. A British (or English/Welsh) Bill will be debated at second reading from 4 p.m. to 10 p.m. on one or more days. A Scottish Bill is lucky to receive two sessions of $2\frac{1}{2}$ hours each in the Grand Committee. Such debates are dominated by the front-bench speakers, who open and close them.

Similarly, Scottish Estimates debates are infrequent in comparison with those for the rest of the country, yet the range of functions covered is great. Two Supply days can be taken in the House for Scottish Estimates, but these lapsed from 1964 to 1970. In all, Scottish Estimates debates do not have the time available to cover in depth the multifarious activities of the Scottish Office; Scottish Matter day debates are also rare and may be remote from the most important political issues in Scotland. In recent years they have covered such subjects as arts, tourism, gale damage and Highland transport. Other debates have been on important subjects, such as housing, agriculture, and local government reform, but even these seem to lack the political impact that a debate in the whole House, or perhaps in Edinburgh, would achieve. The subjects are chosen by the government, and are thus calculated to avoid embarrassment. Violent debates on the floor of the House, such as that on Upper Clyde Shipbuilders (2 August 1971), are unknown in the Scottish Grand Committee, which always seems one stage (at the least) removed from the centre of political power. This may be because it can never involve a vote of confidence in the government.

Another inadequacy is the time available for oral parliamentary questions. Each day, almost one hour is devoted in the House to question time, and departments are taken in rotation. Until October 1970, the Scottish Secretary, or other Scottish Office ministers, answered once in every six weeks. This meant that the opportunities for Scottish M.P.s to get oral answers on such matters as education, health, agriculture, law and order, transport and local government were far fewer than for English M.P.s, who could get oral answers practically every day on one of these subjects.

In October 1970, the position of the Scottish Office in the question time rota was improved, so that it now came up once in three weeks. In April 1971 the government promised to allow Scottish ministers to answer supplementary questions on ministerial statements made by English ministers on matters covering Scotland as well as England and Wales. During that session, the Scottish

Secretary had not been able to reply to questions on three occasions where his name had appeared on joint ministerial statements. Such statements are often made in matters such as the health services, and agriculture, and yet give rise to different problems for Scotland.

It has become more evident in recent years that the machinery of Parliament has been inadequate to cope with the demands of Scottish legislation and the need to oversee the Scottish Office. The congestion in the committees, the strain on the M.P.s, and the farce of co-opting English M.P.s to provide party weight have not enhanced the stature of the Scottish parliamentary system. Scotland has to wait longer than England for some of its legislation, the most recent example being local government reform, which was introduced a year later for Scotland. Law reform has also been slow in Scotland, in part because of the parliamentary situation.[9] Scottish divorce law reform was delayed because the Divorce (Scotland) Bill 1971 was certified as relating exclusively to Scotland, and had to wait in a queue with U.K. Bills.[10] This is despite the fact that legislation had already been passed for England and Wales. Social reforms, such as those relating to homosexuality, Sunday entertainment, and family planning, are delayed in Scotland because of the difficulty of passing separate Scottish Bills, especially as many are private members' measures. It is fair to add, however, that many of the Scottish M.P.s themselves are not anxious to bring Scotland into line with England in these matters, and obstruct their passage. Moreover, ministerial time and concern may be as involved as parliamentary time.

The practice of inserting clauses relating to Scotland into what are essentially English Bills, instead of producing separate Scottish Bills, has been criticised by Scots lawyers. So too has the lumping together of law reforms in 'Law Reform (Miscellaneous Provisions) Bills' in preference to having separate measures with appropriate and clear titles. All these disadvantage the Scots lawyer, in comparison with the English, since the former must subject his reading of the statutes to elimination and amendment.[11]

The surveillance of government departments by M.P.s is not well performed by Parliament as a whole, and perhaps even less so by the Scottish members. Scottish questions are often extremely narrow or parochial, and rarely reach the springs of policy formulation. Where departments other than the Scottish Office are involved, the Scottish M.P.s are swamped by the questions of their colleagues in England and Wales. Even in debates on Bills affecting Scotland, such as the Transport Bill 1967, speeches by Scottish ministers are resented by English M.P.s, who seek to confine them to the Scottish Grand Committee.[12]

The Scottish committees have undoubtedly improved the position of the Scottish M.P.s. The Select Committee on Scottish Affairs has been able to get valuable evidence from civil servants on how policy is made in Scotland. But the M.P.s generally remain remote from St Andrew's House, and raise antagonisms there by the flood of written parliamentary answers which they demand, no doubt as compensation for their weakness in obtaining oral answers and in general debates.[13]

Since the Kilbrandon Commission reported in October 1973, legislative devolution for Scotland has been accepted by all the political parties. The decision by the Labour government in 1974 to set up a directly-elected Scottish assembly has superseded the proposals for reforming the machinery for conducting Scottish business in the House of Commons. The earlier proposal of the Labour Party in Scotland to transfer some Scottish Grand Committee sittings to Edinburgh must now be seen as only an academic alternative to the stronger devolution schemes which involve a separately elected Scottish legislative body. The Grand Committee reform would have had the advantage of retaining the same body of M.P.s for Scottish and U.K. parliamentary business, although it would have increased their work-load. It would have avoided the difficult problem of having two legislative and executive authorities (in Edinburgh and in London), and the potential conflict that might develop between them on policies.

A Scottish assembly or parliament would assume responsibility for all the Scottish business at present conducted through the Scottish committees, Scottish Question-time, and Scottish debates on the floor of the House. The decision as to what is 'Scottish' and what is 'British' would be partly a matter of constitutional arrangement and partly the prerogative of the British government and parliament. For example, important aspects of health and education might be decided on a British basis, while other aspects were devolved to the Scottish parliament.

Whatever the detailed outcome of such matters is, the end of the old system of Scottish parliamentary affairs is now in sight, with the prospect of a new legislative branch in the Scottish political system.

6

Political parties and electoral behaviour

The 'homogeneity' debate

The main features of the party system in Great Britain have traditionally been its simplicity and its homogeneity. Two major parties won nearly all the seats in the House of Commons, and captured over 90% of the votes. Moreover, regional differences within the country were not important, since the principal divisions in electoral terms were derived from socio-economic, not territorial, factors. These divisions reinforced the two-party system, which is based on a bipolarisation of society into the middle and working classes. Thus parties appealing to regional or nationalist sentiment did very badly.

As recently as the 1970 election these features seemed to hold good. The two major parties won nearly all the seats in Great Britain, leaving the Liberals with only 3 seats (7·5% of the vote) and others with 3 seats. The only Nationalist success was a single SNP member, for the Western Isles.

The picture altered considerably in 1974, when the two-party system and homogeneity received a powerful blow. Minor parties won 25% of the vote in both elections, and in October 1974, the SNP took 11 seats with 30% of the Scottish vote.

In this context, it is easy to criticise the validity of the thesis of British homogeneity, which equates British politics with English politics. Books with titles such as *Politics in England* (Rose 1) and *English Party Politics*[1] appeared at a time when stronger regional variations in British politics, notably with regard to electoral behaviour and administration, were already becoming more apparent. Yet these works were not usually intended to distinguish 'English' politics from politics in other parts of Britain. Rather they perpetuated the use of 'England' in place of 'Britain' as a familiar, if inaccurate, substitute-word for the state properly called the United Kingdom of Great Britain and Northern Ireland. In a few instances there is an assumption that English political patterns are reproduced throughout Britain, and may in fact have been grafted on to areas such as Scotland and Wales as a result of political union. Thus Richard Rose, in *Politics in England*, wrote that 'politicians and representatives of Scotland,

Wales and Northern Ireland must work within a political system dominated by Englishmen, and assimilate many of their attitudes in order to prosper. Because the central government rules over all four parts of the United Kingdom in varying degrees, it is still customary and correct to speak of British government in conjunction with English society' (Rose 1, p. 26).

Another writer, A. H. Birch, in *The British System of Government* (1st ed., 1967) maintains that 'the distinctions between the English, the Welsh and the Scots are cultural rather than ethnic and do not have many political consequences'.[2] Graeme Moodie, writing from Glasgow in 1961 (*The Government of Great Britain*), asserted that the British constitutional tradition is 'primarily English rather than British, as the Irish, Scottish and Welsh components of the United Kingdom have contributed little, constitutionally speaking, to the system of government'.[3]

These opinions were all expressed before the wave of Scottish nationalism in the later 1960s. Since that time students of government have been more conscious of the differences between the national units of the U.K., and the renewed troubles in Northern Ireland have emphasised the 'foreignness' of politics in that 'province'. Rose, for example, in 1970, produced *The United Kingdom as a Multi-national State* (Rose 3), which rejected the homogeneity theory, and later produced a book on the politics of Northern Ireland (Rose 4).

It is now difficult to shrug off what happens in Northern Ireland, Scotland and Wales as having no political consequences for the country as a whole. In the case of Ireland, indeed, the course of events has for centuries had a profound effect on the workings of the British constitution. In modern times, the obstruction of the Irish M.P.s led to a drastic revision of the precedure of the House of Commons (1882), and the Government of Ireland Act (1920) re-introduced quasi-federal elements into the British constitution. The existence of a separate legal system in Scotland, and a separate Established Church of Scotland, is also constitutionally significant, and, together with the other constitutional and parliamentary arrangements peculiar to Scotland discussed in earlier chapters, forms an essential part of the British constitution.

In a wider political context, the development of political parties in Britain owes something to Scots and to Scottish political thought. Nineteenth-century Liberalism was largely Scottish in origin, in part because of the 'non-conformist' education which Liberal leaders received at Edinburgh and Glasgow Universities.[4] Gladstone, Rosebery and Campbell-Bannerman were Scottish Liberal Prime Ministers, and Asquith sat for a Scottish seat. The Labour Party may be said to have originated in Scotland, with the formation of Keir Hardie's Scottish Labour Party in 1888.[5] The first Labour Prime Minister was a Scot, Ramsay Macdonald. Although the Conservative Party has appeared more English on the whole, Lord Aberdeen, A. J. Balfour, Harold Macmillan and Sir Alec Douglas-Home are examples of Scottish Conservative Prime Ministers.

The inter-action of all the constituent parts of the U.K. is most clearly seen in the workings of the electoral system. A general election is won by the party which wins the largest number of seats throughout the U.K., not just in England. While this usually ensures that a party with a majority of English seats will also have a majority in the House of Commons, in 1910, 1950, 1964, and February 1974 the Conservative Party won most of the seats in England, yet in each case the combined U.K. result produced a non-Conservative government. In the last resort, then, the English political system (as the Scottish and Welsh systems) is subservient to the British.

These are preliminary correctives to the idea of a self-contained 'English' politics. Yet it is remarkable that Great Britain, despite its 'multi-national' diversity, has usually had a predominantly two-party system, in which minor parties or parties based on region, religion, or occupation present no serious challenge. Moreover, the two major parties are well-disciplined, so that their M.P.s generally obey the party whip in the House of Commons rather than divide into local or other groupings. Far from being a rival to the central party leadership, constituency parties usually support party discipline and reprimand party 'rebels', and these may not be re-adopted at the next election.

Since there is little scope for a back-bench M.P. to influence legislation or government policy, it is difficult for him to build up a strong constituency loyalty, which would support him if he 'resigned the whip'. He can rarely point to anything which he personally has been able to obtain for his constituency, a position unlike that in the United States, where congressmen and senators devote much of their time to promoting the economic interests of their districts or states. Their efforts count, since the loose party discipline in Congress means that they can trade their votes on an issue which does not directly concern their constituents for support in one which does. This 'log-rolling' does not exist in the British House of Commons, where nearly all votes are predetermined, and all give the government a majority.

The reasons for the rigidity of the British party system have been well argued in the literature of political science.[6] The principal ones are the electoral system, which by shunning 'proportional representation', discourages minor parties; the responsibility of the government to Parliament, which leads to the necessity of an assured majority party and a large 'opposition' party; and finally, the homogeneity of the country, which divides the people predominantly on lines of social class rather than by region, ethnic group, religion or urban/rural settlement. Such homogeneity prevents the rise of numerous parties, and has led to two major 'class' parties, supposedly representing the middle and working classes respectively.[7]

While each factor on its own would probably not produce the British party system, the combination of all three seems to be irresistible. The two-party structure has a long history, despite periodic challenges to its stability. One such challenge came in the 1920s, when the Labour Party replaced the Liberal Party as the second largest party, and the latter slowly declined to its present minor position. Then from 1931 to 1945, Britain had coalition government, which made it difficult to talk of two-party competition for office.

Between 1880 and 1918 the Irish Nationalists posed a great threat to the British party system. Their aim was not to become a party of government at Westminster, but to disrupt the British parties in order to achieve Home Rule for Ireland. It is significant that their emergence related to the lack of homogeneity between Britain and Ireland, and their challenge was resolved by most of Ireland becoming independent.

This would seem to indicate that the key explanation for the British party system is the apparent homogeneity of British society. For the electoral system and the responsibility of government to Parliament could not counteract the political consequences of the social separation of Irish society from the rest of the British Isles. Even today, Northern Ireland has remained socially distinct from Great Britain, and possesses its own party system (it has also become painfully obvious that the Unionist Party in Northern Ireland is a different animal from the British Conservative Party).

British homogeneity is not a simple matter, however. We have already seen that it cannot be taken as 'Englishness' spread throughout the land. England itself is intensely regional, with strong social contrasts between south and north, for example. Scotland and Wales add the complexities of national identity and separate political institutions to this diversity. Richard Rose (Rose 3) isolates four major social divisions in the U.K. which serve to separate its national components, England, Scotland, Wales and Northern Ireland. These relate to (1) the division between the central and peripheral areas of the state; (2) religious cleavages; (3) urban/rural disagreement; and (4) class antagonism between manual and non-manual workers in industrial centres. In all these regards, Rose believes, the constituent nations of the

U.K. are in conflict, and from this he rejects the 'thesis of the social homogeneity of Britain' (Rose 3, p. 19).[8] He goes on to reject the 'thesis of political homogeneity' as well, 'because of the historical importance of religious issues and national political differences within the several parts of the United Kingdom'.

The snag with this argument is that, although such national differences undoubtedly exist, there has been no serious challenge to the British political system from any geographic, religious or nationalist force, other than Irish, for at least two hundred years (i.e. not since the Jacobites). And while the Irish question is by no means solved, it remains exceptional. The sharp rise in Scottish nationalism in 1974 may not be such a fundamental or long-lasting threat to the unity of Britain as might appear at first. The SNP's vote is unstable, having risen and fallen once already during the past decade. In 1970, it was only 11% of the Scottish vote. Moreover, only around one-fifth of the Scottish people supported total independence, according to opinion polls conducted in 1974 (see below, p. 136).

This seems to confirm the long-term (if not all the most recent) developments of British political history. Scotland and Wales have shown almost complete loyalty to the British state in times of supreme crisis, such as during the World Wars. It is well-known that Scottish regiments have played an important part in the British army since Napoleonic times. There was very little evidence of disaffection among the Scottish civilian population in the twentieth-century World Wars, although isolated pockets of revolt (e.g. the Clyde in the First World War and some Nationalists in the Second) did exist. On the whole, Lloyd George and Churchill commanded the loyalty of Scotland, as they did of England.

The same is true of peace-time political leaders. The British party leaders are the best-known and most respected politicians in Scotland, and no Nationalist or other Scottish politician can rival them in this respect (Budge and Urwin, p. 129). While this is partly a result of the superior news coverage which the former command, it is principally the result of the sympathies felt by the vast majority of Scots for the 'image' or policies of the major parties and their leaders. Gladstone, for example, was idolised by Scots (he was a Scot himself, although a British politician), and Margaret Thatcher and Harold Wilson, with a somewhat different intensity, are the focus of loyalty of Scottish Conservative and Labour supporters.

The qualifications which must be made to this picture of electoral and party homogeneity come under three headings. First, Scotland (and Wales) differ from England in the electoral strength of the British parties, and in the amount, and sometimes even direction, of the 'swing' from one major party to another between general elections. Second, the British parties are organised separately in Scotland, and to some extent take on a character there which is different from that of the parties as a whole. Third, Scottish nationalism is a direct challenge to British homogeneity, and now commands widespread electoral support.

In this chapter we shall examine the first two of these qualifications to the conventional analysis of British party politics. The third will be dealt with in a separate chapter, since it involves the whole phenomenon of nationalism as well as the specific fortunes of the Scottish National Party.

Electoral behaviour in Scotland

Voters in Scotland have until 1974 overwhelmingly supported the British political parties, rather than purely Scottish ones. It can thus be said that political opinion in Scotland divided along lines similar to the divisions in England and Wales, rather than along lines which divide Scotland from the rest of the country. This was a result of the success of the British parties in integrating the political life of Scotland with that of England, or more accurately, harmonising the special features of Scottish politics with the rest of British politics. Most political issues and political attitudes in Scotland are in fact the same as elsewhere in the country. A large part of social and economic policy-making, and nearly all foreign affairs, is 'British' in the sense that the constituent nations do not form themselves into coherent blocs of opinion which over-ride the divisions between the parties.

There are very few examples in history of the Scottish politicians from different parties coming together to press a Scottish claim in direct challenge to their parties' authority. This is partly because the strength of party discipline inhibits such revolts, but it is also due to the flexibility of the British parties, which can anticipate such demands and accommodate them. Even in the crisis of the Scottish economy in the early 1970s, the Scottish representatives of the Conservative, Labour and Liberal parties showed few signs of 'log-rolling' to the embarrassment of their parties. The Scottish M.P.s (with one exception, the SNP member) accepted that either Mr Heath, Mr Wilson or Mr Thorpe spoke for them.

There are, of course, issues peculiar to Scotland. Such are to be found for example in legal matters, education, the Highlands, and religion. Moreover, 'British' problems such as regional economic imbalance, housing, crime and health, may need special policies for Scotland. Scottish attitudes towards these are polarised within the main parties, and governmental action for Scotland follows. The British parties, rather than separate Scottish parties, have attempted to deal with such problems. Nevertheless, the unity of the British party system obscures the difference in the parties' policies in the nations of the U.K. (further discussion of this point follows, pp. 107–11).

The voters in Scotland, then, are not necessarily expressing the same attitudes as those in England, even when they are voting for the same party. For example, Labour voters in Scotland expect a much higher level of subsidy for council-house rents than do English Labour voters. Scottish parties are committed to the state denominational school system which operates in Scotland, but not in England. In 1970, devolution was much more favoured by Labour supporters in central Scotland than by the Labour Party, according to surveys conducted in March of that year (*Glasgow Herald*, 11, 13, 16, 18 March 1970). An NOP survey in February 1970 showed that 67% of all respondents in over forty Scottish constituencies favoured a Scottish parliament (*Scotsman*, 16 February 1970). Opposition to British entry into E.E.C. was most marked in Scotland in August 1971, according to an ORC survey (62% were against entry, whereas all England except the north and west was in favour (*Glasgow Herald*, 27 August 1971)). (But see below, p. 137.)

The parties in Scotland do not reproduce the strength of the parties which prevails in England. From 1832 to 1918, Scotland voted predominantly for the Liberal Party (the exception is the election of 1900). England in the same period was much more Conservative. Since the First World War, general elections in Scotland have tended to favour the Labour Party. The largest share of the vote has gone to that party at 11 out of 17 elections. England, on the other hand, has voted predominantly Labour at only 4 elections (see table 17).

What is the explanation for the difference in voting behaviour in Scotland, as compared with England? In the period from 1832 to 1918, the predominance of the Liberal Party was bound up with the image which that party presented of sympathy with religious non-conformity in England, Presbyterianism in Scotland, parliamentary reform, and agrarian radicalism. The great strength of Presbyterianism in Scotland, the distaste felt for the 'managed' Scottish political system which existed before the 1832 Reform Act, and the rural distress and individualism of the Scottish countryside, all brought most Scots into the Liberal Party.

After Gladstone introduced Home Rule for Ireland in 1886, many Scottish Liberals (and Liberals elsewhere) deserted him for Joseph Chamberlain's Liberal-Unionist Party. The defection was particularly severe in Scotland, owing to the ties with Ireland in trade and immigrant population. The Conservative Party in Scotland (still 'Conservative and Unionist') has until recently derived

Table 17   *General election results, 1918–74*

	U.K.		SCOTLAND		ENGLAND	
Election	% of vote	M.P.s	% of vote	M.P.s	% of vote	M.P.s
1918						
Coalition	47·1	473	52·3	54	52·5	389
C	6·1	50	2·0	2	3·7	20
L	13·0	36	15·0	8	14·7	25
Lab/Co-op	21·4	58	24·7	6	23·1	43
Others	12·4	90	6·0	1	6·0	8
1922						
C	38·5	344	25·1	13	41·5	307
L	18·9	62	21·5	15	19·6	44
NL	9·4	53	17·7	12	7·3	31
Lab	29·7	142	32·2	29	28·8	95
Com	0·2	1	1·4	1	0·1	0
Others	3·3	13	2·1	1	2·7	8
1923						
C	38·0	258	31·6	14	39·8	221
L	29·7	158	28·4	22	29·9	123
Lab	30·7	191	35·9	34	29·7	138
Com	0·2	0	2·4	0	–	–
Others	1·4	8	1·7	1	0·5	2
1924						
C	46·8	412	40·8	36	47·6	347
L	17·8	40	16·5	8	17·6	19
Lab	33·3	151	41·1	26	32·9	109
Com	0·3	1	0·7	0	0·3	1
Others	1·8	11	0·9	1	1·6	9
1929						
C	38·1	260	35·9	20	38·8	221
L	23·6	59	18·1	13	23·6	35
Lab	37·1	287	42·4	36	36·9	226
Com	0·2	0	1·1	0	0·1	0
SNP	0·01	0	0·1	0	–	–
Others	1·0	9	2·4	2	0·6	3
1931						
Coalition	67·2	554	63·9	64	69·1	455
Ind L	0·5	4	–	–	0·2	0
Lab	30·8	52	32·6	7	30·2	29
Com	0·3	0	1·5	0	0·1	0
SNP	0·1	0	1·0	0	–	–
Others	1·1	5	1·0	0	0·4	1

Table 17 (*contd.*)

Election	U.K. % of vote	U.K. M.P.s	SCOTLAND % of vote	SCOTLAND M.P.s	ENGLAND % of vote	ENGLAND M.P.s
1935						
Coalition	53·3	429	49·8	43	54·5	357
L	6·8	21	6·7	3	6·3	11
Lab	38·1	154	36·8	20	38·5	116
Com	0·1	1	0·6	1	–	–
ILP	0·6	4	5·0	4	0·1	0
SNP	0·1	0	1·1	0	–	–
Others	1·0	6	–	–	0·6	1
1945						
C	39·6	210	41·1	27	40·2	167
L	9·0	12	5·0	0	9·4	5
Lab	48·0	393	47·6	37	48·5	331
Com	0·4	2	1·4	1	0·3	1
ILP	0·2	3	1·8	3	0·03	0
SNP	0·1	0	1·2	0	–	–
Others	2·7	20	1·9	3	1·6	5
1950						
C	43·5	298	44·8	31	43·8	253
L	9·1	9	6·6	2	9·4	2
Lab	46·1	315	46·2	37	46·2	251
Com	0·3	0	1·0	0	0·2	0
SNP	0·03	0	0·4	0	–	–
Others	1·0	3	1·0	1	0·4	0
1951						
C	48·0	321	48·6	35	48·8	271
L	2·6	6	2·7	1	2·3	2
Lab	48·8	295	47·9	35	48·8	233
Com	0·1	0	0·4	0	0·03	0
SNP	0·02	0	0·3	0	–	–
Others	0·5	3	0·1	0	0·1	0
1955						
C	49·7	345	50·1	36	50·4	293
L	2·7	6	1·9	1	2·6	2
Lab	46·4	277	46·7	34	46·8	216
Com	0·1	0	0·5	0	0·1	0
SNP	0·04	0	0·5	0	–	–
Others	1·1	2	0·3	0	0·1	0
1959						
C	49·3	365	47·2	31	49·9	315
L	5·9	6	4·1	1	6·3	3

Table 17 (*contd.*)

Election	U.K. % of vote	U.K. M.P.s	SCOTLAND % of vote	SCOTLAND M.P.s	ENGLAND % of vote	ENGLAND M.P.s
Lab	43·9	258	46·7	38	43·6	193
Com	0·1	0	0·5	0	0·1	0
SNP	0·1	0	0·8	0	–	–
Others	0·7	1	0·7	1	0·1	0
1964						
C	43·4	304	40·6	24	44·1	262
L	11·2	9	7·6	4	12·1	3
Lab	44·1	317	48·7	43	43·5	246
Com	0·2	0	0·5	0	0·1	0
SNP	0·2	0	2·4	0	–	0
Others	0·9	0	0·2	0	0·2	0
1966						
C	41·9	253	37·7	20	42·7	219
L	8·5	12	6·8	5	9·0	6
Lab	48·1	364	49·9	46	48·0	286
Com	0·2	0	0·6	0	0·1	0
SNP	0·5	0	5·0	0	–	–
Others	0·8	1	0·0	0	0·2	0
1970						
C	46·4	330	38·0	23	48·3	292
L	7·5	6	5·5	3	7·9	2
Lab	43·1	288	44·5	44	43·4	217
Com	0·1	0	0·4	0	0·1	0
SNP	1·1	1	11·4	1	–	–
Others	1·9	5	0·2	0	0·3	0
1974 (February)						
C	38·2	297	32·9	21	40·2	268
L	19·3	14	7·9	3	21·3	9
Lab	37·2	301	36·6	40	37·6	237
Com	0·1	0	0·5	0	0·0	0
SNP	2·0	7	21·9	7	–	–
Others	3·2	16	0·0	0	0·8	2
1974 (October)						
C	35·8	276	24·7	16	38·9	252
L	18·3	13	8·3	3	20·2	8
Lab	39·3	319	36·3	41	40·1	255
Com	0·0	0	0·3	0	0·0	0
SNP	2·9	11	30·4	11	–	–
Others	3·6	16	0·0	0	0·8	1

Table 17 (*cont.*)

Key: C   Conservative   ILP   Independent Labour Party
      Com   Communist   Ind L Independent Liberal
      L   Liberal   NL   National Liberal
      Lab   Labour   SNP Scottish National Party
      Lab/Co-op Labour/Co-operative

Note: In elections from 1918 to 1945, the universities seats are excluded (3 were in Scotland).

Sources: F. W. S. Craig, *British Parliamentary Election Statistics, 1918–1970* (Political Reference Publications, Chichester, 1971). *The Times.*

its strength in the industrial west from the remnants of this Liberal-Unionist vote.[9] Liberal-Unionists in the guise of National Liberals or Coalition Unionists have been particularly strong in Scotland. In 1959, six were elected, but since 1964 none have stood. These were rural, rather than urban, Liberal-Unionists who had been Liberal before 1918.

The main feature of British electoral behaviour since 1918 has been the development of class-based parties, with the great majority of the working-class voting Labour and of the middle class voting Conservative (Butler and Stokes, chs. 4 and 5). This alignment of political opinion largely replaced that derived from religious affiliation, and so contributed towards the homogeneity of the country in electoral terms. For one of the basic differences between England, Scotland and Wales is religion, and if this ceases to be reflected in politics, the nations will be drawn together.

At the same time, the development of communications, especially the popular press and broadcasting, broke down localism and focussed attention on the capital and British political issues. It tended to destroy social habits distinctive of the provinces and nations, and thereby consolidated the political trend towards uniformity. Finally, the great increase in government power over affairs previously considered local (e.g. education, health, social security and industrial development) drew all the lines of political activity towards the ultimate point of decision, the centre.

If this is so, it is surprising that Scotland can still not be considered fully merged within the British 'norms' of electoral behaviour. The voting figures and opinion survey research indicate that Scotland is a strong 'political region' with its own patterns of voting, and that it has tended to diverge more from the British national average than other regions since 1955 (Budge and Urwin, p. 132; Butler and Pinto-Duschinsky, p. 397).

The strength of the Labour Party has already been mentioned. In recent elections this has been greatly exaggerated by the number of seats won, since the electoral system has not rewarded the SNP or the Liberals in proportion to the votes they have won. Thus in 1970, the percentage voting Labour in Scotland (44·5%) was not very different from that in England (43·2%), and *less* than the Labour vote in Scotland in 1955 (46·7%) and 1959 (46·7%), when the party was at a low ebb. But the percentage of Scottish seats which Labour won in 1970 (62%) was greatly inflated compared with the English figure (42%). The SNP won 11·4% of the votes, but only 1 seat; the Liberals 5·5% and 3 seats.

Despite these distortions, Scotland was more Labour (and certainly less Conservative) than most of England until 1974. Surveys conducted for the Butler and Stokes study between 1963 and 1966 (i.e. before the SNP reached important proportions) showed that the working class in Scotland was more Labour, and the middle class less Conservative than was the case in seven of nine English regions. The two remaining regions of England (the north-east and Yorkshire), however, as well as Wales, surpassed Scotland in their class-intensified voting (Butler and Stokes, pp. 140–1).

Butler and Stokes are therefore justified in applying the Disraelian usage of 'two nations' to the division between the south and midlands of England on the one hand and Scotland, Wales and the north of England on the other. These two nations are based on economic rather than ethnic criteria, and mark the separation between the prosperous and backward parts of the British economy. Thus such forces as the level of unemployment, wage-rates, and social environment affect the proportion of the working class voting Labour.

So too does the percentage of the population which is working class. If an area is strongly working class, the proportion of that class voting Labour will be greater, and the proportion of the middle class voting Conservative less. Scotland has perhaps suffered even more adverse economic conditions than the north of England and Wales (in terms of unemployment, emigration and housing for example), but it is not so strongly working class, taking the country as a whole. The Clydeside conurbation on its own is as strongly working class as the north of England and Wales, but the social and political differences between the constituencies in Scotland are almost as important as the difference between Scotland and England. Analysis of these constituency differences has just begun (Butler and Pinto-Duschinsky, pp. 376–9, 386–435).

One strong electoral force relates to religion. Budge and Urwin's study (1966) of electoral behaviour in Glasgow, and Bochel and Denver's article (1970)[10] on church and politics in Dundee have brought out the correlation between church affiliation and voting behaviour in these areas. Butler and Stokes (pp. 124–34) and Rose (2) also present evidence relating to the political opinions of those identifying with the Church of Scotland (the evidence for other churches does not isolate Scotland from the rest of Great Britain).

While religion is in general much less political than it was before the 1920s, when the Irish Home Rule issue tended to make Protestants in some areas Unionist and Catholics and other Home Rulers Labour or Liberal, there is still a legacy from the past in the party preferences of those who identify with the various churches. Budge and Urwin found that while 87% of the working-class Catholics in Cathcart (Glasgow) in 1964 supported Labour, only 44% of the working-class Protestants did so. In Govanhill (Glasgow) the proportions were 75% and 56%. Bochel and Denver[10] in a 1968 survey of Dundee strongly confirmed the Glasgow findings. 39.5% of manual workers who were affiliated to the Church of Scotland recollected voting Conservative in 1966, while only 6% of Roman Catholic manual workers did so. Other denominations (a small group) resembled the Church of Scotland, but the non-religious manual worker was 13.5% Conservative.

In Butler and Stokes' survey (1963), those who identified with the Church of Scotland saw themselves as 39% Conservative, 48% Labour, 6% Liberal and 7% others or none (p. 125). The 1964 election vote was Conservative 40.6%, Labour 48.7%, Liberal 7.6%, and others 3.1% (but note, 22.4% of the electorate did not vote). This seems to indicate that the Church of Scotland (here taking in those brought up in a Church of Scotland tradition) resembles the Scottish population in voting behaviour, although the Glasgow and Dundee surveys noted above have emphasised its Conservatism.

Rose (Rose 2, p. 13), reporting a Gallup survey in 1964, says that working-class Presbyterians in Scotland were 60% Labour and 27% Conservative, virtually the same as the working class in England. But Roman Catholic workers were 74% Labour and 11% Conservative. He concludes that the high Labour support among the Scottish working class 'is almost entirely due to the substantial minority of Roman Catholics in its composition'.

Intensity of religious belief (as measured by church attendance) tends to increase the proportion of a church's members who adhere to the party favoured by the majority of the membership. In Scotland, the Roman Catholics are the best church attenders and also the most devoted to the Labour Party. No doubt their attendance in England is comparable, but their Labour partisanship there is much less marked. Scottish Catholics are concentrated in working-class areas, and this amplifies their class voting. There is as much evidence (Butler and Stokes, pp. 124–34) that religion influences voting in England and Wales as in Scotland, for the Church of England is much more identified with the

Conservative Party than is the Church of Scotland, and the non-conformists in England are more Liberal than any sizeable religious grouping in Scotland. (The non-conformist Presbyterians in Scotland, the Free Church and United Free Church, have about 40,000 members between them, and are strong in the Highlands. They may well be predominantly Liberal, as Liberalism is pronounced in the Highlands, but there is no survey evidence available to confirm this.) There is considerable acceptance of the view that religion or quasi-religion divides Scots in parts of Scotland along Catholic-Labour and Protestant-Conservative lines.

The presence in west central Scotland, and to a lesser extent in parts of east Scotland (e.g. in Edinburgh and Dundee) of a large Catholic population (rising to nearly half the total population in some areas)[11] has affected the political behaviour of working-class Protestants in these areas. In some cases, a militant Orangeism has developed, which has swelled the proportion of the working class voting Conservative. Although no survey work has yet been done, it is widely believed by observers that certain constituencies are strongly affected by Orange and Green conflicts, which distort 'normal' class voting behaviour.[12] Similar divisions have been found in England, notably in Liverpool.

In these constituencies too, the influence of events in Ireland itself is present. Contacts are maintained between Northern Ireland and Scotland, and occasionally candidates will take a stand on an Irish issue. The principal football rivalry in Glasgow and the west of Scotland is between a 'Catholic' team, Celtic (which sports the flag of Ireland at its ground), and a 'Protestant' team, Rangers (which flies the Union Jack). Such associations are part of the political culture of the industrial west of Scotland.

Yet the disunity which such religious cleavages bring about should not be exaggerated. 'Orange' Conservatism is less prominent today than before 1955. Both Catholics and Protestants give massive electoral support to the Labour Party in Glasgow. Although over a third of the Labour vote comes from Catholics, a greater part must come from Protestants and others. Around 30% of Glasgow's population are Catholics, and surveys indicate that at least 75% support Labour. In 1970, the Labour vote in Glasgow was 55% of the total. From this it can be deduced that something like 40% of the Labour vote came from Catholics, assuming an equivalent turn-out for Catholics as for others. (Cf. Survey of Glasgow in *Glasgow Herald*, 11 March 1970, showing 33% of Labour supporters Catholic and 46% Protestant.) This shows that, despite the reluctance of many of the Glasgow Protestant working class to vote Labour, many do so, and this helps to produce social harmony and to avoid the hard religious/

political divisions found in Northern Ireland. Evidence on SNP voting and religious affiliation is limited. In the survey just quoted 48% of SNP supporters were Church of Scotland, 7% other Protestant, and 19% Roman Catholic (see also below p. 131).

The most obvious electoral 'deviation' in recent Scottish political history has been the weakness of the Conservative Party. While this was also evident in the period 1832 to 1918, its most modern manifestation dates from 1955. In that year the Conservative Party had a majority (50·1%) of the Scottish vote and 36 out of 71 seats. By 1966 it was down to 37·7% of the vote and 20 seats, and it reached an all-time low in October 1974 of 24·7%, with 16 seats.

This debâcle amounts to a huge loss in Conservative support in Scotland in under 20 years, and is unmatched in any other political region in Britain (for the picture in 1970, see Butler and Pinto-Duschinsky, pp. 356–7). Labour has been only a partial beneficiary of the flight from the Conservatives in Scotland, since it too has declined from its high point of 49·9% and 46 seats in 1966 to 36·3% and 41 seats in October 1974. Much of the decline in the Conservative vote came from the rise of the Liberals in the 1960s. This was soon overtaken by the rise of the SNP, which in 1974 captured 8 seats from the Conservatives. While the Liberals and SNP apparently took more votes from the Conservatives than they did from Labour at general elections from 1959 to 1970, Labour probably lost more to the SNP than Conservative in February 1974. This was redressed in October 1974, when Conservative lost more to the SNP than Labour.

The concept of a uniform swing has been one of the cornerstones of the theories of 'British homogeneity'. At each election, it was found, all parts of Britain produced roughly the same degree of swing between the parties. In 1970, for example, the swing from Labour to Conservative in the regions did not vary from the U.K. figure by more than 1·8%. In no region did the swing actually go in a direction opposite to that prevailing generally.

In 1974, Scotland seemed to demolish the notion of a meaningful U.K. swing which is uniform throughout the country. In the February election, because Labour lost more to the SNP than Conservative, there was a 'nominal' swing from Labour to Conservative of 1·2%. In the whole country there was a 'swing to Labour' of 1·2%. But the figures for swing showed only 'nominal' movements between the two major parties, since they really represented differential loss to third and fourth parties. Thus despite the 'swing' to Conservatives in Scotland at the February 1974 election, that party's share of the vote had dropped 5·1% since 1970, and it lost 4 seats to the SNP. In the October election, Scotland showed a 3·9% 'swing' to Labour, compared with 2·3%

in the U.K. Yet Labour's Scottish total dropped by 0·3% from February, and the SNP's vote rose from 21·9% to 30·4% (see table 17). In this way, one of the pillars of the 'homogeneity' thesis practically collapsed in 1974. For not only did swing lose credibility generally when third and fourth parties increased at the expense of the major parties, but the Scottish results diverged much more markedly from the rest of the country. The SNP became the second party in terms of votes, and the disparity between the Conservative performance in Scotland and in England grew even greater. The Liberals failed to make any breakthrough in Scotland in 1974 (unlike England), and the SNP completely eclipsed them as carriers of 'third-party' voting. While it was possible to see the rise of Liberal voting in England as in some way related to similar 'third party' voting for the SNP in Scotland, by October 1974 it was apparent that the SNP was forging well ahead of the comparable Liberal performance in England. The combined third and fourth party vote in Scotland in October 1974 was 38·7%, while in England the Liberals and other minor parties took only 21·0%. Thus Scotland massively rejected, in its votes, the 'two-party' system and British homogeneity.

Highland political behaviour is probably the least homogeneous with that in the rest of Great Britain (or even Scotland). This is treated in a separate chapter (ch. 12). In Scotland generally there is a separateness in the means of political communication, which gives politics its special 'Scottish' character. Scots learn about politics from their own TV programmes, their own newspapers and their own political conferences – as well as from British ones (see ch. 10). Butler and Stokes have noted (p. 310) that people whose sources of political information are national (i.e. London-based) are more likely to follow the national swing from party to party at an election. Those whose information has been local (and here Scottish newspapers and TV must be considered local) will tend to go against the national tide.

Only a part of the Scottish political behaviour can be explained by differences in political communication, of course. In some elections (e.g. 1950, 1951 and 1966) the Scottish swing has come very close to the U.K. average, while the difference in political communication has remained. This would suggest that other factors, especially the economic situation in Scotland, are as influential. Perhaps it is when economic problems of a regional nature become critical (as they did in Scotland generally in the 1960s and 1970s, and in a special form in the Highlands) that the Scottish (or Highland) means of communication become most important. For they focus on such problems, when the British media are dominated by news from the prosperous (or ailing) south of England. This combination of economic disparity and the publicity which it can get in Scotland may well account for much of the recent idiosyncracies of Scottish political behaviour.

Party organisation and policies

Apart from the SNP, the parties which operate in Scotland are British. In Scotland, however, each takes on a special identity. This identity affects the three cardinal areas of party activity – the making of policy, the choice of candidates and the winning of elections. The Labour Party and the Conservative Party have, in varying degrees, decentralised their organisation so that each plays a part in the Scottish political system which is separate from its other activities. The Scottish Liberal Party is theoretically quite independent of the Liberal Party in England and Wales, although there is only one Parliamentary Liberal Party. The Communist Party is more unitary, but with a Scottish Committee. Although it is relatively stronger in Scotland than in England, in terms of membership (around 7,000 out of the U.K. total of 30,000), votes and seats won (there have been two Communist M.P.s from Scotland), its electoral impact is now negligible (0.3% of the vote in October 1974).

The relationship between the parties in the country and the parties in Parliament adds another dimension to the problem of the distribution of political power within them. Constitutional theory demands that no party organisation outside Parliament should dictate to M.P.s what they must do.[13] In the last resort, then, policy decisions are made in Parliament, not in party conferences. But M.P.s are elected in constituencies, and would not reach the House of Commons at all were it not for their party affiliation and the efforts of party workers. In practice, there is great unity of purpose between local party workers, the Scottish and British party organisations, and the parliamentary party. Only rarely does one section seek to defy another, and the result is fundamental agreement tempered by occasional compromise or even mild dispute.

Scottish M.P.s are a separate group in the House of Commons, on account of the specialised nature of their work (ch. 5). This means that they take the place of their parties as a whole, when for example they are debating Scottish legislation in the Scottish Grand Committee. To facilitate a common strategy in such matters, each party has its own Scottish Parliamentary Group organisation, and the Scottish Labour M.P.s elect their own executive committee, chairman, vice-chairman and secretary.[14] Regular monthly meetings are held to discuss Scottish problems, although these are rarely very influential, or well attended. The major parties, of course, have Scottish whips, who strive to maintain party unity. Scottish M.P.s, like the rest of their colleagues must 'obey the whip', as there is now little room at Westminster for an autonomous group of M.P.s within the major parties (the Ulster Unionists are a special case). Governments make Scottish as well as British policy, and oppositions unite to oppose. The wishes of the Scottish M.P.s on the government side will be closely heeded, as their support is especially needed in committee. The Scottish Labour M.P.s in opposition have proved a formidable squadron of minister-baiters and filibusterers. But they do not embarrass their own leaders: if anything, they work harder for their party than other Labour M.P.s, in terms of committee attendances and votes in divisions.

Away from Westminster, Scottish M.P.s are more conscious that they are part of a separate political system. This is seen most clearly in the development of Scottish party organisations, which have been established independently of the corresponding bodies in England and Wales.

The origins of modern party mass-organisations are to be found in the late nineteenth century. In England, the National Union of Conservative Associations was founded in 1867, and in 1877 Joseph Chamberlain founded the National Liberal Federation. Each body consisted of a conference of constituency delegates, and tried to assist the constituency associations in winning elections. Later, the conferences attempted to shape policy, but this was checked by the parliamentary leaders.

In 1893, the Independent Labour Party was founded, followed by the Labour Party (then 'Labour Representation Committee') in 1900. The Labour Party was an attempt to *create* a parliamentary party on the basis of a mass-organisation, whereas the Conservative and Liberal organisations came after parties had been established in Parliament.

In Scotland, the development of party organisations proceeded in parallel with that in England, but was significantly separate. The Scottish Liberal Association did not owe its formation to Joseph Chamberlain, and dates from 1882. The National Union of Scottish Conservative Associations was founded in the same year. (In 1912 it merged with the Liberal-Unionists to become the Scottish Unionist Association.[15] In 1965 it was renamed the Scottish Conservative and Unionist Association.)[16] Keir Hardie founded the Scottish Labour Party in 1888, which merged with the Independent Labour Party in 1894. The Scottish Trades Union Congress in 1899 sponsored its own Labour Party, which until 1909 operated in competition with the (British) Labour Party.[17] Thereafter, the Scots joined the English and Welsh, and were given some autonomy in the form of the Scottish Council of the Labour Party (established 1915).

The establishment of separate party organisations in Scotland was intended to give the Scots their own conference, where they could discuss Scottish affairs. It was not meant to exclude them from the British conferences of the party, although clearly there would be little time in these for anything exclusively Scottish. In practice, only a few Scottish constituencies could afford to send delegates to England, and to this day Scottish party workers are scarce at the British conferences.

At the Labour Party annual conference in 1970 only 32 out of the 71 constituency Labour parties sent delegates. Most Scottish trade unionists were represented by the British trade unions. At the Conservative Party conference of that year, the party in Scotland was represented by M.P.s, candidates, the principal Scottish officials of the party, 28 representatives of the Scottish Association appointed to the Central Council of the National Union of Conservative and Unionist Associations, and 3 officials of the Scottish Branch of the National Society of Conservative Agents. The Scottish Liberal Party asserts that it is separate from the Liberal Party and does not send delegates to the Liberal Party assembly. Nevertheless, the Liberal Party Organisation Constitution makes provision for the attendance of Scottish delegates, and several Scottish M.P.s and candidates attend (5 in 1970). Russell Johnston, M.P., was chairman both of the Scottish Liberal Party and the Liberal Party Organisation Assembly Committee. In 1961 and 1968 joint assemblies of the Scottish conference and Liberal assembly were held in Edinburgh. M.P.s are the most frequent attenders at conferences held in England, as they feel more united with their English colleagues than do the grass-roots party workers.

The Labour and Conservative Parties have each devised constitutions giving varying amounts of autonomy or independence to their Scottish conferences. (The Scottish Liberal Party conference has been entirely separate since 1946.) The Labour Party's is the most unitary, since it subjects the constitution and programme of the Scottish Council to the rule that these must be 'within the lines laid down from time to time by the British National Conference of the Party'.[18] In fact these lines are not stringent, for the British conference does not wish to sit upon the Scots. In 1968 the Scottish conference took it upon itself to effectively (though unofficially) abolish the rule that only Scottish affairs could be discussed at the conference.[19] This has allowed delegates freedom to cover British and foreign politics as well as purely Scottish matters, and resolutions on such topics have been sent from the Scottish conferences to the National Executive Committee.[20] Most resolutions at Scottish conferences are on Scottish subjects, however, and the British conference does not often express an opinion on these. The Scottish conference does not have any constitutional power to draw up the policy of the party: it remains advisory to the British conference. Only occasionally do important initiatives develop which prove influential: examples are the debates on a Highland Development Board before 1965, and on state Catholic schools in 1971. For many years the Labour Party in Scotland supported legislative devolution to Scotland, but after 1929 this was dropped from its programme. Widespread Labour support for devolution remained, however, but it did not reach official approval until August 1974, when a special conference in Glasgow endorsed the setting up of a directly elected Assembly with legislative powers. The circumstances surrounding this decision were unusual, in that it was the (British) National Executive Committee which had pressed for a Scottish conference on the subject, and which had already stated its support for devolution. This was contrary to a statement of the Scottish Executive rejecting an elected assembly (*Scotsman*, 24 June 1974). Paradoxically, then, London virtually forced devolution on the Scottish Labour leadership, although the policy was subsequently given overwhelming approval by the mass membership and the principal trade unions (*Scotsman*, 19 August 1974, see also below, p. 134).

The Scottish Conservative conference is also relatively unimportant in the counsels of the party. In recent years, however, it has attracted the attendance of more leaders of the party and has obtained more news coverage than any Conservative regional conference in England. This has encouraged a great increase in the number of resolutions submitted for debate. Some of these debates have been important for party policy in Scotland: Mr Heath's speech on Scottish devolution at the 1968 conference, and the substantial majority (3:1) for the Scottish Convention proposal at the 1970 conference, were crucial to the party's policy on these matters. Thereafter, however, the party vacillated. The 1973 conference seemed to reject devolution altogether, while the 1974 one accepted only an assembly made up of local government councillors. Mr Heath's speech at the 1974 conference displayed many new aspects of Conservative Scottish policy (including a Scottish budget and Scottish development fund), and after the October election, the Scottish leadership supported a directly-elected assembly. In this way, the Scottish conference played a subsidiary role to the decisions of the party leaders (see also p. 133).

The Scottish Liberal Party's conference had also dealt with devolution and in 1968 the joint assembly with the Liberal Party Organisation revealed a split between the two Liberal 'Parties'. While the Scottish Liberals supported Home-Rule-all-Round, including an English parliament, the English Liberals preferred to substitute English regional parliaments. This difference of opinion hardened the rift between the Scottish and English Liberals, and emphasised the separation which had taken place in 1937 and 1946.

The Scottish party organisations have the function of helping constituencies choose their candidates, and win elections. This is primarily the task of the professional party workers at Scottish headquarters. Since around 1925, Scottish seats have been contested almost entirely by Scots. This has meant that the Scottish organisations have taken over from the British ones such influence as is possessed by the party 'apparatus' in the nomination of candidates. Constituency associations still jealously regard this as one of their main functions, and resent interference with their wishes. Nevertheless, the Scottish party organisations maintain a register of possible candidates and may press a name on a local party. It is significant that this register is distinct from the one maintained by the parties in England and Wales.

Endorsement of Conservative candidates as 'official' is in the hands of the chairman of the party in Scotland, not the Standing Advisory Committee on Candidates of the National Union of Conservative and Unionist Associations.[21]

Labour candidates are all endorsed by the National Executive Committee,[22] 'with due regard to the recommendation' of the Scottish Executive Committee, which assists in securing such candidates for all Scottish constituencies.[23] A very real power is possessed by the Scottish organiser of the Labour Party, both in influencing nominations and in effecting endorsement. William Marshall occupied this post from 1950 to 1971, and under him the Labour Party's Scottish organisation had more influence over that party's constituency associations than the Conservative Scottish office had over theirs. In the latter, party local disputes broke out which were not easily healed (e.g. Caithness and Sutherland 1959 and 1968, East Aberdeenshire 1962, South Aberdeen 1970).

The winning of votes is the third function of central party organisation. At their Scottish headquarters, the parties maintain a small permanent staff whose job is to gain publicity, raise finance, produce party literature, arrange for conferences and speakers, and improve organisation nationally and in the constituencies (see table 18). Each party responds differently to this task. The Scottish Conservatives and Liberals are financially independent of the London party organisations. Both rely entirely on contributions from individuals and organisations to pay the salaries of their staff, and all running expenses. These contributions come from within Scotland.

In the election year of 1970, the Scottish Conservatives raised £118,350 with a reserve fund of £164,000.[24] Much of this came from wealthy businessmen, and the party treasurer's firm alone (Stenhouse Ltd) gave £25,000.[25] Business contributions are, however, proportionately lower in Scotland than in England. In non-election years, income is somewhat less (1968, £89,000; 1969, £94,000). Grants to constituencies from Scottish Conservative Central Office amounted to £10,000 in 1969–70.[26]

The Liberals have few sources of income, and the total available to the Edinburgh headquarters was around £10,000 for 1970. Individual constituencies get no aid from the central organisation, but some are comparatively wealthy, and three had full-time agents in 1970 (one less than Labour). Despite their financial 'independence', there is a hidden subsidy to the Scottish Conservatives and Liberal Parties from their English cousins. Publicity given to the Conservative and Liberal Parties generally (e.g. broadcasts, press reports and advertising) is consumed in Scotland, but it is not financed by the Scottish sections of the parties. Most of the parties' publicity derives from the British headquarters, not the Scottish sections, which are of marginal importance in this respect. Nevertheless, the parties produce separate Scottish election literature, and occasionally party political broadcasts are directed especially at Scottish voters. In the 1970 election, the Conservatives in Scotland issued *Tomorrow Scotland*, a separate version of their British manifesto. Labour had a Scottish election manifesto (*Labour News*), and devoted part of an election party broadcast to Scottish problems. The Scottish Liberals had their own manifesto, and the Liberal Party dealt with Scottish devolution in one of its broadcasts.

The Labour Party's Scottish organisation is less separate in sources of finance than the Conservatives and Liberals. The Scottish Council of the party has its own income which is largely derived from affiliated trade unions and constituency parties. These pay fees both to Glasgow and to Transport House (just as trade unions in Scotland pay twice if they affiliate both to the TUC and the STUC). This income is not the total expenditure of the Labour Party in Scotland, for the salaries of the Scottish Party officials are paid by the National Executive Committee. Special financial assistance is given by Transport House to selected constituencies at elections. In the 1970 election 20 constituencies in Scotland received £12,400 from head office, a sum equal to that given by the Scottish office. The total Scottish income of the party in 1970 was £21,000, which included special election donations (mainly from trade unions) of £13,200. There was a reserve fund of £3,336.[27] In non-election years, income was of course lower (1967, £4,000; 1968, £5,200; 1969, £11,000).[28]

Table 18 *The Scottish organisation of the Conservative and Labour Parties, and the organisation of the Scottish Liberal Party, 1974*

(a) CONSERVATIVE PARTY

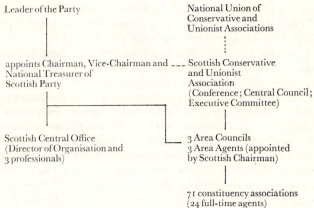

Leader of the Party

National Union of Conservative and Unionist Associations

appoints Chairman, Vice-Chairman and National Treasurer of Scottish Party --- Scottish Conservative and Unionist Association (Conference; Central Council; Executive Committee)

Scottish Central Office (Director of Organisation and 3 professionals)

3 Area Councils 3 Area Agents (appointed by Scottish Chairman)

71 constituency associations (24 full-time agents)

(b) LABOUR PARTY

Labour Party Conference

National Executive Committee

Scottish Organiser Scottish Office (5 professionals)

3 professionals

3 professionals

71 Constituency Labour Parties 4 Central Labour Parties 82 Trade Unions 1 Co-operative Party 5 Socialist Societies 26 Women's Organisations 44 Young Socialist branches

Scottish Council

Annual Conference

Executive Committee

Note: Constituency Labour Parties and trade unions in Scotland are also affiliated directly with the (British) Labour Party, to which they pay separate affiliation fees.

(c) SCOTTISH LIBERAL PARTY

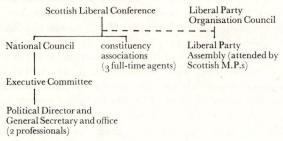

Scottish Liberal Conference

Liberal Party Organisation Council

National Council

constituency associations (3 full-time agents)

Liberal Party Assembly (attended by Scottish M.P.s)

Executive Committee

Political Director and General Secretary and office (2 professionals)

Election expenses per candidate reported for the 1970 election give only a partial picture of how the money was spent. In Scotland Labour and Conservative tied at £854, Liberals were £627 and SNP £644. Labour candidates spent more in Scotland than in England, but not as much as in Wales; the Conservatives spent much more in England and less in Wales; Scottish Liberals spent most of all Liberals (Butler and Pinto-Duschinsky, p. 333).

Success in winning votes is obviously not dictated by finance or even by strength of organisation. The Conservatives have not produced election victories in Scotland by their superiority in these matters, although it could be argued that their poor showing compared with England is partly due to poor organisation. In spring 1970 there were only 29 full-time Conservative agents in Scotland, the lowest number of Conservative agents in proportion to constituencies of any region in Britain (Butler and Pinto-Duschinsky, p. 281). They did, however completely out-class the other parties, whose agents, secretaries and organisers in Scotland numbered 7 (Labour), 4 (Scottish Liberal) and 3 (SNP) (*ibid.*, pp. 270, 262n.).

Discontent over Conservative organisation in Scotland led to a major reform in 1965, when finances and organisation were centralised. Before that time, two Divisional Councils (East and West) had controlled the Scottish finances, and the constituencies had a monopoly of what professional agents there were. The chairman of the party in Scotland was much weaker than the chairman in England and Wales.

In 1965, the two strong Divisional Councils were replaced with 5 Divisions (in 1968 reduced to 4) who received their finance and the services of professional agents from Scottish Central Office. These agents were appointed by the Scottish chairman (who is himself appointed by the party leader). But unlike the situation in England, constituency agents were entirely under the constituency associations.[29]

The Labour Party is run with a minimum of professional or even voluntary activist support. In many rural constituencies, Labour organisation disappears between elections, and even in its stronghold, Glasgow, it was in such poor shape in the late 1960s that Transport House had to appoint a special organiser to improve the situation before the impending general election.[30] The loss of Glasgow, Govan, at the by-election in November 1973, followed by Dundee East and Clackmannan at the general election in February 1974 gave a major shock to the Labour Party in Scotland. Organisation was stepped up in these seats, and in the many others threatened by the SNP. To some extent this was successful, for Govan was regained, and Labour's vote between February and October 1974 held overall. Thus, the challenge of the SNP has awakened the Labour Party from its long lethargy, and has put it on the defensive for the first time.

Liberal organisation has clearly been important in that party's fortunes in Roxburgh, Peebles and Selkirk, where between £3,000 and £4,000 is reported to have been spent in 1970.[31] Inverness is also well organised, and the Liberal M.P. there (Russell Johnston) had the distinction of polling a higher vote in 1970 than in 1966. And, as will be seen in the next chapter (on Scottish nationalism), the financial and organisational strength of the SNP is important to its successes in individual constituencies, but more difficult to sustain when 71 contests are attempted, as at the election in October 1974.

Conclusion

The British party system has until very recently succeeded in aggregating the interests of Scots with the interests of the rest of Britain. Party divisions in Scotland have been similar to those in England and Wales, with only a small minority voting for a 'non-British' (i.e. Nationalist) party.

Today, the theory of British political homogeneity is under considerable strain. Scotland has behaved differently from the rest of the country at the elections in 1974, most notably of course in its strong support for the SNP. This calls into question much of the conventional wisdom regarding British politics.

Even before 1974, Scottish electoral behaviour revealed special features, notably relating to religion, the comparative strength of the parties, the Highlands, and 'swing'. There were also distinctive party organisations, promoting their own conferences and policy resolutions. But all this was within the context of a strong political unity with other parts of the country. The Scottish Conservative and Labour Party organisations, for example, were closely tied up with their U.K. counterparts. To a large degree, they still are. Only the Liberals claim to be 'separate' from the party in England. Moreover, politics in Scotland was concerned largely with 'British' issues, and never departed radically from the British political culture, as did that of Northern Ireland. In Scotland, for example, Catholics and Protestants mixed easily within the parties, especially the Labour Party.

Nationalism has changed Scottish politics, whether permanently or not it is impossible to say at this stage. Its meaning and strength must now be considered, for it is obvious that no account of Scottish parties and voting behaviour is complete without a full discussion of the SNP, and of Scottish nationalism in all its varieties.

7
Nationalism

In one sense, most Scots are nationalists. They are conscious of their nationality, prefer to think of themselves as Scots, and can attribute characteristics to Scots in general which are different from those of other nations (for example, England).

Surveys in recent years have attempted to quantify these dimensions of national consciousness. In some cases (e.g. Budge and Urwin, p. 113) the form of the question asked excluded the possibility that respondents might say they were British rather than (or as well as) Scottish, English, Welsh or Irish. Given this qualification, 76% in Govanhill (Glasgow) and 93% in Craigton (Glasgow) thought of themselves as Scots. In 1970, the *Glasgow Herald* reported surveys in which the option of 'British' was offered. In Glasgow, 18% opted for this ('Scottish' 78%), and in other large towns in central Scotland the totals varied from 16% to 24% 'British', and from 75% to 78% 'Scottish' (*Glasgow Herald*, 11, 13, 16, 18 March 1970). Further evidence is found in the Kilbrandon Commission's *Attitudes Survey* (Kilbrandon 7, p. 47). 94% of those questioned in Scotland accepted as correct for them the designation 'A Scot'. In the North of England, 92% accepted 'A Northerner'.

The 1961 census showed that 92% of those living in Scotland had been born there, which suggests that many of the 'Britishers' are Scots-born and inclined to play down their 'Scottishness'. Characteristics attributed by Glaswegians to Scots and English are also discussed in Budge and Urwin, p. 123. Glasgow schoolchildren show a strong awareness of Scotland and things Scottish, though as they grow older they increasingly fit these into a British framework.[1]

Such subjective awareness of nationality has practical results. It colours the relationship of Scots with other national groups, and even in England or elsewhere most Scots still identify in some way with Scotland. Perhaps as important, they are identified outside Scotland as Scots if they retain a Scottish accent, or if their origins become known in some other way (e.g. when applying for a job).

In Britain, national consciousness is deep-seated, in England as in the more publicised forms in Scotland, Wales and Ireland,[2] and the reception (occasionally hostile) which the 'lesser' nationalities have throughout history faced in England (cf. Hanham 3, pp. 79–80) has fed their feeling of separateness, and at the same time demonstrated the advantages of assimilation to the majority. Similar feelings are felt by members of any minority group of 'outsiders' (e.g. by those from the north of England living in the south, and by 'lowlanders' living in the Highlands), but these groups do not share the emotional loyalty to a separate nation, which a Scottish education and upbringing have imparted.

Yet on the whole, the assimilation of Scots with English has been relatively easy. From the Union of 1707, the Scottish nobility moved the focus of their activities to London, and began to send their children to English 'public' schools. By the late nineteenth century, some of the Scottish upper-middle class were likewise being educated in such schools, or in near-copies in Scotland.

The more general migration of population to England and abroad in the twentieth century has not provided any notable social problems for the receiving countries. As far as England is concerned, Scots have entered the business and professional worlds of London and elsewhere with conspicuous success, and a few have become leading politicians and civil servants. Despite their remaining national identity, they have settled in England in total harmony with the indigenous population, and soon became almost 'as English as the English'.

In Scotland itself national consciousness has far more pronounced results. The whole fabric of Scottish society is now geared to stressing Scottish nationality and the separateness of Scotland from the rest of the U.K. The educational system is one of the strongest influences to this end. Historically derived from the Scottish Reformation, the Scottish parish schools were, until 1872, under the management of the presbyteries of the Church of Scotland. Even today, there is a discernible Church influence in the non-denominational state schools (and a much stronger Roman Catholic influence in the sector of the state system provided for Catholics).

The teaching of Scottish history, social problems and literature was neglected in the Scottish schools until the 1930s and 1940s. The 'Presbyterian' and early twentieth-century schools were barely concerned with these subjects, except in a semi-legendary form. Nevertheless, national heroes such as William Wallace, Robert the Bruce and John Knox were familiar to every Scottish school-child, as were the Battles of Bannockburn, Flodden and Culloden. In this 'history', Scotland faced its enemy England, and was alternately victor and vanquished. Eventually, it merged with England as a partner and became prosperous (very few Scottish historians have attacked the Union and its consequences).

While much of this teaching of history stressed the conflicts between Scotland and England, the period after 1707 (perhaps 1745) was treated as 'non-Scottish'. Anglo-Scottish conflict then became resolved, and Scotland ceased to be different from England. Practically no histories covering modern Scottish developments were used in Scottish schools at this time, and secondary school teaching of history was concerned with 'British' (English in fact), or 'European' history. Similarly, 'English literature' meant what it said. Apart from Robert Burns[3] and a little Scott, there was practically no time for Scottish writers.

What is the explanation for this neglect of national studies (so different from the practice in other nations in the nineteenth century)? In essence it was the desire to assert 'Britishness'. Scots, if they were to succeed (i.e. if they were to prosper in and out of Scotland), must be educated in such a way as to compete with the English on their own ground. They must be conversant at all levels with educated Englishmen, and be eligible for the highest employment in England. To this end, Scotland should be considered as merely 'North Britain'. Even the capital, Edinburgh, should be addressed as 'Edinburgh, N.B.'. In such a climate, there was little room for militant Scottishness in the educational system.

The change to the national consciousness of today is a complex process whose subtleties are beyond the scope of this book (cf. Hanham 2). Even as 'North Britain' was assimilating to England, nationalists were asserting Scotland's 'claims'. In 1853 a group of literary, clerical and romantic notables led a short-lived movement to promote home rule and the revival of Scottish history, literature and heraldry. More important was the nationalist movement of the 1880s which drew inspiration from the Irish Home Rule movement. It found a home in the Liberal Party, which from 1894 became committed to 'Home-Rule-all-Round' (i.e. for Scotland, Ireland, Wales and England).

By this time, most of the radical 'Left' were in favour of devolution. The new Scottish Labour Party and the Crofters Party, in addition to the Liberals, supported it. Not many in the traditional Scottish institutions did so, however. The Church of Scotland, threatened by the Liberal policy of disestablishment, was neutral, and most lawyers (always a Conservative group) stood aside. The nobility, with a few exceptions, were thoroughly North British. Business saw no advantages in home rule, nor indeed did the trade unions, since at this time the Scottish economy was healthy, and seemed to be prospering as a result of Imperial and English trading connections. (The trade unions, however, organised themselves into a Scottish Trades Union Congress in 1897.)

There was thus an insufficient groundswell of popular demand for devolution before the First World War, although Private Members' Bills promoting a Scottish Parliament did pass their second reading in the House of Commons in 1908, 1911, 1912 and 1913. The Liberal government did not give them much support, however (Hanham 3, pp. 97–103; Coupland, pp. 303–6). After the First World War, the Speaker's Conference of 1920 produced respectable home rule schemes for the nations of the U.K. The Irish sabotaged part of that package, and the Liberal Party was no longer there in strength to carry out the rest. The Scots showed few signs of regret at losing their 'Council' (the name given to the legislature in the 1920 schemes), and were soon plunged into industrial unrest and economic depression, which polarised politics along class lines.

Some of the 'Left' still retained their desire for Scottish self-government, and the Scottish Labour Party remained committed to this until 1929. (The STUC dropped its devolutionary policy in 1931. Hanham 2, p. 116.) The Labour governments of 1924 and 1929–31 gave Home Rule Bills no time, however, and most nationalists decided that nothing could be expected from the 'British' parties. In 1928, the National Party of Scotland was formed, followed in 1932 by the Scottish Party. These merged in 1934 to become the Scottish National Party (SNP).

The SNP at its foundation was more in the tradition of the 1853 Scottish romantics than of the only-too-close Irish nationalists of the 1920s. There was a strong literary core from the 'Scottish Renaissance', an eccentric nobleman (the Duke of Montrose), and some lawyers (e.g. Professor Andrew Dewar Gibb and the solicitor J. M. MacCormick). But once more there were few businessmen, trade unionists, churchmen, or 'ordinary people'.

With the advent of the SNP, Scottish nationalism takes on a double aspect. On the one hand, there is the electoral history of the SNP, and the demand for political devolution, while on the other there is the continuing development of Scottish national consciousness in all its forms. The former is a chronicle of 'waves' of support, followed by troughs of decline; the latter is a steady growth to the position today in which national consciousness is to be found throughout Scottish society.

The fortunes of the SNP have of course affected the intensity of national consciousness, but such consciousness is greater than the number of votes won by that party at elections. It is not necessarily concerned, as is the SNP, with 'national self-determinism', or with political devolution. It is rather an assertion of Scottishness on the part of an amorphous group of interests and individuals, whose identity is caught up with that of Scotland.

In the first place, there are the historic 'vested interests' of the

Union. These comprise the Church of Scotland, the legal profession, and the educationists (universities and colleges as well as schools). Following close behind are the local authorities, the Scottish Office, and the Scottish M.P.s. These groups are all intrinsically bound up with the position of Scotland, and each in its different way is threatened with pressures of assimilation with England which would render them or their special functions unnecessary. Numerous other organisations with a lesser pedigree of nationality have adopted a Scottish form. These desire to resist assimilation with English organisations, whether for reasons of convenience or from an actual division of interest (see ch. 10).

The independent position of Scottish football is central to working-class Scottish consciousness (as it is to the teams themselves). The formation of a separate Scottish Football Association in 1873, in contra-distinction to the Football Association (1863), indicated the strong separatist feeling among the Scots. They disliked having to travel to England to play the game, and they feared that in that country they would be little fish in a big pond. Today the intense nationalism of Scots at Scotland v. England internationals preserves a semblance of football Scottish ethnicity which otherwise splits into Irish-Catholic and Scottish-Protestant factions behind Celtic and Rangers respectively. The smaller Scottish teams have a vested interest in maintaining separate Scottish League Divisions, since many would otherwise probably disappear altogether from League structure. As it is, they survive intact within the Scottish League, big fish in a small pond, and Scottish teams find a regular place in international matches. Scottish international representation would be difficult to obtain through membership of the English League.

Cultural nationalists make a small but vociferous contribution to Scottish nationalism. They encourage the use of a Scottish means of expression in literature, and cultivate Scottishness in the other arts. A few support the SNP, or political devolution, but most are uninterested in politics, preferring to change Scottish society through education, and cultural activities. The SNP, for its part, takes little interest in cultural matters. This is not surprising, since, when asked to choose between 'preserving the traditions and culture of Scotland' or 'improving the standard of living for the people in Scotland', 6% of Scots chose the former, and 91% the latter (ORC survey, quoted in *Scotsman*, 13 May 1974).

Some of the efforts of the cultural nationalists have borne fruit in the radical changes in the content of Scottish education and of the mass media over the last forty years. Scottish history and literature have now become more acceptable to the Scottish Education Department as examinable subjects, and their coverage at schools and universities has accordingly increased. There is now considerable emphasis on modern Scottish history and social problems in Scottish education from primary schools to research at universities. The press and broadcasting have become more strongly differentiated from the media in England, and have complemented the educational development (e.g. in the schools broadcasts on Scottish subjects).

The common reference point for most individuals and organisations today is Scottish society, and they defend their interests in terms of the defence of Scotland itself. Thus the Church, law, education, trade unions and even industry use a species of nationalist argument in their public pronouncements. For example, the workers of Upper Clyde Shipbuilders in 1971 frequently stated that 'Scotland' demanded the maintenance of full employment on the Clyde.

But this kind of nationalism has in the past given little political benefit to the SNP. Most Scottish interests found the existing political structure adequate as a channel of communication, and they did not combine to press for a change in the system. This is partly because it was able to deal with a wide range of Scottish demands without reference to the British system. And where reference must be made to that system (as in economic policy), Scottish opinion is able to find sympathy from non-Scottish quarters. Thus in the Upper Clyde Shipbuilders' affair, the whole Labour movement expressed support for the Scottish workers.

Even in areas where 'Anglicisation' is the issue, there is rarely an overt attack on Scottish institutions from England. Instead, there is a Scottish and an English division of opinion among the Scots themselves. Examples are the disputes over educational curricula,[4] bishops in the Church of Scotland,[5] and assimilation of Scots Law to English Law.[6]

The affairs of these 'arenas' of Scottish life hardly bear on the fortunes of the SNP at all. Instead, the state of the SNP depends on the performance of the Scottish economy (actual or potential) in relation to that of England, and to the 'credibility' of using an SNP vote as a pressure on government to improve economic conditions in Scotland.

The waves of nationalism since the founding of the SNP bear out these conditions. The first, in the early 1930s, came at a time of severe depression in Scotland and when the Labour vote had collapsed as a result of the formation of the National (Coalition) government. A vote for the SNP in this confused political situation was as politically effective as a vote for a major party (though not many in fact decided to follow that course in the few seats which the party contested – see table 17, pp. 98–9).

A similar suspension of normal party politics was present at the end of the Second World War, when Dr Robert McIntyre won Motherwell at a by-election (April 1945). The SNP's success was largely due to the war-time party 'truce', which meant that the Conservatives did not contest the seat.

In the late 1940s there was a second nationalist wave, although this time the SNP played a minor role. The principal nationalist body was the extra-parliamentary organisation, the Scottish Convention, which organised a mass petition (the Scottish Covenant) in 1949, to demand a parliament for Scotland 'within the framework of the United Kingdom'. Two million people are reputed to have signed this document.

Once more, the nationalist mood was brought about by economic stringency, in the form of the 'austerity' measures of Sir Stafford Cripps, the Labour Chancellor of the Exchequer. But the two-party system was not weakened as in the 1930s, and the voters in Scotland swung to the Conservatives in the 1950 election, in much the same fashion as those in England (2.6% compared with 3.0%). As for the SNP, all three candidates lost their deposits (so did six other Home Rule candidates). The Conservative Government in 1952 responded to the wider evidence of the Scottish Covenant that something was amiss by establishing the Balfour Commission on Scottish Affairs (1952–4) and minor administrative changes followed its report.

Economic conditions in Scotland in the early 1950s were apparently no worse than in England, nor was the party system so out of joint that an SNP revival could be expected. But the Covenant had shown that nationalism was a powerful sentiment, and could be used successfully for political ends.

The late 1950s was the start of the third nationalist phase. The economic and party-political conditions now came together to help the SNP. Scottish unemployment rose to a level well above that in England, and emigration increased. Wages rose relatively slowly, and the decline of the older, heavier industries was more pronounced than in most parts of England. New industry could not compensate for the loss of jobs which this entailed (McCrone 1, 2). The environment in Scottish cities seemed poor in comparison with that in English cities, especially in housing, school-building and amenities.

Comparisons between the situation in Scotland and that in England were made as a result of the Conservative campaign in the 1959 general election, which stressed the new affluence of British society. The spread of television, particularly commercial television with its advertising appeals to this affluent society, no doubt emphasised the contrast. Scots knew that much of the new affluence had passed them by. In the election, they swung from Conservative to Labour, against the overall trend.

As yet, there was little sign that the major parties would not be able to cope with the discontent. The Labour Party, for example, proved a formidable Opposition from 1959 to 1964, especially in the last two years, and its Scottish M.P.s under William Ross were vehement debaters.

But in fact, Labour only held its ground electorally in Scotland during this period. They did not benefit from the collapse of the Conservatives which had taken place in most industrial seats, and in many rural ones too. Their collapse was accompanied by the intervention of Liberals or SNP candidates, who took votes from them to a greater extent than from Labour, and also brought to the polls people who had previously abstained. The shift in the voting pattern is seen in the results of the by-elections between the general elections of 1959 and 1964 (table 19).

Table 19 *By-elections, 1959–64 (1959 election figures in brackets)*

	Turn-out	C	Lab	L	SNP	Other
	%	%	%	%	%	%
Edinburgh North	53·8	54·2	30·3	15·5	–	–
(19/5/60)	(73·9)	(64·0)	(36·0)	–	–	–
Paisley (20/4/61)	68·1	13·2	45·4	41·4	–	–
	(78·9)	(42·7)	(57·3)	–	–	–
Fife, East	67·3	47·5	26·4	26·1	–	–
(8/11/61)	(75·2)	(69·9)	(30·1)	–	–	–
Glasgow, Bridgeton	41·9	20·7	57·5	–	18·7	3·1
(16/11/61)	(68·5)	(36·6)	(63·4)	–	–	
West Lothian	71·1	11·4	50·8	10·9	23·3	3·6
(14/6/62)	(77·9)	(39·7)	(60·3)	–	–	–
Glasgow, Woodside	54·7	30·0	36·0	22·0	11·1	0·9
(22/11/62)	(75·2)	(49·3)	(43·0)	(7·7)	–	–
Kinross & West	76·1	57·4	15·2	19·5	7·3	0·6
Perthshire	(71·0)	(68·2)	(16·8)	–	(15·0)	–
(7/11/63)						
Dundee, West	71·6	39·4	50·6	–	7·4	2·6
(21/11/63)	(82·9)	(48·3)	(49·6)	–	–	(2·1)
Dumfriesshire	71·6	40·8	38·5	10·9	9·8	–
(12/12/63)	(77·4)	(58·4)	(41·6)	–	–	–
Rutherglen	82·0	44·5	55·5	–	–	–
(14/5/64)	(85·9)	(52·1)	(47·9)	–	–	–

In most of these by-elections, the turn-out was high (except in Edinburgh and Glasgow), and the slump in Conservative support was matched by the new strength of the Liberals and SNP, especially in Labour-held seats. In such seats, many Conservatives must have felt that the most effective challenge to Labour was in voting for a third (or fourth) party. This strategy does not seem to have been adopted to the same extent by Labour supporters in Conservative seats, for although there was some falling off of Labour support, most of the defections again came from the Conservative side, who alongside new voters swelled the Liberal and the SNP vote.

The SNP made its first appearance at the Glasgow-Bridgeton by-election in November 1961, winning 18·7% of the vote. The party's candidate, Ian Macdonald, was so encouraged by the result that he decided to offer his services as full-time organiser of the SNP. From that time, a third factor was added to the economic and political preconditions for Nationalist electoral success – organisation. Macdonald built up the grass-roots organisation of the SNP, by aiding the formation of branches, raising finance, and maintaining an efficient central office. Soon membership was rising fast, and the new activists seemed more practical, and less romantic, than those in the party in former years. One of them, William Wolfe, a local businessman, contested West Lothian in 1962 and received 23·3% of the vote. In 1969, he became chairman of the party.

While later by-elections in this period (1959–64) were by no means equal to this showing (partly because the Liberal revival stole the Nationalists' thunder), in the general election of 1964 there were 15 SNP candidates, a three-fold increase compared to 1959. Wolfe greatly increased his vote in West Lothian, coming second in the poll, but there was as yet no evidence that the SNP was a political force in the industrial heartland of Scotland.

In the only Scottish by-election between the general elections of 1964 and 1966, at Roxburgh, Peebles and Selkirk, the SNP did not stand, and the seat was gained by the Liberals from the Conservatives. Yet this was almost the end of the Liberal revival. In the 1966 election, the Liberal vote in Scotland dropped, and the third-party mantle began to descend on the SNP. That party now approached the Liberals in the number of seats fought, and of votes won. The Liberal appeal remained strong in the rural areas, but it made no progress in the towns. In contrast, the SNP now started to challenge urban seats, although with very little success at first.

The 1966 results gave no indication of what was to come. In the 4 major cities the SNP lost all its deposits, and elsewhere achieved second place in only 3 seats (Kinross and West Perthshire, West Stirlingshire and West Lothian). The average SNP vote in the 23 seats it contested was 14·5%, amounting to 5% of the Scottish total.

The years from 1966 are now legendary in Scottish political history. A substantial literature[7] has been written which describes and analyses the fortunes of the SNP. Much of this literature has been of a polemical nature, written in the heat of battle by protagonists. Other contributions, by political analysts, are often marked by conclusions and predictions which events have since proved false. Perhaps it is even now unsafe to be too certain about the meaning of Scottish politics during that period, or in the mid-1970s.

The chronicle of events is clear enough. The first by-election after 1966, at Glasgow, Pollok, in March 1967, showed an SNP vote of 28%. This had been a marginally held Labour seat, and it now fell to the Conservatives. In May 1967, the municipal elections were contested by a large number of SNP candidates, who won 16% of the votes and gained 23 seats. The climax came at the Hamilton parliamentary by-election in November 1967, when the SNP actually won the seat, with 46% of the vote. In this 'safe' Labour seat, the Labour vote fell from 71·2% to 41·5%. The Conservative vote dropped from 28·8% to 12·5%. Interest in the election was obviously high, for the turn-out (73·7%) was slightly above that at the general election.

The shock this result created in Scottish politics was renewed at the municipal elections in May 1968, when the SNP won 30% of the vote, gaining 100 seats. In Glasgow, the party held the balance of power between the Progressive/Conservative ruling group and the Labour Party.

There then came a decline. No further by-elections took place until October 1969 (Glasgow, Gorbals), when the SNP vote fell to 25%. The local elections in May 1969 had already shown that the tide was turning, with the SNP vote at only 22%, and 20 gains. At the last by-election before the 1970 general election (South Ayrshire) the party polled 20%, and the vote at local elections in May 1970 (12·6%) was similar to that at the general election the following month (11·4%). In that election the SNP lost Hamilton, but gained the Western Isles. Although it lost 43 deposits (a deposit is lost when a candidate gains less than 12·5% of the vote), it came second in 9 seats.

The period immediately after 1970 showed that while the Party had dropped down from its 1968 peak, it was not entering a sharp decline, and was able to make a massive recovery in 1973 and 1974. At the Stirling and Falkirk by-election in 1971 it came second to Labour with 35%, and at the Dundee East by-election in March 1973 was within 1,141 votes of winning that 'safe' Labour seat. Victory finally came at the Govan (also safe Labour) by-election in November 1973, which was won by a majority of 571. The Party's performance in local elections after 1970 was not generally impressive, however, and all the SNP councillors in Glasgow had lost their seats by 1972. At the regional and district elections in May 1974 there were few SNP candidates, and outside the Central Region the Party did badly (5/103 councillors in Strathclyde; 0/53 in Grampian, despite having 3 M.P.s there; 9/34 in Central).

Meanwhile, there had been a big advance at the general election of February 1974. Building on the confidence gained at the 1973 by-elections, and on its strength in seats where it came second in 1970, the SNP was able to mount a campaign in 70 of the 71 seats (the exception being Jo Grimond's Orkney and Shetland). Six seats were gained (Aberdeenshire East, Argyll, Banffshire, Clackmannan and East Stirlingshire, Dundee East and Moray and Nairn) and one (Govan) lost. The Western Isles was held with a greatly increased majority. Four of the gains were from Conservative and two from Labour. Then in October 1974 another four seats were gained from the Conservatives (Angus South, Dunbartonshire East, Galloway, and Perth and East Perthshire), making a total of 11 M.P.s. The Party's share of the Scottish vote rose to 30·4% (it had been 21·9% in February), and it was now the second largest party in Scotland. No deposits were

Table 20 (a) *Growth in SNP vote at general elections, 1955–74*

	No. of votes	No. of candidates	% of Scottish poll
1955	12,112	2	0·5
1959	21,738	5	0·8
1964	64,044	15	2·4
1966	128,474	23	5·0
1970	306,802	65	11·4
1974 (Feb.)	633,180	70	21·9
1974 (Oct.)	839,628	71	30·4

(b) *SNP vote at parliamentary elections, 1966–74*

		% of votes cast
1966	General election	5·0
1967	Pollok by-election	20·2
	Hamilton by-election	46·0
1969	Gorbals by-election	25·0
1970	South Ayrshire by-election	20·3
	General election	11·4
1971	Stirling, Falkirk and Grangemouth by-election	34·6
1973	Dundee East by-election	30·2
	Govan by-election	41·9
	Edinburgh North by-election	18·9
1974	February general election	21·9
	October general election	30·4

lost, and second place was secured in 42 of the 71 Scottish seats. It was easily the biggest nationalist advance in recent British electoral history.

Obviously, an analysis of the SNP 'phenomenon' is essential to an understanding of the Scottish political system. The background to its rise after 1955 is the familiar one of economic 'relative deprivation'. This deepened after 1960, with soaring unemployment, emigration and inferior wages. The return of a Labour government in 1964 brought high hopes that the regional imbalance would be redressed. Stronger regional policies were introduced, but these were quickly modified by 'squeeze' measures curtailing government and private spending. The Hamilton by-election victory of the SNP came at a time of political and economic gloom, in Scotland as in the rest of Britain.

But in Scotland, the SNP offered an alternative to voting for the Conservatives, who were already discredited in Scottish eyes. This was particularly important for disgruntled Labour voters, since the SNP presented something of a 'radical' alternative. Previous abstainers also found the SNP attractive, as long as its policies on general political questions were not spelt out. The poor performance of Britain in world affairs, the decline of the British Empire, and the new found status of small countries in the U.N. may have contributed to the feeling that Scotland could reasonably 'go it alone'. The amount of attention paid to the SNP in the press and TV (see ch. 10) also helped to mobilise opinion in its favour, as did the vigorous campaigning of the party itself.

Such campaigning was a result of the new organisation of the party. The SNP is essentially a decentralised party, and its strength is in local branches (not constituency association). Such branches had been formed in most parts of the country by 1967, although many had small memberships (see table 21 (a)).

The SNP's activists were new men in politics, rather than converts from other parties.[8] They were an untapped political stratum, but one with little staying power. Typically employed in small organisations or on their own account, there were few trade union activists and employees of large business firms. The 'small man' character of the party has occasionally led to a description of it as 'Poujadiste', or anti-authority. While there is something of this in the psychology of many members, the party's official policy has always stressed the importance of strong state action to improve economic and social conditions. Unlike the Poujadistes, it has not supported small shopkeepers against other interests. There has been practically no illegal action in the tactics adopted, and a study of the activists has revealed that they are well adjusted to their position in society.[9]

The identity of SNP supporters at this time is more obscure.

Many voted SNP for a time, while 'identifying' with one of the major parties. Of these, a majority came from the Labour Party (Cornford and Brand in Wolfe, p. 26). At the general election of 1970, most returned to their original allegiance. In that election, the Liberal vote in north-eastern and Highland constituencies was greatly reduced by defections to the SNP. One reason for this was the hostility of many in these areas to the policy of entry into the E.E.C., which the Liberal Party supported. Some Liberals, therefore, switched over to the SNP on this issue.

Table 21 (*a*) *The organisation of the Scottish National Party, 1974*

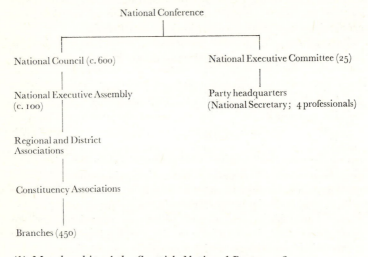

(*b*) *Membership of the Scottish National Party, 1962–74*

1962	2,000	1966	42,000
1963	4,000	1967	80,000
1964	8,000	1968	120,000
1965	16,000 (June)	1971	70,000
1965	20,000 (November)	1974	85,000

A survey in six Labour-held seats in Scotland, taken at the end of 1968,[10] found that only 15% of the sample said they would vote SNP if a general election were to take place immediately. These were drawn mainly from three roughly equal sources: 27% from Labour voters in the 1966 general election, 25% from Conservative and Liberal voters, and 20% from those who were too young to vote in 1966.

The attitudes towards policies of these SNP supporters bore a striking resemblance to the attitudes of electors in England at that time who were not consistent Labour or Conservative supporters,

A parallel English survey showed that this group agreed closely with SNP supporters in its evaluation of the Labour government's performance on various issues, its assessment of whether the Conservatives would have done better, and its identification of the most urgent issues facing the government (these were mainly socio-economic, such as 'holding down prices', 'full employment', 'increasing exports').

Even on purely Scottish issues there was no unity in the SNP ranks. Only 40% desired a fully independent Scotland, with 59% seeking only control over internal affairs. The main advantages of a Scottish parliament were seen as control over the Scottish economy and a better handling of local politics. Yet only 53% thought that Scotland had been treated worse than the rest of the U.K. under the Labour government.

In both England and Scotland between 1967 and 1969 there were a large number of people who changed sides politically, or were 'don't knows'. In both countries, their reaction to the performance of the Labour government on economic issues was the cause of this state of flux. In England, however, Labour lost more support, and the Conservatives less, than in Scotland. The surveys quoted show that in England Labour retained only 53% of its 1966 support, while the Conservatives retained 90%. In Scotland, the totals were 67% and 78% respectively. The main movement from Labour in Scotland was not to the Nationalists but to the ranks of the 'don't knows'.

It is therefore important to see the political situations in England and Scotland as subject to common influences, and producing common reactions in terms of political attitudes. But in terms of party preferences, the Scottish electorate moved into a pattern of its own, partly because of the SNP and its unique appeal to Scots, but also because of the special weakness of the Conservative Party in Scotland (see ch. 6).

This became more clear in 1974, when the Conservative Party sank even further (to 25% of the vote), while the SNP rose to 30%. The Labour and Liberal parties also suffered from the SNP's advance. Labour dropped from nearly 50% of the Scottish vote in 1966 to 36% in 1974. While the Liberals greatly increased their vote in England in February 1974, they were unable to make progress in Scotland, and stuck at 8%. This is partly because in Scotland the Liberals were badly organised, and partly because peculiar 'Scottish' issues were present in Scotland which the Liberals could not effectively capitalise on. Clearly, there was no room for both the SNP and the Liberals in most Scottish seats, and by October 1974 there was doubt as to whether there was room for the Conservatives either.

It would appear, then, that the SNP took votes from all other parties. A more detailed analysis would suggest that the character of the SNP's support varies considerably from place to place, and from election to election. In the 1970 election, for example, the seats where it did best were rural 'fringe' seats, with a few 'specialities' in the industrial belt in which prominent candidates stood. In February 1974 it seemed that the SNP was taking more votes from Labour in the Conservative-held rural seats in the north, and more from Conservative in the urban Labour-held seats in the central belt (see article by J. M. Bochel and D. T. Denver, *Scotsman*, 27 September 1974). This conclusion was based on a comparison of the net losses of the major parties. In October 1974, the Conservatives lost more than Labour, presumably to SNP. One explanation for the variations in voting patterns is the phenomenon of 'tactical voting'. In this a Labour voter votes SNP when that party seems to have a better chance of ousting the Conservative, and a Conservative does likewise in a Labour-held seat. This has some plausibility, but it would need to be supported by survey evidence. It makes an interesting variant on the previous 'protest vote' description of SNP support, which presumably had no such calculation in mind, and merely represented rejection (pro tempore) of the major parties. It is, of course, true that many voted SNP because of positive attraction to that party, either because of sympathy with the aim of Scottish independence (surveys indicate around 20% backed this in Scotland in 1974, see for example the ORC surveys in the *Scotsman*, 13 May 1974 (17%), 4 October 1974 (21%)), or because of desire for devolution, or because the SNP 'gets things done' for Scotland.

In the north of Scotland, where the SNP did particularly well, its strength was massed in the small towns which made up a considerable proportion of the constituencies. Here, Dr Michael Dyer of Aberdeen University has analysed the SNP vote in terms of the realisation of a latent 'anti-Conservative' majority, thwarted for historical and political reasons (see 'Why Tory stronghold crumbled', *Scotsman*, 24 October 1974). After the decline of the Liberals, who dominated the area up to 1918, the 'anti-Conservative' vote either abstained or was split between the Liberals and Labour. The last could make little headway in a society which distrusted trade unions and industrialisation. But it was anti-landlord and anti-deferential, as well as strongly parochial. The SNP produced a majority from these and other disparate elements in 1974. In some places, about half of the SNP voters were voting for the first time (Dyer's survey of North Aberdeen in February 1974, reported in the *Press and Journal* of 19 March 1974). In North Aberdeen, nearly all the converts from other parties were from Labour, and the SNP was particularly strong in the under-35 age group, and among women.

The picture in Scotland generally emerges from the System Three Scotland poll conducted in 38 Scottish constituencies at the end of May 1974, when the SNP was supported by 26% of the respondents (it was 30% in the October election).

| | Total | Class | | | | Age | | | Sex | |
		AB	C1	C2	DE	18–34	35–54	55+	Male	Female
	%	%	%	%	%	%	%	%	%	%
Conservative	29	57	41	21	19	19	31	36	21	35
Labour	38	13	21	43	49	35	36	43	42	35
Liberal	8	10	8	10	6	8	10	5	8	8
SNP	26	20	28	25	27	37	24	15	28	24
Others	1	—	1	1	1	2	—	1	2	—

Source: System Three Scotland, Dundee.

This shows the SNP's strength in the youngest age group, and its very even support throughout the social classes and between the sexes. In October 1974, System Three found that the SNP was getting support from the other parties in the following proportions: 13% of former Conservative voters, 14% of former Labour voters, and 14% of former Liberals (*Glasgow Herald*, 10 October 1974). In the North of Scotland alone, the proportions were 18% of Labour voters, 18% of Liberals and 9% of Conservatives (*Glasgow Herald*, 8 October 1974). (In the event, the Conservative vote throughout Scotland dropped more than the Labour vote.) Survey-evidence for religion and SNP support relates to 1970. Roman Catholics made up 19% of the SNP's support in Glasgow (they are about 30% of the population there),[11] with lower figures for Hamilton, Rutherglen and Stirling.[12] There is some evidence that Orangemen in 1974 supported the SNP, out of disillusionment with the Conservatives' 'soft' policy on Ulster. In the industrial field, shop stewards were being increasingly attracted to the SNP, and nationalism was blamed for some strikes in 1974.

The October 1974 election established the SNP as the second party in Scotland in terms of votes (30.4%). Its 11 seats were mainly outside the central industrial belt (Dundee East, Dunbartonshire East and Clackmannan were the exceptions), and Labour preferred to call the SNP 'Tartan Tories'. This description, however, does not tally with the analysis quoted above which sees the Nationalists in North East Scotland as anti-Conservatives, nor does it take account of the strong support coming from former Labour voters. In many industrial seats the SNP did better against Labour than any Conservative candidates had done.

The SNP policy, while opposed to nationalisation, included many radical proposals,* and some candidates such as Winifred Ewing and Margo MacDonald in Govan were socialist in sympathy. George Reid, the Clackmannan SNP M.P., was a former Labour Party member. On the other hand, most SNP candidates were middle class, and the Party's links with the official trade union movement were tenuous. The conversion of Sir Hugh Fraser, the Scottish millionnaire businessman, to the SNP in April 1974, linked capitalism with nationalism, and brought the Party financial support.

Explanations for the new phase of the 'phenomenon' are somewhat different from those applying in 1967–8. In the earlier period, 'relative deprivation' seemed the most plausible hypothesis, with Scots protesting at the deprived economic state of Scotland compared with that in the prosperous parts of England (the result, it seemed, of neglect by London government).† By 1974, the potential of the Scottish economy was transformed by the discoveries of North Sea oil, and its relationship to the British economy was now seen as 'saviour', since it would solve the balance of payments deficit. The combination of successive British governments' failures to manage the economy, and the reliance on oil to redress this failure played into the hands of

---

*The SNP's manifesto at the October 1974 election (*Scotland's Future*) included the following: a Scottish constitution, covering the Crown, National Assembly, and Judiciary. The Assembly is to have one chamber, elected for four years (fixed term) by the 'alternative vote' method. All land will be Scottish-owned, but security of tenure to non-Scots is guaranteed. Land badly used will be specially taxed. An Industrial Development Corporation, financed partly from oil revenues, will stimulate industry. Oil production is to be slowed down, with Scottish participation in oil companies rather than nationalisation. Scotland is to decide by referendum whether to join the EEC, and is to seek an 'Association of British States' and membership of the British Commonwealth. A minimum wage and higher social security payments are promised. Gaelic is to have 'equal official status' with English.

† But see Roger Brooks, 'Scottish Nationalism: Relative Deprivation and Social Mobility'; Unpublished Ph.D. thesis, Michigan State University, 1973. Brooks argues that SNP supporters are not as conscious of personal relative deprivation, and many see themselves as upwardly mobile. Yet they share a feeling that Scotland *collectively* is deprived. This fits the hypothesis that the SNP does best in areas of fast social change (New Towns, oil-boom areas), where incomes are higher and class divisions less important, and least well in more static communities (e.g. large towns in central Scotland). Support for the SNP is particularly strong in social class C1 (skilled non-manual), and most of the activists are middle class.

nationalists and devolutionists, since if Britain could be saved by oil, how much more would Scotland stand to benefit if that country controlled it? Thus 'relative deprivation' was matched by the prospect of 'relative affluence' under a Scottish government. Arguments that Scots would suffer if they were cut off from London 'subsidies' no longer retained credibility when matched against the new-found wealth off the Scottish coasts. Thus, in 1974, businessmen and economists were to be found supporting devolution or independence on economic grounds (e.g. Jack McGill, *Scotland's Goals*, Collins (Glasgow and London, 1974); the Scottish Council Research Institute's Report, *Economic Development and Devolution*, Edinburgh, June 1974; the Hudson Institute (Europe) Report, *The United Kingdom in 1980*, Associated Business Programmes (London, 1974); D. I. MacKay and A. G. Mackay, *The Political Economy of North Sea Oil*, Martin Robertson (London, 1975)).

The effect of Scottish nationalism on political opinion is seen in the acceptance of devolution by the major parties. While this is directly related to the electoral threat posed by the SNP, it also derives from a more general 'conversion' of opinion in Scotland to devolution, and to a generally heightened national consciousness in Scotland since the 1960s.

The response of the two major parties to the SNP 'wave' of 1967–8 was to institute inquiries into the devolution question. The Conservative Party in Scotland set up a study group in 1967, which reported in favour of a Scottish Assembly at their conference in 1968. Edward Heath, the party leader, endorsed this at the conference, and set up a 'Constitutional Committee' to provide definite and detailed proposals. The result was the Report on Scottish Government (March 1970), which recommended a 'Convention', directly elected, to take on the work of the Scottish committees of the House of Commons. This was accepted by the Scottish conference in May 1970, by a three-to-one majority, and became official Conservative policy. It did not, however, pay any obvious electoral dividend, and when the SNP showed signs of decline the party conference reneged on the proposal (May 1973). At the following conference, however (May 1974), an assembly indirectly elected from local councillors was accepted. After the October 1974 election, the Conservative leadership in Scotland came out in support of the Labour Government's proposal for a directly-elected assembly (*Scotsman*, 16 Oct. 1974).

While this was the position taken by Labour after August 1974, it was in marked contrast to the party's earlier pronouncements. The response to the SNP's earlier challenge was the announcement of setting-up of a Commission on the Constitution in December 1968 (the 'Crowther' later 'Kilbrandon' Commission).

133

At the same time, the party spokesman in Scotland (in particular, Scottish Secretary William Ross) denounced nationalism and devolution as 'shabby' and 'irrelevant', and proposed no major alteration to the government of Scotland other than that Edinburgh sittings of the Scottish Grand Committee 'could be tried' (*The Government of Scotland.* Evidence of the Labour Party in Scotland to the Commission on the Constitution, Glasgow, March 1970, p. 19).

Meanwhile, some Labour M.P.s and activists renewed Labour's traditional 'Home Rule' policy, which had been practically shelved since the 1920s. In the 1960s, John Mackintosh was the most prominent of these (see Mackintosh 1), but by 1974 a 'ginger-group' of M.P.s led by James Sillars (M.P. for South Ayrshire) was demanding 'substantial' devolution (*Scottish Labour and Devolution,* A discussion paper, 1974). The crucial voice in the Labour Party, however, was that of the trade unions, and Alex Kitson of the Transport and General Workers Union (formerly leader of a Scottish trade union), and a member of the Labour Party's National Executive Committee, persuaded that Committee to support devolution. The Executive of the Scottish Council of the Labour Party was not in favour, but at a special conference in Glasgow on 17 August 1974, the party in Scotland overwhelmingly adopted the devolution stance. Powerful unions such as the TGWU, AUEW and NUM were all in favour, as were about half the constituency parties. This led on to the Labour Government's formal support for an elected Scottish assembly (*Democracy and Devolution: Proposals for Scotland and Wales* (HMSO, Cmnd. 5732, Sept. 1974)).

All this has to be seen in the background of the changing climate of opinion in Scotland regarding devolution and nationalism, and the widespread support for an assembly which had been seen in the evidence to the Commission on the Constitution. The Report of that Commission (Kilbrandon 5) published at the end of October 1973 may also have been influential in shaping opinion. Eight of the eleven Commissioners who signed the majority Report favoured a form of legislative devolution for Scotland in which 'transferred' matters would come under a Scottish assembly. These matters would be basically those pertaining to existing Scottish legislation and Scottish Office functions. The U.K. Parliament would retain the ultimate right to legislate on all matters, but by convention it would seek the consent of the Scottish government if it entered the 'Scottish' sphere. (Kilbrandon 5, p. 337.) It was this scheme which appealed most to the Scottish organisations who were canvassed during 1974 for their reactions and which was basically adopted by the Government. Other schemes supported were a 'deliberative and advisory' assembly with limited legislative powers (one Commissioner) and 'executive devolution' in which a Scottish Assembly would 'execute policies within a framework set by U.K. legislation (Kilbrandon 5, p. 252) (two Commissioners). The Minority Report, signed by two Commissioners, objected to 'transferred' powers, and wanted decentralisation of all central government functions to the regions (Kilbrandon 6). It is important to note that all thirteen Commissioners supported an elected assembly of one kind or another for Scotland.

The Kilbrandon Report by itself would probably not have inspired the Government to move quickly on devolution, and indeed the Report was not given a debate in the House of Commons (devolution was not debated until 3–4 February 1975). Although civil servants did start to study the implications of devolution before the February 1974 election, it was that election, with its SNP successes, which brought the matter forcibly on to the agenda. The increased size of SNP representation in the House of Commons during 1974 (11 M.P.s after October) and the swelling of the SNP vote to 22% in February, followed by 30% in October, made it seem that Scotland was now on a collision course with the rest of the United Kingdom.

But how accurate would that assessment be? In the first place, Scottish opinion on home rule has not apparently changed in recent years. A comparison of the responses to identical questions in surveys conducted for the Kilbrandon Commission in the summer of 1970 (Kilbrandon 7, p. 62) with the ORC survey reported in the *Scotsman* on 13 May 1974, shows that support for the status quo *rose* between 1970 and 1974, while the home rule sympathies apparently dropped.

	Kilbrandon survey (1970)	ORC (May 1974)
	%	%
Leave things as they are at present	6	14
Keep things much the same as they are now but make sure that the needs of Scotland are better understood by the Government	19	20
Keep the present system but allow more decisions to be made in Scotland	26	24
Have a new system of governing Scotland so that as many decisions as possible are made in the area	24	23
Let Scotland take over complete responsibility for running things in Scotland	23	18
Don't know	1	1

In the Kilbrandon survey, Scotland was clearly more dissatisfied with the status quo than other regions of Great Britain, but some doubt is cast on the credibility of the answers by the fact that 21% in the South of England wanted complete responsibility for running things there. Additional evidence comes from questionnaires which pose alternative forms of government for Scotland in more specific terms, and these produce a somewhat different result. (ORC surveys reported in the *Scotsman*, 13 May, 4 October 1974.)

	ORC (*May 1974*)	ORC (*October 1974*)
	%	%
Keep the present system	21	21
Have a Scottish Assembly, not directly elected but made up of representatives of the new regional councils, which would handle some Scottish affairs and would be responsible to Parliament at Westminster	19	14
Have a directly elected Scottish Assembly which would handle some Scottish affairs and would be responsible to Parliament at Westminster	24	17
Have a Scottish Parliament which would handle most Scottish affairs, including many economic affairs, leaving the Westminster Parliament responsible for defence, foreign affairs, and international economic policy	16	24
Make Scotland completely independent of the rest of Britain, with a Scottish Parliament which would handle all Scottish affairs	17	20
Don't know	4	4

This shows a clear rise in the support for the stronger forms of home rule during 1974, with that for the status quo remaining constant at about one-fifth. It is significant that in October 1974 44% supported independence or what could be described as federalism.

Support for devolution is not a matter of great intensity for Scots, according to the surveys. Only 11% considered 'more power-sharing for Scotland and Wales' to be 'one of the most important problems that the Government should do something about' (*Scotsman*, 10 October 1974). And this was higher than the figures in previous surveys (e.g. *Scotsman*, 15, 22 February, 27

September 1974). But a survey published in the *Scotsman* on 6 March 1975 (but conducted in 1974), found that 60% of Scots rated devolution as 'an important issue'.

The paradoxes are increased when further survey responses are examined. In the ORC survey (*Scotsman*, 4 October 1974), 68% in Scotland believed that 'the oil in the North Sea should be used to benefit all of Britain and not just Scotland alone'. But 58% supported the view that 'the oil in the North Sea belongs to Scotland, and the tax revenue from it should be used for the benefit of the Scottish people'. 68% thought that Scotland would probably get very little from the North Sea oil discoveries, since it would all go to the oil companies and the British government. Yet, despite the new-found wealth in Scotland, 49% thought that Scotland would not soon be strong enough economically to be independent of the rest of Britain, with only 39% 'optimists' on that score. Nevertheless, 57% thought that Scotland had much better economic prospects than other parts of Britain. On the EEC, 70% wanted Scotland to have its own representatives in the Common Market, but only 44% were definitely in favour of staying in. (In the Referendum on 5 June 1975, 58% voted YES, compared with 67% for the U.K.)

While there is ample evidence of confusion and uncertainty in the minds of Scots about devolution and independence, there is undoubtedly an increasingly general and vociferous assertion of national identity in Scotland, coupled with specific demands for devolution or independence from 'opinion-leaders'. This latter development is of the greatest significance, since it contrasts with the finding of the Kilbrandon Report that 'the overwhelming opinion among those involved in public life in Scotland was in favour of preserving the *status quo*' (Kilbrandon 5, p. 112, par. 364). This could not be maintained in 1974, as Table 22(*b*) below shows. Nearly all 'spokesman' groups and all the political parties had come out for devolution by the end of 1974, and many newspapers and prominent individuals were voicing devolutionist sentiments, where before they had been silent. The *Daily Record*, the top-selling newspaper in Scotland, and staunchly Labour, campaigned vigorously for a Scottish Assembly before the Scottish Labour Party conference in August 1974 (see *Daily Record*, 16 August 1974), and attacked the Scottish Party leaders for not granting such an Assembly strong economic powers, including control over the Scottish Development Agency (10 February 1975). Its sister-paper, the *Sunday Mail*, did likewise. *The Scotsman* continually promoted devolution, or, as it preferred, federalism (e.g. *Scotsman*, 22 February 1975). Even the 'unionist' *Glasgow Herald*, under a new editor in late 1974, began to treat devolution sympathetically (30, 31 October, 1 November 1974).

137

Some significant statements were made by prominent individuals, which marked a shift in opinion among the Scottish 'Establishment'. Sir William McEwan Younger, chairman of the Conservative Party in Scotland from 1971 to 1974, and a leading businessman, attacked the Department of Trade and Industry under the Conservatives, as having 'displayed in matters relating to off-shore oil a mixture of ignorance and arrogance which demonstrated over-centralisation at its worst' (*Scotsman*, 2 November 1974). James McGuinness, now retired from his position as top Scottish Office economic planner, sought for Scottish Ministers and departments 'a much stronger point of entry (both in Whitehall and in Brussels) into major policy-making on the economic front' (*Scotsman*, 20 May 1974). As for the legal establishment, Lord Hunter, chairman of the Scottish Law Commission, attacked Whitehall departments for their 'lack of knowledge of, or any real feeling for, the private Law of Scotland', and he thought that a single department covering all aspects of the law of Scotland 'should have been set up long ago' (*Scotsman*, 3 March 1975). These are straws in the wind, no doubt, but they show a significant shift in attitudes and in the method of their expression.

The 'key issues' relating to devolution are summarised in Table 22(*a*), and the general proposals of the principal Scottish organisations during 1974 in Table 22 (*b*).

The array of bodies (collective and individual) shown in table 22(*b*) in favour of some kind of devolution has out-voiced in quantity those who have spoken against it, but the opinions of the latter are important. In Notes of Dissent to the 'Scottish Constitutional Committee's' Report, *Scotland's Government* (inspired by the Conservative Party), Sir Charles Wilson, Principal of Glasgow University, and Professor J. D. B. Mitchell of Edinburgh University (Constitutional Law) write forcibly in opposition to the proposed 'Scottish Convention'. The former says, 'I am against parliamentary devolution as likely to impair the efficient political unity of Great Britain', and the latter, 'I do not believe that there is adequate political living-space for such a body' (*op. cit.*, pp. 69–72).

These sentiments have been echoed by the Labour Party (Scottish Council) and the Confederation of British Industry (Scottish Council), in evidence to the Constitutional Commission. They have also been found in editorials in the *Glasgow Herald* before 1974. In essence, they provide a counter-claim to that of Scottish nationalism. The counter-claim asserts that Scotland and England are essentially one society, and so require only one government and legislature. Such differences as there are between them are minor, and are adequately taken care of under the present arrangements. If Scotland were to be separated off further, it would lose influence at the central decision-making centre, and gain no real power by way of compensation. Although the remoteness of government is a feature of modern society, it can be met by strengthening local government, granting further

Table 22(a) *Key Issues in Devolution*

1. *Type of division of powers.* Will powers be 'transferred' to a Scottish legislature, or 'delegated'? Will Westminster have a 'veto' over Scottish legislation, or will it have a positive power to legislate itself in areas within the Scottish sphere?

2. *Legislative spheres.* What subjects will be within the competence of the Scottish legislature? Will it have 'all' of education, health, etc., or merely 'part' of these functions (e.g. omitting the school-leaving age, teachers' pay and the universities from education)? What about industry, energy, transport and employment?

3. *Secretary of State for Scotland.* Will this office be retained, and if so, will the Scottish Secretary exercise functions (e.g. over the Scottish Development Agency) for which he will be responsible to Westminster, not Edinburgh?

4. *Finance.* Will there be an 'expenditure'-based system (i.e. a block grant from the Treasury, to be spent by the Scottish government), or a 'revenue'-based system (i.e. taxes raised in Scotland). Or a mix of the two? Will there be any revenue from North Sea Oil?

5. *Scottish–U.K. relationship.* Will Scotland be represented in the U.K. Cabinet (see Secretary of State for Scotland, above)? Will finance be regulated by an Exchequer Board or by inter-governmental negotiation? Will 71 Scottish M.P.s be retained in the House of Commons? Will they be allowed to vote on English, Welsh, or Northern Irish matters?

6. *Type of Scottish Government.* Will the executive be a Cabinet-type, with Prime Minister, or a local-authority-type with a fused executive-legislative committee structure? Will there be proportional representation, and fixed legislative terms? Will Westminster and Edinburgh elections be held on the same dates? Could the U.K. Prime Minister dissolve the Scottish legislature? Is it to be a 'Parliament' or an 'Assembly'?

7. *The EEC.* Should a Scottish government be directly represented in the EEC?

Note: by early 1975, the Government had already come to a decision on many of these questions. See for example, *Democracy and Devolution*, Cmnd. 5732, Sept. 1974, and speech by Edward Short in the House of Commons, 3 Feb. 1975, and to the Labour Party (*Times*, 6 March 1975). Westminster was to remain 'sovereign' in all legislative matters; the Secretary of State for Scotland was to be retained, as were the 71 Scottish M.P.s; finance was to follow the 'expenditure' pattern, but without an Exchequer Board. Most of the other 'key issues' were unresolved.

Table 22(b) *Proposals relating to Scottish devolution, 1974*

Labour Party (Scottish Council)	Directly-elected legislative assembly.
Conservative Party	Scottish conference supported indirectly elected assembly of local councillors (May), but leadership subsequently supported Labour scheme (October).
Scottish Liberal Party	Federal system; U.K. Exchequer Board; some taxes and 50% of oil revenues to Scottish parliament.
Communist Party	Assembly and government, with income tax and corporation tax powers.
Scottish National Party	Sovereign state, but prepared to support devolution *pro tem*.
Co-operative Party	Rejected devolution (13 April).
Church of Scotland	An 'elected national authority' for Scottish affairs.
Free Presbyterian Church	Opposed devolution (1 July).
Scottish Trades Union Congress	Assembly; Government; U.K. Exchequer Board (limited Scottish taxes).
Confederation of British Industry (Scotland)	Assembly 'irrelevant' (5 August).
Scottish Landowners' Federation	Advisory Scottish council.
Scottish Council (Development and Industry)	Assembly with strong industrial powers.
Scottish Council Research Institute	Assembly and Government with 50% of all public revenues including oil revenues, and wide economic powers.
Scottish Chamber of Commerce	Scottish 'Senate' with minor powers.
Highlands and Islands Development Board	Kilbrandon majority report.
Law Society of Scotland	New Scottish department equivalent to Lord Chancellor's Office. Perhaps Scottish Standing Committee on Law Reform, to meet in Edinburgh.
Glasgow Corporation	Rejects Scottish assembly.
Strathclyde Region	At first rejects, then accepts assembly.
Edinburgh Corporation	Would 'discuss' assembly with local authorities.

administrative decentralisation, and establishing new forms of control over government (e.g. a system of administrative law).

Another argument put forward by anti-devolutionists is that Scotland is itself divided politically and socially, and if left to itself would produce an Ulster-type situation, with one-party rule and the re-emergence of religious conflicts. Northern Ireland has offered an awful precedent in devolution, according to this school of thought, and a similar situation could develop in a Scotland under home rule.

The anti-devolutionist argument, where it refers to Scotland, seems to be at this point largely groundless. Certainly, since 1959 the Labour Party has appeared secure in Scotland, and a system of proportional representation would be appropriate to ensure adequate representation of minorities. But the party system in Scotland has no overtones of 'dominant' majority rule, as in Ulster, nor is it as static. As for religious strife, what there is is on quite a different scale from that in Ireland, and ought not to be affected by home rule. The Scottish state system of Roman Catholic schools, inaugurated in 1918, was created essentially by Protestant Scots, and shows generosity on the part of the Protestant majority to the Catholic minority in Scoland.

A more fundamental objection to devolution is that much of the nationalism of recent years has been an expression of protest unrelated to support for devolution. The mobilisation of Scottish opinion in favour of a separate parliament, convention or assembly has been part of a 'band-wagon' based on the SNP's electoral successes, themselves largely based on a 'protest vote'. Had such a demand been deeply felt, it would have been voiced continually, not just in the late 1960s.

In reply, historians of Scottish nationalism are able to trace political demands for national self-determination or devolution for over 100 years, in which the same arguments have been used repeatedly (Hanham 3). As recently as the early 1950s, the evidence to the Balfour Commission on Scottish Affairs, anticipated in most respects that to the Commission on the Constitution.

These developments, repeated in cycles, have made Scottish nationalism a most unreliable political force. While it is ever-present in Scottish society, in the form of national awareness and a multitude of Scottish organisations, the very security and fulfilment of such nationalism which these organisations represent has made political nationalism less relevant. Scottish interests can be preserved without national self-determination.

Nevertheless, nationalism is of first-order importance to the Scottish political system. It sustains the Scottish Office and the other institutions of the system, which could hardly exist without it. It colours the speeches of Scottish M.P.s in the House of Commons, and permeates the demands of interest groups. It makes Scotland a framework of reference for the mass media, education and research.

It is too much to expect that the nation should speak with one voice. Scotland is a nation sub-divided into the interests of locality, region, class, religion, and political party. If it were united, and consistent, this would no doubt suit some of the politicians and most of the civil servants. It would certainly clarify the situation for many in England who want to learn what would keep Scotland quiet.

There is now a wide consensus that Scotland lacks a legislative branch of government which can balance its executive and judicial branches (represented by the Secretary of State for Scotland, and the courts). Over 10,000 civil servants operate a purely Scottish administrative structure and a large contingent of lawyers, the Scottish legal system. With them, Scottish local authorities, interest groups and other organisations have an on-going relationship.

But this is not enough for democratic government. Scotland has its own law, is separately administered, and is a separate community. Its political system can only be made complete with the establishment of a separate legislature, directly elected by the Scottish people, to make law for Scotland and control Scottish administration.

8

Local government

New systems of local government have been introduced through-out the United Kingdom. The process of reform involved two Royal Commissions on Local Government: Redcliffe-Maud for England (*Report*, Cmnd. 4040),[1] and Wheatley for Scotland (*Report*, Cmnd. 4150). The new structures were established by Acts of Parliament, that for Scotland being the Local Government (Scotland) Act, 1973. Scotland was one year behind England in changing over to the new system, and the first elections took place in May 1974. The transfer was completed in May 1975, when the system became fully operational.

It is pertinent to ask why Scotland and England should have different systems of local government. In part, the reason is historic. Each country developed its own self-governing local communities from medieval times, and in Scotland these were the royal burghs. They were typically small towns, or villages, and represented isolated pockets of trade and civilisation in a some-what barbarous environment. Only after 1889 were county councils established, and the present (pre-reform) structure dates from 1929.

While a belief in the virtues of local government has undoubtedly been part of Scottish political culture, there has also been an equal emphasis on the efficient performance of functions. Where the structure of authorities stands in the way of efficiency, Scots have been ready to change it, and there does not seem to be the almost mystical belief in local democracy which has dominated English thought (derived in part from John Stuart Mill, a Scot whose ideas on this subject are based on English experience).[2]

In Scotland, the 'intermediary' tier of government, the Scottish Office, has taken over some of the area occupied by local government in England, and has played a stronger directing role than have the local government ministries in England. In education, for example, local authorities have been subject to much more detailed controls in Scotland, and the Scottish Education Department soon after its inception in 1872 produced a uniform system covering curricula, examinations, training of teachers and school buildings. Most of these controls remain today.

The physical characteristics of Scotland also contribute to a different approach to local government. Scotland has only five million people – the population of two large English counties. It must nevertheless support numerous local authorities, since its territorial area is so large, and its communities scattered and distinct. While 80% of the people live in the central belt, the remaining 20% are spread over two-thirds of the land. In the Highlands and Islands (seven old counties), a distinct region composed of many self-contained communities, 281,000 people live in an area stretching the length of Scotland, from Shetland to Kintyre.

There is thus no possibility of producing a scheme of evenly matched local authorities, equal in size and area. This can be attempted in England, where the distribution of the population is less askew. In Scotland, there are few large cities which can act as the focal point of a regional authority. Only four (Glasgow, Edinburgh, Dundee and Aberdeen) are over 150,000, and three of these are in the central belt. The great majority of towns in Scotland are small, and compared with England, there are relatively few of over 50,000 people.

There is one large exception to the pattern of small towns. Glasgow has just under one million people, and its surrounding country forms a conurbation (the 'Central Clydeside Conurbation') of over one and three-quarter millions.

The main problem for Scottish local government can thus be simply stated: how to produce a structure which provides equably for both Clydeside and the Highlands.

The pre-reformed structure will only be briefly described here, as a preliminary to a discussion of the Wheatley Report and the new system. In it, there were four counties of cities, Glasgow, Edinburgh, Dundee and Aberdeen (all-purpose authorities); 21 large burghs (exercising all powers but education and valuation); and 176 small burghs (with functions of housing, sanitation, streets, licensing of public houses and amenities). These were the urban authorities. In addition there were 33 county councils and joint county councils, whose authority was shared with the burghs. The counties provided only education and valuation within the large burghs, and all the functions within the small burghs except those mentioned under 'small burghs' above. In the non-urban 'landward areas' the counties exercised all functions, although some minor ones were delegated to district councils, of which there were 196.

Apart from this basic structure there were various bodies, made up of delegates of several local authorities, which were appointed to perform specific functions. There were 13 water boards, 11 fire authorities and 20 police forces. This process of functional co-operation in local government had gone further in Scotland than in England, and was an indication of the difficulty of matching the function to be performed with the authority to perform it. The Scottish Office has been a powerful force in promoting the setting up of such bodies.

The Scottish Office, indeed, has been the master-mind behind the whole local government reform movement. When economic planning began to dominate its thought, in the early 1960s, it became acutely aware of the shortcomings of the local government structure. The attraction of industry to Scotland required the provision of a suitable 'infrastructure', such as housing, roads, water supply and schools. Factories could not be built without these, yet local authorities were not anxious, or always able, to incur the necessary expense. Nor were they very willing to co-ordinate their activities. The arrival of BMC (now British Leyland) at Bathgate and Rootes (now Chrysler) at Linwood in the early 1960s highlighted these problems, for both developments were hampered by inadequate local response.

One way round such difficulties was to set up New Towns. These could provide the resources for industry without the problems facing local authorities. By 1971 there were five New Towns in Scotland, East Kilbride, Glenrothes, Cumbernauld, Livingston and Irvine. East Kilbride had local authority status as a large burgh, and Cumbernauld and Irvine were small burghs.

Another institution peculiar to Scotland is the Scottish Special Housing Association, a government-financed body which builds houses at low rents where industry is being developed, or where a local authority is proving inadequate. In the Highlands, the Highlands and Islands Development Board (1965–) acts as a complement to local government in planning and the attraction of industry.

But these measures could not cope with all the shortcomings of the 1960s. Scotland's economy was lagging badly compared with most of Britain's, and declining industries, high unemployment and emigration led the government to attempt stronger remedial action. The 1963 Central Scotland Plan (Cmnd. 2188) and various other regional plans, called for the development of 'growth areas' involving close co-operation between central and local government, and a new degree of joint action between the authorities of the growth areas.

But it became evident that *ad hoc* arrangements would not be sufficient to cope with the situation in Scotland as a whole. Although growth areas did not involve all local authorities, the problems they presented drew attention to the general inadequacies of the system, which had been brought about by movements of population, poor local resources and duplication of authorities. The Scottish Office thus proposed in June 1963 a 'modernisation' of local government in a White Paper (Cmnd. 2067). This gave a two-tier system, comprising around 15 combined counties and counties of cities as the top tier, and about 50–60 burgh and rural councils as the lower tier (population of around 40,000). Most functions would go to the top tier, and minor functions, including housing, to the lower.

While this scheme met with some opposition, especially from the small burghs, its adoption at this stage would have saved much time and effort subsequently expended on the Wheatley Commission. The Scottish Office was here ahead of the English departments and local authorities, and could have brought in a reformed system ten years before it will in fact be established.

The delay was largely due to the advent of the Labour government in 1964, which introduced the whole problem of English local government reform, and so halted a unilateral solution for Scotland. Scotland had now to go back to square one and follow the slow and tortuous road to reform via a Royal Commission.

The Wheatley Commission's Report (September 1969, Cmnd. 4150) and the evidence submitted to it, could hardly discover anything fundamentally new, since the subject had been argued over since 1963 (at least). But the mass of material, including some special research papers, did give the discussion some depth. During the same period (1966–9), other documents were issued dealing with *Social Work and the Community* (1966, Cmnd. 3065); a *Report on the Staffing of Local Government in Scotland* by a working party of central and local officials (Edinburgh, 1968); and *Administrative Reorganisation of the Scottish Health Services*, a Green Paper of the Scottish Home and Health Department (December 1968). The principal practical result of these subsidiary reports was the Social Work (Scotland) Act 1968, which set up social work departments in counties, cities and large burghs. These departments contain the probation, child care and social welfare services of local government, and operate under social work directors.

The Wheatley proposals were that Scotland should have a two-tier system of local government. The top tier ('regions') would consist of 7 authorities, and the lower tier ('district') 37. Nearly all important functions would go to the top tier, but minor aspects of local planning and of housing and amenities, as well as libraries, licensing and administration of justice would be for the lower tier. Voluntary community councils, outside the structure of local government, could be set up. Each authority would be independently elected and levy its own rates. The Commission, however, did not have the power to consider any reshaping of local government finance, and this was to be decided by the central government itself.

The reasoning behind these proposals was squarely in the Scottish tradition of attempting to provide for the efficient local administration of functions. 'It is when local government operates at the scale which its services demand that true local democracy emerges' (Wheatley 1, p. 50). The services demanded one Highland regional authority (seven counties) and one West of Scotland authority (2½ million people). The old conundrum of the shape of Scotland and the distribution of its communities was thus forcibly resolved in the Wheatley Report in favour of centralisation.

Its implications for the Scottish Office were not discussed. If one local authority contains half the population of Scotland, and another almost half the area, what is the residual role of the Scottish Office? If new powers are to be given to local government (as Wheatley asserted but did not elaborate), then surely fewer can be retained by the Scottish Office. Thus not only the old local authorities but the intermediary tier also, stood to lose power by these proposals. Because if a strong regional structure of local authorities were established, these authorities might well deal directly with the Treasury in London for finance, and not bother with Edinburgh.

Even more important was the effect on local government of devolution to Scotland. If Scotland were to have a parliament or assembly, and an executive, what effect would this have on the structure of local government? Would large regional authorities still be necessary, given that much of their power would be shared by the Scottish Parliament? Because local government reform came first, and devolution second, the regions were a *fait accompli*, and devolution had to be grafted on to it. Yet the two reforms were not necessarily consistent with one another.

The original Wheatley Commission recommendations were not accepted in detail by the Conservative government or by Parliament, although the principles were. Strong pressures were immediately mobilised in Scotland to resist certain aspects of the Report, some of which were party-political, some communal, and some related to various 'vested interests' of councils and officials. In the islands, the Borders, and in Fife, vigorous campaigns were mounted to preserve, or achieve, independent status as local authorities. By February 1971, the Government conceded the cases of Orkney and Shetland to be separate 'island authorities', and by December 1971, the Western Isles was recognised for the first time as having a claim to its own local government (previously, the Western Isles had been split between Ross and Cromarty and Inverness-shire). Thus the large

Highland Region of Wheatley was dismembered. Nevertheless, it remained a huge authority in terms of area.

The Borders and Fife also put up a great fight for recognition. The Borders won in 1971, but Fife was resolutely resisted until pressure within Parliament itself during the passage of the Local Government Bill resulted in the restoration of its identity. At the same time, suburban areas around Glasgow (Bearsden, Milngavie, Clydebank and Bishopbriggs), which had been included in the Glasgow District, were removed by the House of Lords to form three new Districts, and the Commons did not overturn the decision. Meanwhile, some other departures from the Wheatley Report had been made in the distribution of functions between the Regions and Districts. Housing became primarily a District function, a change which gave the Districts a much-needed political and administrative boost.

Thus some important alterations were made, not only to the Wheatley scheme, but to that of the Government in its draft legislation. The final Act did not satisfy everyone. The Labour Opposition, led by Mr Ross, campaigned during the passage of the Bill for the abolition of the Strathclyde Region, on the grounds that it was too large. They preferred to split it into four regions, with an overall metropolitan authority for strategic planning and some other functions. But some Labour M.P.s seemed quite happy with the reforms, and divisions did not take a strictly party line. Indeed, it was because of cross-party pressures that so many changes were made during the passage of the legislation.

Certain aspects of local government were left over to be dealt with later. Community councils were to be established by the Districts and Islands by May 1976. A community council would express community viewpoints and 'take such action in the interests of that community as appears to it to be expedient and practicable' (1973 Act, s.51(2)). Financial arrangements for the new authorities, although dealt with in outline in the Act, had to be worked out further in practice. No new sources of revenue were given, and the only substantial innovation was the establishment of a Commission for Local Authority Accounts in Scotland. No salaries for councillors were introduced. A local government 'Ombudsman' was a matter for the future. More important innovations were to come in the management of the new authorities, as the result of a report by an advisory group under the chairmanship of I. V. Paterson, the County Clerk of Lanarkshire (*The New Scottish Local Authorities: Organisation and Management Structures*, HMSO, Edinburgh 1973). In line with the corresponding 'Bains Report' in England, the Paterson Report recommended 'corporate management' arrangements in both the elected-councillor and official sides of the authority. In the former, a Policy and Resources Committee would head the committee structure of the council, and would lay down over-all policies for other committees. On the official side, a Chief Executive would be appointed to oversee the administration and lead a team of Directors of functional departments. By 1975, most authorities had adopted the 'Paterson' structures. In Strathclyde Region, for example, a Policy and Resources Committee, consisting entirely of Labour councillors, was formed. This type of one-party committee is new in local government, for committees under the old system were multi-party. While co-ordination of policies throughout the authority is achieved, the contribution of the minority parties to the top level of policy-making is lost. In the case of Strathclyde, the huge predominance of the Labour Party at the elections of 1974 makes the danger of 'one-party' rule more severe. On the official side, the restructuring has involved the creation of many new posts and office-buildings, with consequent public complaint at the expense involved for rate-payers. Conservatism in appointments of chief executives has moderated the degree of innovation implied in the new structure. Most chief executives are former town or county clerks, with no educationists, social workers or planners. Similarly, the new councillors are drawn largely from the ranks of the old, despite hopes that the reforms would attract a 'new breed of men'. While many of the latter came forward to the parties for adoption as candidates, those chosen to run were usually established party stalwarts. The elections of May 1974 posed some new political problems (see Table 23). The city Districts of Aberdeen, Dundee and Edinburgh had different party profiles from their surrounding Regions (Grampian, Tayside and Lothian respectively), with opposing parties leading at the different levels. This seemed a recipe for conflict. There was also a danger of indecision, since many authorities lacked overall control by any one party. While some parts of Scotland were converted to party politics, others retained the old 'non-partisan' approach (e.g. Highland, Borders, Dumfries–Galloway and Islands). The SNP was very poorly represented, despite its importance at parliamentary elections. Labour was overwhelming in Strathclyde and Glasgow. In a variety of ways, then, the new system represented a mixture of old and new, with many unsolved problems for the future.

The work of the councillor will change. Officials will take on more administration, as the time-consuming committee system is progressively abolished. Clearly, the greater distance between home and council will reduce the amount of time a councillor (at least of a regional authority) can spend in the chamber.

Table 23 *The reformed structure of local government*

	Population (1971)	May 1974 elections (councillors)						
		Lab	C	SNP	Lib	Ind	Com	Others
Regions (9)								
Highland	175,449	3	2	1	3	38		
Grampian	437,231	13	28		2	10		
Tayside	396,766	15	22			9		
Central	263,284	17	4	9		3		1
Fife	328,028	26	10			3	1	2
Lothian	742,257	24	19	3	1	2		
Borders	98,782		9		3	11		
Strathclyde	2,578,314	71	21	5	2	4		
Dumfries/Galloway	143,530	2				33		
Island Areas (3)								
Shetland	17,596					22		
Orkney	17,256					23		
Western Isles	30,570					30		
Districts (53) including								
Glasgow	983,548	55	17					
Edinburgh	472,224	29	30	1	3	1		
Dundee	197,537	22	19			2		1
Aberdeen	208,356	29	17		2			

Community Councils: provision is made for these to be established.

Regions and island areas (elected every four years):
Major planning and related services, including strategic planning, industrial development, transportation, roads, water, sewerage.
Education; social work; regional housing; police; fire; community centres, parks and recreation;* museums and art galleries;* registration of births, deaths and marriages; registration of electors. In the island areas, police, fire, aspects of education and social work are administered jointly with other authorities.

Districts (elected every three years):
Local planning and associated services, including urban development and countryside;† building control;† housing; community centres, parks and recreation,* museums and art galleries;* libraries;† environmental health, including cleansing, refuse, Shops Act, burials; regulation and licensing, including cinemas and theatres, betting and taxis.

* Exercised concurrently by regional and district authorities.
† Except in Highland, Dumfries/Galloway and Borders regions, where the function is regional.

Conversely, his contacts with his constituents will have to be catered for in improved 'consulting-rooms' at the grass-roots level. Decentralisation of administration by officials will also be necessary, and is strongly recommended by the Commission.

The wider aspects of the changes are perhaps lost in these details. The avowed aim of the Wheatley Commission, and of the government in the White Paper of 1971 (*Reform of Local Government in Scotland*, Feb. 1971, Cmnd. 4583), is to strengthen local government by transferring some authority to it from central government. There would, for example, be fewer calls on the professional skills and technical advice of central departments, since the staff of the new local authorities would be so much better. The numerous controls exercised by St Andrew's House over local decisions would be relaxed. In finance, the authorities would be more 'viable', and would therefore escape some of the financial bondage to central government.

It is doubtful whether many of these aims will be realised. The Wheatley Commission was not allowed to consider the transfer of specific functions from central to local government, although it hinted that such a thing was possible. Instead, it reported within the context of existing local powers. The White Paper of 1971 did not mention any transfer of functions, and went out of its way to exclude local control over the National Health Service (p. 13), which had seemed possible under a regional structure.

The improvement in the staff of local authorities will still not bring them up to the standard of central government. For example, town and country planners will be required in 12 regions and islands and 37 districts. (Districts in the Highland, Borders and Dumfries/Galloway regions will not have planning powers.) They will continue to be largely dependent on the skills and over-all view of the Scottish Development Department.

In finance, the present dependence of Scottish local authorities on the central government, to the extent of over half of their income (as much as 80% in the Highlands) and 75% of rate-borne expenditure, will not fundamentally change in the reformed structure. The rates will continue to be the principal source of revenue, and the special needs of Glasgow and the Highlands will remain, calling for large government subventions. Such aid has already been given to these areas in the early 1970s.

One innovation is the deal concluded between Shetland County Council and the oil companies, which should give the authority £3m. per annum from an oil barrelage tax and rates by 1980 (*Scotsman*, 19 June 1974, 7 March 1975).

Finally, there are strong political reasons for ensuring the continuance of central control over local authorities. In Britain, local government has always been seen as the agent of central government. Where local authorities stand in the way of such wishes, they must be over-ruled. In the early 1970s, this remained as true as it has ever been. For example, the Labour government in 1970 sought to coerce the local authorities in Scotland into accepting comprehensive and non-fee-paying public schools. In 1972 the Conservative government introduced a scheme to make local authority council tenants pay much higher rents, despite the fierce opposition of many councils. They also prevented them from providing free milk in schools to those over seven, except on medical grounds. National policy now covers more areas previously considered local, and this trend will inevitably lead to the continuation and even strengthening of central direction.

In the context of the Scottish political system, 'national' policy includes those aspects of central government which are specifically Scottish, and which are dealt with at St Andrew's House. The reform movement in local government provided an opportunity for the setting-up of an elected Scottish Parliament, which could add the democratic element to the otherwise mainly administrative arrangement of the Scottish Office. It would recognise the fact, acknowledged in the Wheatley Report (p. 166), that 'Scotland as a whole forms a community'.

The development of Scotland, whether in economic planning, law reform, social services, transport, agriculture or education, requires an over-all strategy which covers the whole country. The importance of co-ordination in the areas of transport, power, health and social security has been pointed out in a previous chapter. It is also uppermost in the minds of the Scottish Office reformers and appears in the White Paper of 1971 at several points (e.g. 'the entire road network must be planned as a whole', Cmnd. 4583, p. 10). But to achieve such co-ordination, a strong all-Scottish authority is needed, at both the political and administrative levels. Only devolution can satisfy that need.

9
Organisations and interest groups

The process of representation in Britain includes the activities of organised groups as well as those of M.P.s and political parties. Parliamentary representation serves to reflect the shared opinions and interests of people over a wide range of policies, for these are channelled through the medium of the parties. It also has the function of ensuring that the wishes of the 'governed' are taken into account by the 'governors', since in Britain governments require the support of a majority of M.P.s in the House of Commons. Finally, it gives an element of geographic representation, in that M.P.s must look after the general interests of their constituencies, and of the individual constituents within them. Scottish constituencies have a special status within Parliament (see ch. 5), and in many of them local sentiment is strong.

Organised groups represent specific economic or occupational interests, or shared attitudes on some particular aspect of policy.[1] Some are formed specifically to put pressure on government (e.g. trade unions whose members are employed by government departments or public bodies), while others exist primarily for other purposes, but turn to political pressure on occasion (e.g. churches). They are not involved in the general function of governing, nor do they usually seek to provide a comprehensive programme of political action in areas which do not directly concern them. (The exceptions to this are churches and trade unions, which tend to take a broad view of their role in representing their members' interests.)

A Glaswegian, who is also a railwayman and a Roman Catholic, is represented in at least three different ways. As an elector in a parliamentary constituency, he can look to his M.P. to safeguard his interests at Westminster. As an employee of British Rail, he may join a trade union, which will negotiate on his behalf with the management and the government. As a Catholic, he is under the care of his priest, and ultimately the Hierarchy of the Church, who speak for him in religious and educational matters.

It would be difficult to say which of these three channels of representation is the most important for him, or whether each is in harmony with the other. The example indicates that, even at the level of an individual person, there are difficulties in producing a simple, consistent picture of interests and demands.

It is even more difficult for the entity called Scotland. The parliamentary representation of Scotland has already been discussed, and here it must be re-emphasised that the Scottish M.P.s themselves do not on their own constitute a legislative body. They are essentially part of the House of Commons, with no legislative powers of their own. Nevertheless demands are channelled to government from Scotland via the Scottish M.P.s, who play a distinctive role in 'representing Scotland'. For example, on 29 October 1971, the front-page headline in a Scottish newspaper read 'Scotland says "No" 36 times', above a report of the vote in the House of Commons on British entry to the E.E.C. In that vote, 36 Scottish M.P.s had voted against entry and 32 for. The paper concluded that 'Scotland as a nation' was in opposition to entry ((Glasgow) *Evening Citizen*, 29 October 1971).

The other channels of representation are the interest and attitude groups,[2] the government and public bodies in Scotland (which 'speak for Scotland' within the machinery of government itself), and an amorphous Scottish 'public opinion' expressed in the media and in opinion polls.

Since policy-making for Scotland is formulated and executed at two centres of power, Edinburgh and London, the representative process of the Scottish political system is concerned with two 'access' points, while the English political system must concern itself with only one. Table 24 shows in diagrammatic form the various channels and their principal directions.

The arrows shows the main 'flow' only. All the points are interconnected to some extent, and in the case of the channels 3 and 4 it depends on the subject-matter whether the Scottish Office will become involved. For example, trade unions concerned about industrial closures will exert most pressure on the Department of Industry in London, and not on the Scottish Office, since the latter has no powers of decision (though it may have influence) in that field.

The diagram is also over-simplified in that it assumes that all flows are in one direction – to the government. In fact, the flows are circular, with the government providing impetus or 'feedback' to the entire system. Thus governments inspire the formation of consultative groups, so that they may learn what different interests think about policy. A large number of such groups has been set up on a Scottish basis, and these communicate the wishes of government to their constituent members, as well as *vice versa*.[3]

Much of the flow of information may not deeply involve the government at all, except as 'arbiter'. In certain areas of public life, for example, law, education, medicine and other professions, the principal organisations carry on a discourse among themselves which is as important as the discourse between them and government. The government often allows these professions virtual autonomy over their own affairs, ratifying decisions reached by their official representatives.

Table 24 *Channels of representation of the Scottish political system*

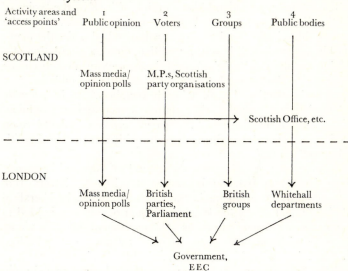

In the Scottish context, such practices take on a special form of their own. For it is common to allow Scots to settle their own disputes without reference to London. The plethora of Scottish organisations representing Scottish interests is an indication of this, for if decisions had to be taken in England, there would be a need for British organisation on the grounds of realism and convenience, and the pressure of assimilation of Scotland to England would inevitably increase. As it is, outside, the industrial arena, Scotland is remarkably self-contained in its range of organised groups, and by inference, its own decision-making network.

The 'historic' Scottish institutions of Church, law and education play a 'quasi-governmental' role in that they perform tasks on behalf of the state. For example, the Church of Scotland runs 'approved schools' for young offenders, is represented on local education committees and is part of the Constitution through its position as the Established Church of Scotland. The Church of

155

Scotland, unlike the Church of England, is virtually free from formal political influence. It is completely self-governing, and there are no Crown appointments. While a small amount of revenue comes from unextinguished teinds (English: tithes), the Church is almost totally supported by voluntary contributions. Lacking bishops, it has no official representation in the House of Lords, and its ministers are ineligible to be M.P.s. The Crown is represented at the annual General Assembly of the Church of Scotland by the Queen or the Lord High Commissioner.

The Church of Scotland likes to think of itself as the 'voice of Scotland', and its General Assembly has some claim to be the nearest thing in Scotland to a representative body. Yet the membership of the Church is only 1·2 million, out of a population of 5 million (adults c. 3½ million), and the procedure used to choose delegates to the General Assembly bears little resemblance to a democratic election by all Church members.[4] It is arguable whether Assembly deliberations represent accurately the opinions of the Church members, and no 'general elections' take place on the issues discussed, which range over a wide conspectus of political as well as religious matters.

Despite these qualifications, the Church of Scotland has sometimes had great political influence. Its views on Africa were listened to by governments in the late 1950s, when its liberalism (derived largely from the large contingent of missionaries) led to the support of such causes as self-government for Nyasaland. Assembly debates have been attended by government leaders, such as Iain Macleod in 1959 and Harold Wilson in 1969.

Some Scottish government members have been active churchmen, notably William Ross (a Church elder and Secretary of State for Scotland, 1964–70 and 1974–). Ross reflected the Conservative wing of the Church in such matters as liquor licensing, Sunday observance, homosexuality, family planning and divorce. In all these, the Church as a whole tends to conservatism, and parliamentary legislation on the above subjects was either not forthcoming or seriously modified in its application to Scotland. It is likely that such variations between Scots and English Law owe much to the influence of powerful voices in the Church of Scotland, and their political allies.

Ross did not follow his Church in its devolutionist sympathies. In the late 1960s, resolutions calling for a Scottish legislative body were accepted by the General Assembly, and the Church and Nation Committee gave evidence to the Commission on the Constitution to this effect. Other notable policy stands were: opposition to Sunday Entertainment Bill (1967); acceptance of homosexual law reform (1968), which had been opposed in 1967; proposals for divorce law reform (1969); support for providing unmarried women with contraceptive pills (1970); support for the Scottish Council's 'Oceanspan' development project and criticism of the Conservative economic policies for Scotland (1971). The Church opposed entry to E.E.C. in October 1970 and May 1971, but supported entry in October 1971. The inconsistencies sometimes revealed owe much to the rotating membership of the Assemblies and Commissions of Assembly.

The position of the Roman Catholic Church on many of these questions reinforces the pressure exerted by conservative Presbyterians. The failure of the Divorce (Scotland) Bill 1970 and the restrictions on free family planning in the late 1960s gave as much satisfaction to the strong Roman Catholic faction within the Scottish Labour Party as it did to the Presbyterians. But the Catholic interest in licensing restrictions and Sunday observance is much less marked than that of the Church of Scotland.

The Roman Catholic Church is a quasi-governmental body as a result of its position in the state educational system. Under the Education (Scotland) Act 1918, Roman Catholic schools were transferred to the state, which maintains them as an integral part of the public provision of education. This is unlike the position in England and Wales, where the Roman Catholic Church is still in charge of buildings, appointments and curricula, although in receipt of government grants covering nearly all running expenses. The merger of Catholic schools within the state system in Scotland was the result of the relative poverty of Catholics in Scotland, who could not afford the finance necessary to pay for their own schools.[5] The bargain then struck gives the Catholic community 100% financial support for their schools, which are officially controlled by the education committees of local authorities. Appointments of teachers are made in accordance with the wishes of Church representatives, and a Catholic content is retained in the curriculum.

Today, the position of such denominational schools is under attack from a section of the Labour Party in Scotland. This group wishes to abolish the separate Catholic schools, as a corollary of the comprehensivisation of education. Such a change is strongly resisted by Catholic spokesmen and their allies in the party who point to the potential loss of the Catholic vote in such areas as Glasgow.

Both Labour and Conservative governments tend to stand aside from this issue, and await a settlement of differences between the relevant interests. While the Catholic leadership is reluctant to agree to change, there is some evidence that the laity is not strongly in favour of separate schools,[6] and such schools have in recent years been unable to recruit a sufficient number of Catholic teachers.

Indeed, there is a general teacher shortage at these schools, with a consequent decline in standards. Public opinion is moving against 'segregation' in education, whether religious, racial or meritocratic, and the Labour Party's policy of favouring comprehensive schools has had special repercussions in Scotland on account of the religious division of the state system. The Labour Party in Scotland has accepted that total integration is desirable in the long run, but it is in no hurry to precipitate a clash with the strong Catholic element in the party.[7]

The strong links between the churches and education should be borne in mind when considering the organised groups concerned specifically with the teaching profession. Nevertheless, these groups help to break down religious distinctions, since they recruit their members from both the non-denominational and Catholic schools. There are no teachers' associations specifically for Catholic or Protestant teachers.

The principal teachers' association is the Educational Institute of Scotland (EIS) with over 40,000 members. This includes three-fifths of all Scottish teachers, and is the principal spokesman group in consultations with the government. Its organ, *The Scottish Educational Journal*, appears weekly, and is read by a large number of teachers. The *Times Educational Supplement* started a Scottish edition in 1965, with about half of its content separate from the London edition.

Other important teachers' organisations are the Scottish Secondary Teachers Association (7,000 members) and the Scottish Schoolmasters Association (3,500 members). These bodies claim that the EIS does not adequately represent the views of certain types of teacher, being dominated by primary women teachers. Along with the EIS, they make up the teachers' side of the Scottish Teachers' Salaries Committee, which negotiates with local authorities and the government on teachers' pay. A smaller body with its own special interests, and outside the official 'charmed circle' is the Scottish Honours Graduate Teachers' Association.

The whole sphere of Scottish education is an autonomous 'arena', with the government represented by the Scottish Education Department. The autonomy of the arena was strengthened in 1965 by the establishment of the General Teaching Council for Scotland, a body which has no counterpart as yet in England, and which is intended to provide the teaching profession with a measure of self-government.

The General Teaching Council (GTC) registers qualified teachers in Scotland (their qualifications are different from those of English teachers), advises the Secretary of State for Scotland on the conditions for registration, and exercises professional discipline. It consists of 49 members, of whom 25 must be teachers and elected by registered teachers in Scotland. Fifteen are appointed by local authorities; 4 elected by the principals of colleges of education; 4 nominated by the Secretary of State; and 1 elected by college of education teachers. In 1970, the EIS secured 19 of the 25 teacher seats, SSTA 5 seats, and the Scottish Further Education Association 1 seat. In 1974, the EIS did not sponsor candidates.

The first five years of the GTC's history were marked by bitter fighting among the teachers' associations, and between the teachers and the government. At first the teachers' representatives were not given a majority on the Council, but as a result of vigorous pressure from the teachers' organisations this was granted in 1970, by Act of Parliament. Disputes continued, however, about the rules for teacher registration, with the SSTA considering these as a means of diluting the profession by the acceptance of unqualified teachers, since for a time unqualified teachers might be registered with the GTC if they fulfilled certain requirements, and passed a reference panel. The EIS, on the other hand, was much more allied to the government's position, and had indeed suggested the setting-up of the GTC in the early 1960s.[8]

The relationship between the Scottish and English education 'arenas' is spasmodic and at times tinged with suspicion. Scottish teachers consider their professional qualifications superior to those of English teachers, largely because graduates in England until very recently could become qualified teachers there without possessing a professional certificate from a college or institute of education. This led to the exclusion of English teachers without professional qualifications from Scottish schools. As a result, there has been little coming and going between the staffs of schools in England and Scotland.

Pay settlements for Scottish teachers are made separately from those for English teachers, and the rates for the various categories of teacher are different. Thus graduate teachers earn more, and women non-graduates less, than their counterparts in England. Nevertheless, Scottish teachers watch the outcome of pay settlements in England very carefully, and demand parity, or superiority, of treatment with regard to the overall percentage award. This illustrates the typical duality of the Scottish political system: an assertion of independence, coupled with a demand for equality with England.

The Scottish universities stand somewhat on one side of this arena. About 70% of their students are from Scottish schools, and their entrance requirements and courses derive from Scottish traditions. But they come principally under the University Grants Committee and the Department of Education and Science, not the Scottish Education Department. In 1971, most of the Scottish universities and colleges withdrew from the Scottish Union of Students, to join the (U.K.) National Union of Students. The SUS was then wound up, and by 1975 all Scottish universities except Glasgow were affiliated to the NUS. The NUS maintains a separate Scottish organisation and holds a Scottish conference. This is paralleled by the Association of University Teachers (Scotland) on the staff side.

The legal profession in Scotland is more interested in maintaining its independence from the English legal profession than in ensuring comparability. It is more exclusive than the teaching profession, for all practising lawyers in Scotland must be qualified in Scots Law. This means that part of their education must have been spent in Scotland.

Law and politics have always been closely intertwined in Scotland, and after 1707 the Court of Session and the Scottish Bar took over Parliament House in Edinburgh. While the Church of Scotland General Assembly makes claims to be the 'voice of Scotland' in the absence of a Scottish parliament, the Scottish bar and judiciary can reasonably claim that it was for nearly two centuries the effective government of Scotland. And we have seen, until 1885, when the office of Secretary for Scotland was established, the Lord Advocate looked after the affairs of Scotland in the government, and even to this day the influence of lawyers in Scottish public life remains great.

The importance of Scots Law in the Scottish political system has already been stressed (cf. ch. 2). The Act of Union, as far as the position of the law is concerned, has continued undiluted to the present time. So too has the part played by Scottish judges, advocates and solicitors in quasi-governmental activities. For example, numerous public bodies include one or more judges, and such official organs as the Council on Tribunals have Scottish committees, appointed in this case by the Secretary of State for Scotland.

The principal professional organisations are the Faculty of Advocates, representing the Scottish Bar, and the Law Society of Scotland, representing the solicitor branch. The latter has its own *Journal*, and there are several other periodical publications concerned with Scottish legal matters (the most well-known being the *Scots Law Times*). The scales for legal aid are determined by the Law Society, and it also regulates solicitors' fees.

Although few Scots lawyers are M.P.s or peers, their influence in legislation is considerable. The drafting of law relating exclusively to Scotland requires parliamentary draftsmen qualified in Scots Law, and law reform is largely inspired by the Scottish Law Commission, composed in 1971 of a judge, an advocate and three law professors. It issues periodic reports on aspects of law in need of change. On occasion, joint reports with the English Law Commission are produced, one indication that much modern law is common in principle to both Scotland and England.

On the whole, the relationships between the legal profession and the other sections of the community, and between it and government, are harmonious and somewhat detached. The historic clash of Law and Kirk in the 1830s, leading to the Disruption of the Church of Scotland in 1843, is now forgotten, as is the subsequent Free Church case in 1904 (for an account of these, see Kellas, *Modern Scotland*, Pall Mall Press (London, 1968), pp. 53, 60). The self-government of the legal profession, which is probably greater than that of the medical profession, and much greater than that of the teachers, means that it rarely has to negotiate with the government about pay or conditions of service. At the same time, the structure and staffing of the courts and the other sources of politico-legal patronage loom large in the horizons of many lawyers, and for them the relationship with government must be close and profitable.

The three historic Scottish institutions of Church, education and law are to a large extent the basis of the national identity of Scotland. Their separateness ensures the survival of the Scottish nation. Yet there are numerous other organisations which are Scottish in form, and contribute to the Scottishness of organised group activity.

The old Scottish local government system gave rise to bodies such as the Convention of Royal Burghs and the Association of County Councils. In 1975, a Convention of Scottish Local Authorities was formed, to represent both the new regions and the new districts. The authorities themselves are important influences in the shaping of policy, and it is significant that Scottish local authorities are almost entirely confined, in their dealings with government, to putting pressure on the Scottish Office, as the department concerned with local government. This makes their appearances on the English political scene minimal. In recent years, however, concern about industrial development and rail closures has brought them into contact with Whitehall ministries, and they have always had dealings with the Scottish officials of the Department of Industry on the siting of factories.

Next in importance in terms of Scottish identity are the 'omnibus' associations, comprising a number of organisations which have combined to form a Scottish spokesman body. The Scottish Trades Union Congress (STUC) dates from 1897, and includes trade unions and trades councils (the latter are excluded from the

British TUC). It has over 815,000 affiliated members from around 70 unions.

Although few trade unions are purely Scottish today,[9] in contrast to the situation when the STUC was founded, the Scottish members of British trade unions often face employers whose associations are Scottish, or who maintain that Scottish conditions are different from those elsewhere. This necessitates separate negotiations in Scotland. For example, local government officers, electricity workers and newspapermen are members of British unions, but their employers are the Scottish local authorities, the Scottish electricity boards and the Scottish Daily Newspaper Society, respectively. This has led to specifically Scottish industrial disputes, and some insulation from English disputes. When London newspapers are on strike, their counterparts in Scotland often continue publication (the same is of course true in reverse, when the Scottish papers are on strike).

In its evidence to the Royal Commission on Trade Unions and Employers' Associations (1966–8) the STUC described itself as 'spokesman for Scotland' on the industrial, economic and social scene 'and not only within the trade union movement'. As such, it is another attempt to fill the gap left by the absence of a Scottish legislature. It claims that it has

> provided a service to organised labour in Scotland which it is doubtful if the Trades Union Congress could have performed so effectively. The texture of Scottish life with its separate traditions in Law, Church, Education and Government is such as would have compelled the establishment of a separate Congress ...
> As the most representative organ of Scottish opinion it has assumed a growing role at a time when the tendency towards regionalism may well continue to develop.[10]

This role can be seen in the large number of Scottish public bodies and advisory committees which include one or more members nominated by the STUC (see appendix to this chapter, pp. 169–170). And its position as a leader of Scottish opinion was given expression on 14 February 1972, when it organised a 'Scottish Assembly' in Edinburgh to discuss Scottish unemployment and industrial development. Over a thousand delegates were present, representing bodies such as the political parties, local authorities, Scottish Council, the Confederation of British Industry, the Church of Scotland, and the universities. There was widespread support for devolution and for a strengthening of the Scottish Office's functions in industrial matters. A permanent Commission of 18 was established to represent the views of Scotland in the future, and the whole exercise was another example of the desire to fill the vacuum in the Scottish political system which is caused by the lack of an elected legislature or representative body (*Glasgow Herald*, 15 February 1972). A subsequent meeting of the Assembly took place in January 1973.

The outlook of the STUC seems at first sight to be strongly nationalist, but this should be seen in the context of the increasingly British character of industrial relations generally. The Industrial Relations Act 1971, the 'social contract' of 1974 and the disappearance of most purely Scottish unions indicate in different ways a shift away from Scotland as a focus of industrial decision-making.

The STUC remains an active pressure group on behalf of Scottish workers' interests, and its lobbying in London is vigorous. Its annual congress receives considerable publicity in Scotland, and throughout Britain when Labour Party leaders speak at it. It is more to the left than the TUC, and so are such unions as the Scottish Area of the National Union of Mineworkers, in which Communist influence is strong. The STUC has fewer bureaucrats in its organisation than the TUC, and its congress is made up of rank-and-file union members to a greater extent than the official-laden congress of the TUC. Being more remote from government, the STUC has struck an independent line earlier on such subjects as the prices and incomes policy (1967), and entry to the E.E.C. (1970).

But the real power has slipped to the big unions and the TUC, and trade unionists in Scotland increasingly look to them for support. This is all the more necessary as the control of industry in Scotland shifts to non-Scottish firms or public corporations, whose headquarters are in England, or abroad.

Scots want equal wages with workers in England and they stand to gain from British unions negotiating British rates. This tends to leave purely Scottish spokesmen somewhat on the sidelines.

At the same time, the STUC does draw attention to the particular needs of Scottish industry, which might otherwise be swamped within the all-British organisations. In the campaigning over Upper Clyde Shipbuilders and the Hunterston steel development in 1971, the STUC added an extra dimension to the activities of the unions involved by emphasising the needs of the whole Scottish economy. Thus particular Scottish disputes became enhanced with the aura of a national struggle.

A similar approach is adopted by the Scottish Council (Development and Industry). This is an 'omnibus' body, made up of representatives of employers, unions, local authority associations, civil service 'assessors', and individuals. It originated in the 1930s, when Sir James Lithgow, the shipbuilder, established the Scottish Development Council to attract industry to Scotland.

During the Second World War, a semi-official Scottish Council on Industry was set up by Thomas Johnston, the Scottish Secretary, as a substitute for a Scottish Board of Trade. These two bodies merged in 1946 to form the Scottish Council (Development and Industry).

Although not a government agency, it appears as such in the *Handbook on Scottish Administration* (HMSO, Edinburgh 1967). This illustrates the ambiguity of its position. It is a private body, supported largely by subscriptions from its members, but also in receipt of considerable government grants. In 1971 these amounted to £70,000, earmarked for a campaign to attract German industry to Scotland.

The Council's terms of reference include the making of surveys of industrial trends, the promotion of Scottish trade by publicity, trade missions, and 'research into particular problems affecting the well-being of Scotland'. It published until 1972 a glossy monthly magazine, *Scotland*, to advertise the attractions of the country, and run features on Scottish business (now *Business Scotland*). Thus the Council does unofficially what the Scottish Office might be expected to do officially

That department has at times used the medium of the Scottish Council to promote its ideas, most notably in the publication of the Council's *Report on the Scottish Economy* ('Toothill Report') in 1961. In form the work of the Council, the report was in fact written by Scottish Office civil servants, and one of its principal recommendations was the setting up of a Development Department within the Scottish Office. This was done in 1962.

The Labour governments from 1964 to 1970 did not co-operate as closely with the Council as the Conservatives had done, largely because William Ross, the Scottish Secretary, distrusted its business connections and disliked its semi-nationalist pronouncements. At this time, Douglas Crawford, one of the Council's chief executives, joined the SNP as director of communications and in general the Council has based much of its campaigning on the thesis that Scottish industry and Scottish society should be disentangled from English and foreign control.[11]

The Council has produced ambitious plans for the development of the Scottish economy, including the Oceanspan and Eurospan projects of 1970 and 1971. These envisage the central belt of Scotland as a bridge between North America and the continent of Europe, with part developments at Hunterston and Greenock on the west coast, and Grangemouth and Leith on the east. Between these ports various industries would grow up to utilise the materials which would be passing through.

While the Scottish Office has supported these plans in general terms, their implementation is clearly not within its powers, but rather within those of British ministries such as the Departments of Trade and Industry and the Treasury. To these ministries, the Scottish Council is just another regional development association, and its claim must be set beside those of spokesmen from other parts of the U.K. Even the Scottish Office cannot be seen to be too much influenced by the Scottish Council, for its policies on industrial development would then appear to be geared to the special benefit of Scotland alone, and not necessarily to that of the whole country. No British government department can afford to appear to be a 'clientèle' department. For the Scottish Council, 'what is good for Scotland, is good for the U.K.', a sentiment which cannot command widespread support in Whitehall. The Scottish Council's recommendation in 1970[12] that the government alter its system of industrial incentives to benefit existing firms in Scotland as well as incoming industry met with resistance in the Treasury and Department of Trade, although many in the Scottish Office supported such a change. Lord Clydesmuir (R. J. B. Colville, director of the steel firm of Colvilles Ltd), the chairman of the Council, and Sir John Toothill (director of Ferranti Ltd, Edinburgh), a vice-president, were both outspoken critics of government policies for Scotland in 1971, and they argued for investment grants, the retention of the regional employment premium and higher public expenditure in Scotland.[13] In March 1972 the government succumbed to this pressure, and reintroduced investment grants covering both new and existing projects.

While such demands may embarrass the Scottish Office at times, they probably strengthen its position in Whitehall. Armed with evidence that important pressure groups in Scotland are restless, the men from St Andrew's House can often extract concessions from the Treasury and other departments which many other regions are unable to obtain, since their interests are usually less well organised and less prominent in the communications media.

The Scottish Council is not the only business-related group with a Scottish organisation and Scottish policy. The Scottish Council of the Confederation of British Industry issues annual surveys of Scottish industry, and makes recommendations which, like those of the Scottish Council, call for special incentives for Scottish industrial development. So too do those of the Scottish Chamber of Commerce.

Scottish agriculture has been separately organised for many years. In part this is the result of the Scottish Office's responsibilities for the industry in the Department of Agriculture and Fisheries for Scotland. The department administers most of the agricultural support expenditure in Scotland, regulates farming and fishing, and even manages smallholdings and crofting estates of its own.

Scottish farmers have their own association, the National Farmers' Union of Scotland, which, along with the National Farmers' Union of England and Wales and the Ulster Farmers' Union, negotiates with the government on the annual farm price review. In this negotiation, the Scottish Office is a participant. Farm workers are normally members of the Transport and General Workers' Union, although their wages are regulated by the Scottish Agricultural Wages Board. The rates have been higher than those in England in recent years.

Complaints are sometimes heard that Scottish farming interests tend to be swamped in the review by the dominance of the English farmers, whose produce (e.g. wheat and pork) may not be important in Scotland. There are no separate subsidies for Scotland, and if the money goes on, for example, wheat, then oats and barley tend to suffer. Lately, however, Scottish farmers have appeared more content with the support schemes, and the strength of the Scottish Office here may be indicated by the fact that the ministerial team conducting negotiations for entry into the E.E.C. in 1971 included the Scottish Office minister for Agriculture and Fisheries, Alick Buchanan-Smith. Much of the Scottish interest was in the question of the fisheries' limit, a subject which exercised the fishing organisations in Scotland (mostly local) and the two public boards, the White Fish Authority and the Herring Industry Board. All of these were highly critical of the proposed terms for British entry to the Common Market.

Hill farmers have also been sceptical of their prospects in the E.E.C. The Crofters' Union represents that unique category of Scottish farmers, the Highland crofters, whose rights are laid down in the Crofters Acts, and whose system of farming is administered by the Crofters Commission, an autonomous public agency. The Crofters' Union is markedly cool about entry to the E.E.C., while the National Farmers' Union of Scotland has supported entry, with the proviso that the Scottish NFU be directly and fully represented in Brussels.[14] The Farmers' Unions of the U.K. now have a joint office in Brussels.

Apart from these major economic interest groups, there are a whole host of Scottish organisations related to particular trades, businesses and professions. That these should have a Scottish form is one of the minor puzzles of modern Scotland. The Glasgow telephone directory for 1971 lists 290 entries under 'Scottish . . .', ranging from the Scottish Opera Centre to the Scottish Bookmakers' Protection Association. While some of these can be related to a peculiar Scottish interest (e.g. the Scottish Football Referees' Association), others seem to have no Scottish character other than location (e.g. Scottish Window Cleaning Co.).

The reasons for using the word 'Scottish' vary from one body to another. The principal ones are (*a*) that the organisation is located in Scotland; (*b*) that the organisation's activities are confined largely to Scotland; (*c*) that the tag 'Scottish' is a trading advantage in a country with strong national consciousness; (*d*) that there are actual differences in the interests or services involved as between Scotland and elsewhere, and (*e*) that it is an expression of Scottish nationalism.

In some cases, only one of these factors is relevant, while in a few all characteristics are present. Many groups adopt a Scottish organisation because it is more convenient to do so than to be part of a British one. There is a close-knit pattern of trade and communication in Scotland, which is broken by the sparsely populated Border region between Scotland and England. Commercial and travel links in Scotland converge on Edinburgh and Glasgow, not on the main cities of England. Thus a Scottish network of organised groups develops almost naturally.

The relevance of convenience is clearly seen in such trade associations as the Scottish Commercial Travellers' Association and Scottish Federation of Meat Traders' Association. These bodies illustrate points (*a*) and (*b*), above. Under (*c*), it is possible to trace a trading advantage in the use of 'Scottish' in enterprises such as the *Scottish Daily Express*, and in the various insurance companies such as Scottish Amicable, Scottish Provident and Scottish Widows. The newspapers wish to impress their Scottish readers that they are predominantly devoted to Scottish affairs, while the insurance companies perhaps believe that they can attract customers on the strength of the popular belief in Scottish thrift and business acumen.

National differences in the interests or services of an organisation (point (*d*)) occur principally among the historic or public sectors of Scottish life, such as the churches, education, law and administration. Some of these have been discussed earlier in this chapter. They combine considerations of convenience with nationalist sentiment, and range very widely indeed from the relatively 'neutral' (as far as nationalism is concerned) promotional groups such as the Royal Scottish Society for the Prevention of Cruelty to Children,[15] to the intensely nationalist Scottish Football Association and Scottish Football League.

It is obviously convenient to organise football on Scottish lines, as most of the teams are in the central lowlands of Scotland and would have to travel long distances to play English teams. But the origins of the Scottish Football Association (founded 1873) owe as much to the nationalism of Scottish football enthusiasts, who preferred to have nothing to do with English football. Football rivalry between Scotland and England is of course a large determinant of the nationalism of the working class in the twentieth century (cf. ch. 7).

It might be deduced from this account of organised groups in Scotland that almost all the interests of the people of Scotland have taken on a Scottish form. As a corrective, it is necessary to balance the picture of apparent strength of such Scottish groups with an assessment of their importance relative to British groups operating in Scotland.

Interesting as it may be to discover that Scottish plumbers, motor traders and tobacconists have their own national associations, and that those concerned about cruelty to children and animals also assert their Scottish identity, such facts tell us little about the real differences between these groups and the corresponding English groups.

In reality, a large number have identical interests and aims with those in England, and their Scottishness is the least important of their characteristics. It is doubtful whether it would make any difference if many of them merged with English groups, and some might gain financially if they were to do so. We have seen that Scottish trade unions have declined rapidly in recent years, as the benefits of membership of British unions have become apparent.

It is therefore true to say that the economic interests of the vast majority of the industrial working class of Scotland are represented and protected by British organisations, and that the Scottish bodies which remain are largely those of employers, farmers and professional people. These three categories usually have good reason to preserve their Scottish identity, either because they pay their employees lower wages than the average rates in England, or because they themselves have vested Scottish interests which they wish to maintain. Thus lawyers, teachers and church ministers in Scotland defend a 'closed shop' which effectively excludes the English. In this way then, Scottish groups are predominantly middle class, with working-class Scottishness expressed in organised form through football, and the STUC.

As far as government and policy-making is concerned, the Scottish 'arena' is composed mostly of the former (middle-class) category of spokesmen. The vast apparatus of advisory councils and committees is dominated by professionals and businessmen (with an occasional STUC representative). On the other hand, Scottish working-class interests merge in the British 'arena', where the big, British unions negotiate for the Scottish workers in London, or at the factory.

Such variations in the process of making policy for Scotland must now be examined in detail in selected activity areas, for these show the organised groups in action.

APPENDIX

Public bodies and advisory committee on which the STUC was represented in 1971
Source: *STUC 74th Annual Report*, pp. 165–74.
Scottish Economic Council
Regional–Consultative Groups of Scottish Economic Council (4 Groups)
West Scotland Plan Steering Committee
Highlands and Islands Consultative Council
White Fish Authority
Aberdeen Harbour Board
Clyde Port Authority
Forth Estuarial Authority
Local Employment Committees (17)
National Youth Employment Council
National Youth Employment Council Scottish Committee
National Advisory Council for the Employment of the Disabled
Scottish Gas Board
South of Scotland Electricity Consultative Council
Electricity Consultative Council for the North of Scotland
Scottish Advisory Committee for Civil Aviation
British Productivity Council
Industrial Tribunals
Ministry of Social Security Local Tribunals
Supplementary Benefits Appeals Tribunals
War Pensions Committees
General Teaching Council for Scotland
Scottish Committee for Central Training Council
Scottish Association for National Certificates and Diplomas
Scottish Council for Commercial, Administrative and Professional Education
Scottish Technical Education Consultative Committee
Boards of Governors and Boards of Management of Colleges of Further Education
Scottish Schools/Industry Liaison Committee
Open University
Newbattle Abbey College
Regional Health Boards (5)
Hospital Boards of Management (73 boards, 166 STUC nominees)
National Health Service Executive Councils (35)
Scottish Health Services Council and Standing Advisory Committees (9 nominees)
Scottish River Purification Advisory Committee

River Purification Boards (nominees on 5/8 boards)
Central Advisory Committee for Scotland on Justices of the Peace
Social Work (Scotland) Act 1968 – Children's Panels and Hearings (ensures application from trade unionists for membership)
Parole Board for Scotland
Borstal and Young Offenders Visiting Committees
Scottish Tourism Consultative Council
Transport Users' Consultative Committee for Scotland
Scottish Food Hygiene Committee
Cinematograph Films Council (nominated by TUC in consultation with STUC)
Post Office Users' Council for Scotland
Meat and Livestock Commission – Advisory Council
Race Relations Board Conciliation Committee
British Council Scottish Advisory Committee
Scottish Civic Entertainment Association

Political communication and the mass media

Scotland has a strongly differentiated mass communications network, which reflects and emphasises the particular characteristics of its society and its political system. It is one of the most active centres of newspaper-publishing outside London, with 6 daily morning, 6 evening, 2 Sunday, and over 100 weekly or twice-weekly newspapers. Many of these papers are independent, or are autonomous members of London publishing companies.

There is also a vigorous broadcasting output in Scotland, derived from BBC Scotland (Glasgow, Edinburgh and Aberdeen), Scottish Television (STV) (Glasgow and Edinburgh), and Grampian Television (Aberdeen). Border Television, which operates from Carlisle in England, transmits programmes to parts of the south-west of Scotland and the Borders, as well as to the extreme north-west of England and the Isle of Man. Independent local radio stations are Radio Clyde (1974) and Radio Forth (1975).

All the communications media in Scotland assert varying degrees of independence from London, and they are able to achieve it to a greater extent than any other media output centre in Britain. Scots demand, and support, a separate newspaper press and separate broadcasting, and their tastes are reflected in the strongly Scottish content of the press, TV and radio. The newspaper structure is shown in table 25.

Table 25 (a) gives the circulations (1973) of the principal newspapers in Scotland. The proprietors and dates of foundation are also given, where known. Table 25 (b) gives the figures for adult newspaper readership (1973), covering Scotland, Great Britain, London, and north-east and northern England.

The Scottish newspaper press has a long history, with four of its morning dailies dating back to the eighteenth or early nineteenth centuries. While few major papers published in Scotland are now Scottish-owned, all display distinctly Scottish characteristics. The *Scottish Daily Express*, though printed in Manchester, uses Scottish material for two-thirds of its contents, taking from London only major British and foreign stories, and some features. Editorial comment is shared between London and the Scottish edition, with effective power to differ where the Scottish editor

Table 25 (a) *Place of publication, circulation (1973), founding date, and proprietor of principal Scottish Newspapers*

	Circulation	Founding Date	Proprietor
DAILY MORNING			
Daily Record (Glasgow)	569,137	1895	IPC
Scottish Daily Express (Manchester)	565,000	1928	Beaverbrook
Courier and Advertiser (Dundee)	(122,657)	1801	D. C. Thomson
Press and Journal (Aberdeen)	107,910	1748	Lord Thomson
Glasgow Herald (Glasgow)	85,141	1783	Outram
Scotsman (Edinburgh)	80,113	1817	Lord Thomson
EVENING			
Evening Times (Glasgow)	181,056	1876	Outram
Evening News (Edinburgh)	148,474	1873	Lord Thomson
Evening Express (Aberdeen)	76,288	1879	Lord Thomson
Evening Telegraph (Dundee)	(66,617)	1877	D. C. Thomson
Greenock Telegraph (Greenock)	24,938	1857	Orr, Pollock
Paisley Daily Express (Paisley)	18,825	1874	Outram
SUNDAY			
Sunday Post (Glasgow and Dundee)	over 1,000,000	1920	D. C. Thomson
Sunday Mail (Glasgow)	753,880	1914	IPC
Scottish Sunday Express (Manchester)	(340,000)	1940	Beaverbrook
PRINCIPAL WEEKLY			
Weekly News (Glasgow, Dundee and Manchester)	(1,312,217)	1855	D. C. Thomson
People's Journal (6 editions) (Dundee)	(133,000)	1858	D. C. Thomson
Sporting Post (Dundee)	(57,689)	n.a.	D. C. Thomson
Hamilton Advertiser (Hamilton)	45,704	1856	Hamilton Advertiser
Perthshire Advertiser (Perth) (twice weekly)	36,287	1829	Outram
Dumfries and Galloway Standard (Dumfries) (twice weekly)	34,071	1843	Outram

Sources: Newspaper Press Directory 1974 (Benn, London 1974) and independent inquiries. Figures in brackets are pre-1973.
Note: In May 1975, the *Scottish Daily News* commenced publication, with a circulation of c. 200,000.

Table 25 (b) *Readership of newspapers in Scotland,* January–December 1973 (percentage of adults over 15 who read the following newspapers)*

	Scotland	G.B.	London	North-east and North England
Daily Record (asked about in Scotland only)	48	4	–	–
Daily Express (incl. Scottish)	43	23	20	19
Sun	6	26	30	26
Glasgow Herald	6 (Glasgow alone: 12)			
Scotsman	5 (Edinburgh alone: 20)			
Daily Mail	4	13	14	10
Daily Mirror	3	33	42	32
Daily Telegraph	2	9	13	5
Times	1	3	6	1
Guardian	1	3	4	2
Financial Times	1	2	4	1
Evening Papers	41	47	42	58
Sunday Post	77	11	1	17
Sunday Mail	52	6	11	4
Sunday Express (incl. Scottish)	24	26	28	21
News of the World	23	39	41	40
Sunday People	16	32	32	37
Sunday Mirror	9	33	42	28
Sunday Times	9	10	14	7
Observer	5	6	11	4
Sunday Telegraph	2	5	8	3

* The Surveys did not cover Scotland north of the Caledonian Canal. The *Courier and Advertiser* and *Press and Journal* are very strong in Dundee and Aberdeen respectively. In northern Scotland, the *Press and Journal* was read by 64% of adults in the early 1960s. *Readership Survey of North Scotland* commissioned by the Thomson Organisation, May 1963.

Sources: National Readership Survey 1973 (Jan.–Dec. 1973), vol. 3, Table 7; *Readership Survey of Glasgow*, commissioned by Glasgow *Evening Citizen* (now defunct), October 1969, table 1; *Readership Survey of Edinburgh*, commissioned by the Thomson Organisation, October 1965, table 1A.

thinks fit. The London editor does not see the *Scottish Express* before it is published, while the Scottish editor can pick and choose from the London edition. This arrangement had political significance during the 'D' notices affair in 1967, when the *Scottish Daily Express* printed the story about 'cable-vetting' before the English editions of the paper.[1]

The *Scottish Sunday Express* is less markedly Scottish, and uses more London features. The *Daily Mail* was published in Scotland as the *Scottish Daily Mail* until December 1968, but its poor circulation led to a retreat to Manchester. No other daily newspaper published in England amounts to more than 6% of the Scottish adult readership (table 25(*b*)). Such stalwarts of the English popular press as the *Daily Mirror* and the *Sun* are replaced in Scotland by the *Daily Record* (sister-paper of the *Mirror*, but almost totally Scottish in content), the *Express*, and (in their place) the Dundee *Courier* and Aberdeen *Press and Journal*. The middle class in Scotland forsake the *Daily Telegraph*, *Times* and *Guardian* for the *Scotsman* and *Glasgow Herald*. Thus all social groups adhere on week-days to the native press. On Sundays, the *News of the World* and *People* break through successfully, but no English Sunday matches the *Sunday Post* (77% of adults) and *Sunday Mail* (52%).

In the Highlands, the strength of community interests, and the delay experienced in receiving newspapers from the south, makes the local press peculiarly important. The principal Highland newspapers are:

> *Highland News* (Inverness) (1883) in a group with *Caithness Courier* (Thurso) (1866) and *John o' Groats Journal* (Wick) (1836). Circulation of group, 28,376.
> *Ross-shire Journal* (Dingwall) (1875) (16,000)
> *Inverness Courier* (1817) (twice weekly)*
> *Oban Times* (1861) (25,291)
> *Stornoway Gazette* (1917) (12,566)
> *Orcadian* (Kirkwall) (1854)*
> *Shetland Times* (Lerwick) (1872) (8,080)
> *The Buteman* (Rothesay) (1854)*
> *Campbeltown Courier* (1873)*
> *West Highland Free Press* (Kyleakin, Skye) (1972) (7,000)

These papers are widely read in the Highlands (and even outside) and pay much attention to political reporting of constituency or regional matters. All are locally owned, and although most are independent politically, the *Stornoway Gazette* and *Shetland Times* describe themselves as Liberal, and the *Ross-shire Journal* is Unionist (*Newspaper Press Directory*, 1970). The Stornoway paper has recently been sympathetic towards Scottish nationalism, and is an exponent of Gaelic culture. The *West Highland Free Press* is socialist.

The politics of the principal Scottish newspapers have become less static in recent years. Until the late 1950s, all except the *Daily Record* and now-defunct *Bulletin* (Glasgow) were Conser-

* Circulation not available.

vative. After Lord Thomson took over the *Scotsman* in the mid-1950s, that paper became sympathetic towards the Liberal Party, and in the 1970 and 1974 general elections it favoured the SNP. Another Thomson Group paper, the Aberdeen *Press and Journal*, deserted the Conservatives in the late 1960s for the Scottish Nationalists.

The *Scottish Daily Express* exhorted its readers to vote for Mrs Winifred Ewing, the SNP candidate, at the Hamilton by-election in November 1967. By the general election of 1970, however, it had returned to the Conservatives, while stressing that devolution along the lines of the Party's Scottish Convention was essential. Its principal political columnist, Charles Graham, wrote on election day (18 June) of the refusal of Labour to support devolution and 'recognise that Scotland is a nation, and a part of the U.K. that is very different in many respects from the rest of Britain'. (Mr Harold Wilson, the Labour Prime Minister, for his part, wrote in the *Sunday Mail* (7 June) that 'Scotland is a nation in her own right. Different from the English and the Welsh. But not apart from them.')

The D. C. Thomson papers (including the Dundee *Courier* and *Evening Telegraph* and *Sunday Post*) found the Nationalists attractive for a time. The last named's colossal circulation (over 1 million; 77% of Scottish adult readership) requires some comment. The *Sunday Post* is probably the most 'Scottish' of the Scottish papers, although it circulates widely in the north of England (see table 25(*b*)). Some of its writing and comic material is in Scots dialect. Most of the content consists of every-day stories about ordinary people. Politically, the paper is very right-wing. It abhors socialism, the welfare state, and trade unions (it will not recognise them among its own employees). But it stresses the peculiar virtues of Scottish character and independence of mind. This no doubt brought it close to the SNP, and in general the paper helps to keep alive the differentiation between Scottish and English society, and the assessment of politics in terms of 'what is done for Scotland'.

Most Scottish newspapers take this line, and even Tory papers such as the *Glasgow Herald* have on occasion proved critical of Conservative governments' Scottish policies; in August 1971, for example, the paper persistently demanded more favourable treatment for Upper Clyde Shipbuilders, and the siting of a steelworks at Hunterston (Ayrshire).

Scottish economic interests are identified and pursued by the Scottish press. Both the *Scotsman* and *Glasgow Herald* run Scottish financial supplements and trade reviews, and maintain industrial and agricultural correspondents. All Scottish papers are part of the economic log-rolling of the Scottish interest groups (among them the trade unions, employers associations and the Scottish Council (Development and Industry)), who seek further government-aided development in Scotland. The political affiliation of the papers then becomes somewhat irrelevant.

The political line-up of the principal Scottish papers is as follows:

Scottish Daily Express	Conservative
Daily Record	Labour
Courier (Dundee)	'Anti-socialist'
Press and Journal (Aberdeen)	Vaguely SNP
Glasgow Herald	Conservative (but no explicit recommendation on how to vote)
Scotsman	Liberal/SNP
Evening Times (Glasgow)	Liberal/non-committal
Sunday Post	'Anti-socialist'
Sunday Mail	Labour
Scottish Sunday Express	Conservative

During the election campaign of 1970 (as in other elections) a Scottish consciousness pervaded the press. In the two quality papers (*Scotsman* and *Glasgow Herald*), all the Scottish constituencies were analysed, with profiles of the candidates. Thereafter, constituency reports were given, and the prospects weighed up. The dividing line between Scotland and England was again evident: the Scottish press had Scotland for its 'parish', and the English press, England. There were of course some overlapping interests, and the principal political speeches in England were reported in Scotland. But the Scottish campaign was seen as a unity, and was the main material for the Scotland readers.

The party leaders were interviewed by the Scottish press on their policies for Scotland (e.g. Harold Wilson, 'Why I'm proud of our record in Scotland', *Sunday Mail*, 7 June 1970. 'Mr Wilson: My Pledges to all Scots', *Scottish Daily Express*, 17 June 1970. Edward Heath, 'Outlook Scotland', *Evening Citizen*, 17 June 1970). There were also features on special Scottish problems such as the Highlands, Scottish nationalism, devolution, unemployment, and Scotland and the E.E.C.

At non-election periods, too, the Scottish press presents a continuous service of reporting and commenting on Scottish political affairs. There is full coverage of Scottish parliamentary debates, parliamentary questions and even House of Commons Scottish committee work in the *Glasgow Herald* and *Scotsman*, who maintain their own parliamentary correspondents at Westminster. The popular papers also have parliamentary correspondents, and some have columns written by Scottish M.P.s. For the first year of her stay in the House of Commons (from

November 1967), Mrs Winifred Ewing, the SNP M.P., wrote a weekly column in the *Daily Record*, and had one written *about her* in the *Scottish Daily Express* ('Winnie at Westminster'). Other prominent M.P. columnists in the Scottish press in recent years have been W. Hamilton (Labour) in the *Sunday Mail* and Edward Taylor (Conservative) in the *Evening Citizen*.

Such journalism transmits the activities of the 'detached' portion of the Scottish political system in London to the grass-roots in Scotland. The reverse, however, is rarely the case. London prints very little political news from or about Scotland, except during such 'crisis' events as the collapse of Upper Clyde Ship-builders (1971). The separate organisation of the press in Scotland is partly responsible for this, since it caters fully for Scottish readers. But a division of political interest between Scotland and England is also evident. What appears important in Scotland may have no meaning in London (recent examples are the disputes over the General Teaching Council for Scotland, the licensing laws, the Highlands Board, and local authority rates). So the press illustrates the separation of the Scottish and British segments of politics.

Table 26 *Broadcasting in Scotland*

TV	Coverage	Hours per week originating in Scotland
BBC Scotland	Most of Scotland	10
Scottish Television	Central Scotland	10
Grampian Television	North-west Scotland	6
Border Television	South-west, Borders	4 (from Carlisle)
Radio		
BBC Scotland	All Scotland	40
Radio Clyde	Glasgow area	140
Radio Forth	Edinburgh area	130

Scottish broadcasting does this also, although it is more homogeneous with that in the rest of the country. The main sources are BBC TV, Independent TV, and BBC radio, in ascending order of 'Scottishness'.

The BBC's TV output in Scotland consists of around 130 hours a week (BBC-1 and BBC-2 combined). Of this, only about 10 hours originates in the studios at Glasgow, Edinburgh and Aberdeen. Nevertheless, about half of the Scottish output has a bearing on politics. There is a daily Scottish news bulletin and magazine (25 minutes) at 6 p.m., and a late-night summary around 11.30 p.m. These programmes include grass-roots and parliamentary material, with interviews of Scottish M.P.s and interest group spokesmen. For nine months in the year there are two weekly current affairs programmes, devoted to Scottish problems. Special programmes are produced to report the party conferences in Scotland, the STUC conference, the Scottish local elections, and the general campaigns and results (in the last case, Scotland 'opts out' of part of the network programme). Scottish schools programmes have series on Scottish history and affairs.

The BBC's Scottish headquarters in Glasgow maintains several experienced news and political commentators, whose contributions are equal in importance to those of the journalists in the Scottish press, if less partisan.

The ITV output is split between Scottish Television (STV) covering central Scotland, Grampian Television covering Aberdeen and the north of Scotland (not the north-west), and Border Television covering the south-west and Borders. The programme hours produced by these companies average 10, 6 and 4 hours respectively. As with the BBC, about half the programmes are concerned with news, current affairs and education. Unlike the BBC, however, ITV fragments Scotland into three, and combines the south-west with part of England and the Isle of Man. Moreover, about half the land area of Scotland (including most of the Highlands) does not receive ITV at all. Thus ITV programmes reflect a regional audience rather than an audience spread throughout the whole of Scotland. Grampian caters for Aberdeen and the north-east, STV for central Scotland, and Border for its 'multi-national' community.

STV is the largest and most vigorous company, with an extended Scottish news programme daily (30 minutes for nine months of the year and 15 minutes for the remainder). It has a weekly 45-minute political magazine programme, and as good a coverage of the annual political 'events' and elections as the BBC. It has one experienced political commentator, with supporting industrial and news staff.

Grampian and Border do not offer the same output of current affairs or political programmes, nor do they usually attempt to cover all the political conferences or elections. Border rarely bothers with the Scottish conferences, but Grampian and STV have reciprocal arrangements for reporting them. Local elections are badly served on Grampian and Border. The 1971 local elections in Scotland, for example, were not given full-length reporting on either station. The 1970 general election campaign, however, was given extended local coverage on BBC Scotland, STV and Grampian (see table 27).

The smaller companies' strength lies in the news coverage and local magazine programmes. In 1971 Grampian offered a 10-minute news (Monday to Friday) and a weekly magazine programme on the life of the area. It produced a monthly political programme, involving a discussion between Scottish M.P.s. Other regular programmes were about farming, religion and education. There was also a considerable emphasis on Scottish-style light entertainment, with overtones of nationalism.

Table 27   *The 1970 election. Scottish TV programmes*

BBC Scotland

9, 10, 11 June	*Election 70 – Question Time*: 3 45-minute programmes from different parts of Scotland, with journalists and representatives of 5 parties.
10, 11, 12 June	*Reporting Scotland*: 3 constituency reports (60 minutes).
14 June	*Scottish Viewpoint*: Scottish churches and the election (45 minutes).
16 June	*Current Account*: campaign report (4 marginal seats) (50 minutes).

STV

22, 29 May; 5 June	*In Camera*: 3 programmes using representatives of 5 parties, with analysis (90 minutes).
8/12, 15, 16 June	*Scotland Now*: daily constituency reports (70 minutes).

Grampian

10, 11, 12 June	*Grampian Voter*: 3 programmes using representatives of 5 parties, with 3 constituency reports (155 minutes).
16 June	*Grampian Election Special*: 4-party representatives (59 minutes).

Border

15, 16 June	*Border General Election Report*: 2 programmes covering 10 constituencies (4 Scottish). Analysis and candidates' statements (90 minutes).

Note: all Scottish channels gave election reports in their nightly news programmes, and all except Border had opt-outs on 18 June during the results service. The BBC and STV election studios in Glasgow were elaborately equipped to cover all Scottish results. In the elections in 1974, a very similar pattern prevailed.

Border cannot afford to involve itself in Scottish nationalism, since 60% of its viewers are in England or the Isle of Man. In general, it does not offer a distinctively Scottish output, whether in news, politics, sport or light entertainment. Nevertheless, its nightly news and magazine programme is very popular, as is its light entertainment. These programmes draw on local community interests. For 'Scottish' programmes Border viewers must turn to the BBC, especially for politics, sport or religion.

BBC Scotland has a prolific radio output (around 40 hours a week), which is unmatched by any other region. Some of this is taken by the network, especially the considerable amount of music. About 13 hours is Scottish news, comment or educational material. The breakfast programme *Good Morning Scotland* (two editions) is important as it has a large audience and is an opt-out from the London programme *Today*. There is also an hour-long magazine and news programme at mid-day. Radio caters for the Gaelic minority, with about 3 hours weekly on VHF, and occasional programmes on television. Since 1974, Radio Clyde (an independent station) has captured much of BBC Scotland's radio audience, and has produced several political programmes. Radio Forth (1975) is the other independent radio station in Scotland.

The BBC has not in Scotland, as in England, largely replaced its regional broadcasting with local radio stations. This is because the National Broadcasting Council for Scotland vetoed such a proposal, as being destructive of the national unity of the country.[2] The Council is charged with controlling BBC broadcasting in Scotland, and it is a buttress of national identity. At the same time, it is very much part of the Scottish Establishment, and consists of respected representatives of the Church, university, local government and Gaelic communities. Its chairman is Lady Avonside, wife of a Conservative judge. At the height of the SNP's electoral success (1967–9) it refused to entertain the party's request that its political broadcasting time be increased beyond the five minutes on TV and radio per year granted in 1965, although the ITA favoured this.

Party political broadcasting time is fixed by the Committee on Political Broadcasting, which consists of representatives of the Conservative, Labour and Liberal Parties and, since 1974, the SNP, and of the IBA and BBC (Butler and Pinto-Duschinsky, p. 201). The Committee meets annually to review, in the light of election results and other evidence, the ratio of time which will be allotted to the parties. It also devises separate ratios for Scotland and Wales, in view of the existence of nationalist parties in these areas.

The formula for party political broadcasts during a general election campaign states that if a party nominates 50 candidates or more at a general election it is entitled to a five-minute broadcast (Butler and King, p. 126). The Communist Party qualified for a broadcast in this way in 1966 and 1970. The SNP did not so qualify in 1970, however, although it had 65 candidates. The reason given was that it did not put up candidates outside Scotland, and so it was inappropriate to give it a U.K. broadcast.

The decision was of course attacked by the SNP, who sought the maximum publicity. As for the major parties, the formula gave 13 broadcasts in the 1970 election, in the ratio of Labour 5, Conservative 5 and Liberal 3 (Butler and Pinto-Duschinsky, p. 201).

In the election of October 1974, party political broadcasts were as follows: Labour 5, Conservative 5, Liberal 4, and SNP 2. Labour and Conservative produced two special Scottish broadcasts each, on both TV and radio, and the Scottish Liberals produced one for TV and radio. The Communists no longer had a broadcast, but the National Front, whose candidates with one exception (Govan) were in England, had one.

On political programmes other than 'party politicals' yet another formula is in operation. In 1966 it was agreed that if a party contested one-fifth of the seats in a region, it was entitled to equal representation on programmes featuring party spokesmen. U.K. programmes were similarly dealt with, leaving the three main parties with assured seats on network coverage. As far as Scottish programmes were concerned, the formula secured representation for five parties in 1966 and 1970 since the Communists just qualified, with 15 candidates both times. Despite the fact that there were three ITV companies operating in Scotland, Scotland was treated as a unit for this purpose. This meant that Grampian and Border had to have Communist representation on all 'spokesmen' programmes despite the absence of Communist candidates in their areas. In other regions, each company's territory was used to compile the ratio. In October 1974, the Communists did not qualify.

Outside election campaigns, political discussion programmes are largely free from such formulae, although fairness, impartiality and party balance must be observed. From 1966 to 1970 the SNP complained that their appearances on current affairs programmes were fewer than their popular support warranted (in 1968 they received 30% of the vote in the local elections). It is true that BBC Scotland veered away from all political subjects on TV after mid-1968, and that SNP spokesmen were not seen for a year on that channel. While pressure from the major parties may have been partly responsible for this, there was also a feeling, reflected throughout the mass media, that the SNP was less newsworthy than it had been. The number of broadcasts and newspaper articles devoted to nationalism had been high to that point, and the subject was becoming over-exposed (see table 28). Nevertheless, the building-up of the SNP by the media, followed by its comparative neglect, may have contributed to the rapid rise and fall of the party's fortunes at that time.

Scotland has a volume of broadcasting about politics in its area, both at election and non-election times, which is unmatched

Table 28 *Principal TV broadcasts about Scottish nationalism, 1967–1970*

BBC network	
12 June 1968	*The Disunited Kingdom*: From London, Glasgow and Cardiff

BBC Scotland

13 October 1967	*Checkpoint*: The Hamilton by-election
3 November 1967	*Checkpoint*: Interview with Mrs Ewing
12 January 1968	*Checkpoint*: Do we need a Scottish Parliament?
9 February 1968	*Checkpoint*: The 1320 Club (a nationalist body)
5 April 1968	*Checkpoint*: Where do we go from here? (Economics of nationalism)
2 June 1968	SNP Conference Report
1 June 1969	SNP Conference Report
6 June 1969	*Current Account:* Economics of nationalism
10 October 1969	*Current Account*: Gorbals by-election
31 October 1969	*Current Account*: Scottish budget
22 January 1970	*Current Account*: Liberal/SNP pact
20 March 1970	*Current Account*: Scottish Convention
10 April 1970	*Current Account*: Scotland and the Common Market
15 March 1970	*Left, Right and Centre*: Ayrshire by-election
8 May 1970	Evidence to Commission on the Constitution (50 minutes) (other programmes 30 September 1969, 55 minutes; 21 November 1969, 15 minutes)

STV

3 November 1967	*In Camera*: Mrs Ewing's journey to London
1967–70	*In Camera* (weekly): used SNP spokesmen on one-fifth of programmes
June 1968	SNP Conference reports
June 1969	SNP Conference reports
1 November 1969	*In Camera*: The Scottish budget (one hour)

Grampian

1967–70	*Points North* (monthly): M.P.s' discussion programme; occasionally included SNP representative
1966–7	*Country Focus* (fortnightly): Did intensive study of effect of entry into E.E.C. on north-east Scotland (SNP was the only party campaigning against E.E.C. entry in 1970)

Border

1967–70	*Border News and Lookaround*: Included interviews with SNP spokesmen about the party's conferences and local election results (c. 5 minutes each). Other programmes included interviews about devolution with Liberal M.P.s David Steel and Jo Grimond, and with Conservatives Sir Alec Douglas-Home and Edward Heath

by any other part of Britain. It does not seek to produce programmes about other regions, or about British politics in general. Indeed, only a small proportion of Scottish programmes are seen outside Scotland. In 1969–70, 62 hours out of the 534 hours of TV originating in BBC Scotland went to the network. This should be compared with BBC Midlands (318 out of 551 hours to the network), BBC North (243 out of 574) and BBC South and West (241 out of 543).[3] Even smaller network contributions are made by STV and Grampian. Such insularity reinforces the separation of Scotland from England, and emphasises the identity of the Scottish political system.

But there are strong forces for homogeneity as well. Scottish broadcasting is a small percentage of the total number of hours of TV and radio consumed in Scotland. Scots watch network or other non-Scottish programmes for nine-tenths of the time. They are well accustomed to such programmes as the network news and network political features (e.g. BBC's *Panorama* and *Midweek*, ITV's *World in Action* and *This Week*). These programmes emphasise the British, not Scottish, aspects of politics, and during election periods rarely mention parties such as the SNP, or Scottish political issues. Broadcasting therefore goes some way to counteract the otherwise divisive influence of the Scottish media, especially the press, which is much more completely Scottish.

The quality of Scottish political broadcasting is not equal to that of the best network productions. Its popularity in terms of audience ratings is also lower. There is a high rating for Scottish news productions, however, and Scottish light entertainment and sport programmes are as popular as those from the network. The expense and difficulty of producing good programmes in Scotland is greater than that of producing good newspapers. So there is more reliance on London in broadcasting than in the press. Both branches of the communications media in Scotland play a vital part in the Scottish political system. Political information is now principally conveyed by TV, and the Scottish channels have developed their own news and current affairs programmes. In the Scottish press, a vigorous and partisan political commentary is available, with the two 'quality' papers (*Scotsman* and *Glasgow Herald*) providing comprehensive reporting and analysis. There is ample support in the communications media for the operation of an autonomous Scottish political system.

And the links between the communications network in Scotland and the decision-making machinery are also close. Scottish decision-makers in central and local government are as influenced by the *Scotsman* and the *Glasgow Herald* as their English counterparts are by *The Times*, *Guardian* or *Daily Telegraph*.

The prominence given to Scottish politics in the Scottish press shapes the attitudes of the electorate and the interest groups. Campaigns in Scottish newspapers (such as that to 'Save the Argylls' and attack the Highland Board in the *Scottish Daily Express*) have been important politically, and Scottish M.P.s avidly read the Scottish newspapers in the Library of the House of Commons for reports of their speeches. They are rarely disappointed, for Scottish papers carry an ample coverage of Scottish parliamentary activities. It must be presumed that the Scottish public shares at least some of their interest.

11

The policy-making process

The process of making policy is central to the working of a political system. In a democracy, it converts the political demands of society into governmental actions. If this job is done properly, the political system will be stable, and its activities will be beneficial to the social system (or systems) as a whole.[1]

The components of the Scottish political system have already been dealt with. They include those means which Scots have developed for articulating and aggregating their interests, such as the Scottish M.P.s, organised groups and the media; those institutions which respond to such demands within the governmental structure, such as the Scottish Office; and those institutions which execute the decisions of government, or adjudicate disputes (i.e. the public service and the Scottish legal system). It is the thesis of this book that such activities constitute a Scottish political system, since the degree of interaction and interdependence of the components defines a boundary between the Scottish and English political systems, and that the range of activities which is involved makes it a relatively more important political system than those which could be analysed at (for example) the regional level in England or at the local (i.e. sub-state) level in countries such as the United States. It thus has feature of 'macro-politics', as well as 'micro-politics'.

In analysing these components, some attempt has been made to describe how they work, and to illustrate their dynamic qualities within the system. The question has been, 'What is the place of these institutions/organisations/people in the Scottish political system, and what are their characteristic activities?

In this chapter, the question is rephrased to shed a different light on the system. Instead of asking what makes up the system, the enquiry is directed to the question of how decisions in certain fields of policy are made, and by whom. This involves a re-examination of the parts of the system, and reintroduces more forcibly the place of actors outside the system who are important to it. In particular, it shows the place of the British political system in the decision-making process affecting Scotland.

Three broad areas have been chosen, for their importance and contrasting nature. They are (a) economic planning, (b) social services, and (c) law reform. Each has a measure of documentation, and a lively history. And in each there is a different relationship between Scottish and British decision-makers.

(a) Economic planning

From February 1969 to June 1970 the House of Commons Select Committee on Scottish Affairs investigated economic planning in Scotland. It published a report and two volumes of evidence, taken at the hearings which the Committee held in Scotland and in London (SCSA 1–3). The Commission on the Constitution also took evidence in Scotland at this time, some of which was concerned with the same problem (Kilbrandon, 2, 4). The evidence to these two bodies is the principal published source of information on how economic policy in Scotland is formulated, and the findings are central to an understanding of the Scottish political system. Much use will be made of them in this section.

The Select Committee was as concerned with the content of economic policies for Scotland as with the decision-making process. These policies were the responsibility of the Labour governments of 1964–70, and the Committee contained a majority of Labour M.P.s (There were 9 Labour M.P.s, 5 Conservatives, 1 Liberal and 1 SNP. The SNP member, Mrs Winifred Ewing, issued her own minority report.) To some extent, its report reflects the desire of the majority not to embarrass the Labour government, but the Committee was genuinely interested in the way in which its policies were formulated. The Kilbrandon Commission was more involved with questions relating to the machinery of government, though the Commissioners raised issues of substantial policy on occasion.

Regional economic planning in Britain has developed over the years from the piece-meal financial inducements given under the Special Areas Acts of 1934 and 1937 to encourage industry to come to depressed areas, to the armoury of regional policies which have been tried since the 1960s (see McCrone 1–3, especially 3, p. 12). From being a minor aspect of economic policy between the wars these regional incentives have become a central interest of politicians and economists today.

Today, the main features of regional economic policies are controls over industrial expansion in congested areas and financial incentives to industries in development areas. The administration of the controls was by industrial development certificates, and the incentives were various grants, payroll subsidies and loan facilities. It should be noted that there was no direction of industry to needy regions, rather pressure to develop there.

The impetus for regional policy has been the changing attitude towards the economy, especially towards the part played by government in its regulation. Since the Second World War, it has been accepted that the state must seek to maintain full employment, promote economic growth and ensure a minimum standard of living throughout the country. If a region lags behind in these respects, the state must seek remedial measures. The Labour and Conservative Parties differ about the degree of state intervention here, but each is committed to the general principles of regional policy which have evolved since 1945.

The background to this policy is the shifting distribution of wealth in Britain between different regions, and the unwillingness of the people in the poorer regions to tolerate 'relative deprivation'. There have always been rich and poor areas in Britain, but until the 1930s these were considered to be the result of market forces, which it would be unwise to upset. While it was permissible to redistribute wealth (up to a point) between individuals (e.g. through a progressive income tax), it was less laudable to redistribute the country's wealth between its different regions.

The trouble came when previously wealthy regions now found themselves poor. Such areas were the central Lowlands of Scotland and the north of England. In these, the traditional heavy industries of coal, steel and shipbuilding, as well as other industries such as textiles, were in decline, causing high unemployment, low incomes and heavy emigration. While the inhabitants of traditionally poor areas are more inclined to suffer their poverty in silence, or to leave home, those of the 'new-poor' regions tend to be vociferous and resentful. The spokesmen of these places soon began to make their influence felt in government circles, so that stronger economic policies had to be adopted to satisfy public opinion.

The combination of forces derived from economic theory, changing economic circumstances in the regions, party-political philosophy, and political pressure from the grass-roots, makes up the explanation for the development of regional economic policy in Britain.

What part did the Scottish political system play in its formulation? The contribution of individual Scottish economists or economists working in Scotland to the theory of regional policy as it developed in the 1950s and 1960s, was considerable. Academics such as Professor (now Sir) Alec Cairncross[2] and Professor Thomas Wilson[3] of Glasgow University were fore-runners in the field, and economists in the Departments of Political Economy and Social and Economic Research at Glasgow University made major contributions.[4] So too have economists in Edinburgh University and Aberdeen University. Many economists working in Scotland feel an involvement in the problems of the Scottish economy, and play an active part in advising government on regional policies. Some of their efforts have proved extremely influential, not only in the Scottish Office, but in the Treasury and other Whitehall departments.

Reports such as the 'Cairncross Report' of 1952,[5] and the 'Toothill Report' of 1961 (Toothill), helped to shape government policies regarding the Scottish economy and the 'growth areas' within it (McCrone 3, p. 209). According to Sir Douglas Haddow, then Permanent Under-Secretary at the Scottish Office, 'it is not in the least unfair to say Scottish thought and Scottish practice pioneered in this country regional development policies' (SCSA 2, p. 23. Q. 54). Examples of Scottish initiatives were the *Central Scotland Plan 1963* (Cmnd. 2188) and the formation of the Scottish Development Department in 1962. Another innovation which owed much to Scottish inspiration was the setting up in March 1972 of regional development offices within the Department of Trade and Industry. These offices, which included the Scottish Industrial Development Office in Glasgow, were given financial and administrative responsibility over regional development grants. In 1975, this responsibility was transferred to the Scottish Office.

In the 1960s, five economics professors of Glasgow, Strathclyde, Edinburgh, Dundee and Aberdeen Universities became economic consultants to the Scottish Office, and were closely involved in the sub-regional plans[6] which were then being produced, and in other specific research projects. They met in Edinburgh with the Permanent Under-Secretary of State and others at the Scottish Office, and took it in turn to attend meetings of the Scottish Economic Planning Council (SCSA 2, p. 6). In 1972, the number of professor-consultants was three, with a panel of others called on as required.

In May 1970, Dr Gavin McCrone, the Glasgow and Oxford economist, whose works on regional planning have already been quoted, was appointed as head of the Economics and Statistics Unit at the Scottish Office. There were only a few economists and statisticians at this time in the Scottish Office, but by July 1971 the unit had a staff of ten economists and two statisticians, and was producing its twice-yearly *Scottish Economic Bulletin*.[7]

The formulation of the major decisions in economic policy is, of course, largely the prerogative of the Treasury and other Whitehall economic departments. The former fixes the rates of taxation, industrial financial incentives and the level of government spending in the different departments. Clearly, the Scottish Office's functions and the general responsibility of the Scottish Secretary for the Scottish economy are here subsidiary to the powers of Whitehall, though Edinburgh has a hand in the decision-making.

The amount of consultation which the Scottish Office has with these departments depends on the subject-matter. As far as taxes are concerned, the Chancellor of the Exchequer consults no other minister (except the Prime Minister) before he lays his Budget proposals before the Cabinet. But arguments between ministers do take place over taxation, and one can be sure that the Scottish Secretary was vocal about the implications for parts of Scotland of the selective employment tax (introduced 1966), and about regional incentives. In 1967, a regional employment premium was brought in, which benefited manufacturers in development areas.

Contacts between the Scottish Secretary and the economics ministers are maintained through Cabinet meetings (including Cabinet committees) and informal talks. It is difficult to evaluate these, since personal considerations (as well as secrecy) loom so large in their operation. A popular (and politically strong) Scottish Secretary can influence policy here, while a weak minister cannot.

The evidence to the Select Committee and the Kilbrandon Commission shows that frequent consultations take place at the official (civil service) level, in such bodies as the Scottish Economic Planning Board (an inter-departmental committee chaired by the Scottish Office: see p. 192). As far as these committees in Scotland are concerned, the Scottish Office is the dominant partner. Viewed from Whitehall, however, Scotland is only one of many claimants for scarce resources, and in terms of skilled negotiators the Scottish Office is no more than the equal of powerful departments like Trade, Industry, the Environment, and Employment.

The Select Committee was told by the Board of Trade (now part of the Departments of Trade and Industry) that it did not have to consult with the Scottish Office on a day-to-day basis over the location of industry, although it got in touch about major problems. It did not attempt to encourage industry to go to the Scottish Office's 'growth areas', nor even to Scotland in particular (SCSA 2, pp. 172, 220). Neither was the Department of Economic Affairs (now defunct) concerned about these (*ibid.* p. 158). The DEA looked at the problems of industries as a whole rather than the purely Scottish aspects, and was not usually operative on projects in Scotland (p. 190). The Minister of Technology (now within Industry), too, thought in terms of industries rather than in terms of the needs of particular locations (p. 240). The Ship-building Industry Board was not governed by regional policies (p. 269), and the Ministry of Power's Scottish Controller was seen by that department in part as 'a sort of ambassador representing the Minister of Power's interests in Scotland' (p. 284). Nevertheless, the Minister of Power was better informed about Scotland than he was about the English regions because since 1959 the Ministry has had no nationwide English regional organisation (pp. 284–5).

There was close consultation between the Scottish Office and British departments on colliery closures (p. 161), and rail closures. In the latter the Scottish Region of British Rail had ministerial support from the Scottish Office which was not present for English regions (p. 313). The case for retaining an uneconomic line in Scotland for social reasons is made by the Scottish Office to the Minister of Transport, although the expense of such a subsidy is not borne on the Scottish Office vote.

The Select Committee reported that the Scottish Office had 'full opportunities for a distinctively Scottish view of administrative questions to be formed and to be pressed at all levels of central government from the Cabinet downwards', but it added that 'this is not to say that co-operation between the Scottish Office and the Great Britain departments is as effective a method of administration for Scottish purposes as that implied by the transfer of further functions to the Scottish Office' (SCSA 1, p. 21).

The evidence before the Committee showed that while inter-departmental co-ordination for Scottish economic planning has increased greatly since the early 1960s, the major British departments are still very much London-bound, and do not shape their policies to fit the needs of the Scottish economy as a whole, as opposed to the needs (as they see them) of particular industries throughout Britain, or of the general requirements of the British economy.

The Scottish Office may therefore find it difficult to present a convincing case for special expenditure in Scotland in the location of industry and the placing of government contracts. While the principle of parity of services throughout the U.K. is accepted by governments today, even if it means spending more in some parts of the country in proportion to population, it is not generally accepted that there should be equality of employment opportunities or of incomes as between all regions. The most favourable locations for some types of industry may be outside Scotland, and it would be economically foolish (in the conventional wisdom) to force industry into areas where it could not make a profit. If the growth industries are unwilling to come to Scotland, for reasons of distance from markets or lack of suitable labour, the regional policies of British government cannot compel them to do so, despite a wide range of regional incentives, and the Industrial Development Certificates system.

The Scottish Office, as the department held responsible for planning the Scottish economy, must involve itself in the decisions

of the British departments and public corporations which determine or influence the location of industry. Quite often it has to
fight a 'rear-guard action' against a decision which has ignored
the interests of Scotland. In many instances, the Whitehall department or public corporation leaves the advocacy of the Scottish
case to the Scottish Office, and presses for economic development
in England. For example, the Ministry of Transport employed
American consultants in 1967 to advise on the location of a con-
tainer port. The ports examined were all in England, so the Scottish Office had to undertake its own survey, to make the case for a
Scottish port. Its vigorous campaigning (and that of the Clyde
Port Authority) for Greenock won the day, partly through the
use of experts such as shipbuilder Kenneth Douglas, but also by
the skill of Scottish Office civil servants, and the eternal nagging
of Scottish Secretary William Ross. Ross and Barbara Castle, the
Transport Minister, settled it between them.

Similar confrontations, at all levels of government, are repeated
whenever a big decision has to be taken about industrial development. The energies of the Scottish Secretary, his Minister of
State, and his top civil servants, are devoted to bringing more
employment to Scotland, and to pressurising the departments
which have it in their power to do so. The classic cases in recent
years have been the motor-vehicle factories at Linwood and Bathgate, the Fort William pulp-mill, the Ravenswood steel strip-mill,
the Invergordon aluminium works, the Dounreay fast breeder reactor, Upper Clyde Shipbuilders, and the Hunterston deep-water
port and steel-mill. For each, there is a story of reasoned persuasion, threats ('Scotland must have it or its economy will collapse'),
political blackmail ('votes will be lost if it does not come'), and
personal influence ('you know that I am one of your most stead-
fast allies, Mr Prime Minister'), almost monotonous in their simi-
larity. More recently, the development of North Sea oil has involved the Scottish Office in a tussle with the Department of
Energy. The Scottish Office handles infrastructure (housing,
roads, water), local government and planning permissions for on-
shore development, while the Department of Energy controls the
oil production side. But the interaction of these responsibilities
has given rise to many conflicts, for example, over planning permissions. The Scottish Office has to bear in mind sensitive Scottish
opinion, while the London-based Department is concerned mainly
with the rapid development of the energy supply. To moderate
this problem, two Scottish M.P.s (Gavin Strang and John
Smith) were appointed ministers at the Department of Energy
in 1974.

Who are the key figures? Undoubtedly, the Secretary of State
for Scotland is of the utmost importance in the decision-taking

process. No other region (not even Wales) has so powerful a figure in the Cabinet, or can any other Cabinet Minister claim to influence such a political fiefdom (71 seats). In return for getting his way on a development in Scotland, a Scottish Secretary will often pledge support for his Prime Minister in his battles in Cabinet, and will promise to deliver the votes of Scotland at the next election.

Next come the top civil servants in the Scottish Office, who brief their ministers and negotiate with other departments. The itinerant crew who commute from Edinburgh to London twice-weekly, and the 'Embassy' of 100 at Dover House, Whitehall, argue the case for Scotland in innumerable committees, Cabinet meetings, and through speeches prepared for ministers. In economic policy, the influence of civil servants such as Sir Douglas Haddow (Permanent Under-Secretary, 1964–73, biography on p. 74), and J. H. McGuinness (head of the Regional Development Division, 1964–72[8]) has been great. They have helped transform the Scottish Office from an administrative department into a planning department, and have added in effect to the responsibilities of the Scottish Secretary.

Then there are the other Scottish Office administrators who use the powers given directly to the Scottish Office. The development and range of these functions has already been discussed (ch. 3). It is important to note that they cover several important activities such as roads, electricity, transport (except rail and air), local government, agriculture, and since 1975 industrial incentives and development.

Since 1962, special development agencies have been established, such as the Scottish Development Group (SDG, 1962–4), the Regional Development Division (RDD, 1964–), the Scottish Economic Planning Board (SEPB, 1965–), and the Scottish Development Agency (1975–). The SEPB is the successor of the SDG, and consists of officials of the Scottish Office and other departments concerned with the economic and physical development of Scotland (e.g. Trade, Industry, Employment, Environment, Defence). It formulated the five-year plan for the Scottish economy (Cmnd. 2864, 1966), and is 'the main official instrument for ensuring that the separate developments which contribute to economic growth are kept in step' (SCSA 2, p. 3). It is not an executive agency with powers of its own, for each department represented on it retains the right to take its own decisions. The Scottish Development Agency is an autonomous body concerned with promoting industrial development.

Up in Inverness, the Highland and Islands Development Board (1965–) has statutory executive powers to assist industry in its area (the seven crofting counties), and receives a grant-in-aid from the Scottish Economic Planning Department. It is not staffed by civil servants, but has close liaison with the Department. Projects costing over certain sums must be sanctioned by that department or by the Treasury. (SCSA 1, p. 46.) Physical planning powers (land use, housing, roads, etc.) are left to local authorities (see also ch. 12).

Outside the network of official bodies are the consultative groups and councils. At the top is the Scottish Economic Council, chaired by the Scottish Secretary. It has 24 members and meets occasionally. It used to delegate most of its work to three committees (industrial, regional and transport) but these have now been discontinued. So too have the consultative groups in four sub-regions, but the Consultative Council for the Highlands Board remains. In recent years, these bodies have been downgraded, and play a very small part in the decision-making process.

Policy formulation also involves the 'pressure groups' such as the Scottish Council, CBI, and STUC, described in chapter 9. The Scottish Council, in particular, has been closely associated with economic planning through its various reports (e.g. Toothill, 1961, and Oceanspan, 1970–1), and with the promotion of trade in missions to foreign countries undertaken jointly with the Scottish Office (e.g. Attraction of German Industry, 1971–1972).

In examining the process of decision-making in Scottish economic policy, it is thus necessary to distinguish between the different types of decision. At the level of physical planning, the local authorities have discretionary powers to build council houses, schools, roads and advance factories, within the limits set by law and the supervision of the Scottish Office. They must draw up development plans to determine the use of land under the Town and Country Planning Acts. Some local authorities have cooperated in producing regional plans (see note 6), usually with the assistance of the Scottish office and outside consultants.

Disputes between local authorities, or between local authorities and central government (including the Highlands Board), as to how development should take place, have hampered sub-regional planning in Scotland. In the Borders, the opposition of local authorities to the Scottish Office's Central Borders Plan (1968), coupled with litigation by a private landowner, effectively killed the development of a new town in the district. Confrontations took place between Ross and Cromarty County Council Planning Department, local farmers and the Highlands Board over industrial sites in Easter Ross in 1967. In the west central Lowlands, economic planning was made difficult by the lack of a unified planning authority to cope with the problems of the Clyde area.

In October 1970, a West Central Scotland Plan Steering Committee was established (composed of members of 32 local authorities and nominees of the Secretary of State for Scotland), to produce a plan for the sub-region. The rivalries between the authorities involved continued, however, and the administrative difficulties are only now being settled under the new local government structure (the Strathclyde region).

The Scottish Office possesses controls over local government (e.g. through grants and planning approvals), and can itself provide major public works such as roads, bridges and hospitals (through hospital boards). While all these expenditures require the sanction of the Treasury, the formulation of specific proposals is very much in the hands of Scottish civil servants and ministers. Moreover, the Scottish Office possesses a limited power of 'virement', that is, the right to transfer expenditure authorised for one subject to another. For example, it can make adjustments in the order of £1m. between the roads programme and the housing programme (SCSA 1, p. 24). When one considers the range of functions possessed by the Scottish Office, the degree of choice is theoretically great. 'There is no formal limit to the amounts that may be transferred or the time at which they may be transferred' (SCSA, loc. cit.). But the practical possibilities are limited by on-going commitments, which make it difficult to save on one service to benefit another.

The proposed expenditures of the Scottish Office are made in detail to the Treasury and the Public Expenditure Survey Committee (an inter-departmental committee), and the latter plans over a period of five years. Hard decisions are taken for three years ahead. The result is that 'when ministers consider the allocation of public expenditure each year, the choices before them relate to marginal changes' (SCSA 2, p. 59). This is particularly relevant to the scope of 'virement' in the Scottish Office.

The Scottish Office makes requests for money to run individual services (e.g. education, housing, roads), rather than for a global sum to cover all its activities (there is no 'general grant' but 'specific grants'). The argument then turns on comparability with services offered in England. As a starter, the Scottish Office usually demands parity with England ('any marked divergence in standards would be unacceptable to public opinion', SCSA 2, p. 60). But it explains, diplomatically, that Scottish needs are somewhat different from those of England. For example, there are more slums, and a large public sector in housing. As a result, the Scottish allocation covering housing activities in the public sector is about one-fifth of the allocation for England and Wales (as compared with the population proportion of one-ninth) (Kilbrandon 2, p. 5).

Again, the population is scattered thinly over much of the land area, which is costly in terms of social services, transport and public administration. Thus the *per capita* expenditure for these services must be relatively higher than in England (cf. Kilbrandon 4, p. 111, for the actual expenditures in 1967–8).

The Treasury does not determine the amount to be spent in Scotland on the basis of population, or on the amount of revenue received from Scotland (Kilbrandon 4, p. 25). Up to 1959, the 'Goschen' formula[9] was applied in the estimates for education (except universities) in Scotland. This gave Scotland eleven-eightieths (13·7%) of the expenditure for English and Welsh education (Kilbrandon 2, p. 5). It became a generous proportion in terms of population (Scotland was 11·3% of England and Wales in 1961) and gave the Scottish Office an assured sum each year. Now the educational estimates are negotiated annually, and the resulting Scottish share is somewhat lower. Nevertheless, in 1967–8, expenditure on education in Scotland (central and local authorities), other than universities, was 11·2% of the total for Great Britain (population 9·6%) (Kilbrandon 4, p. 111). This shows that the Scottish Office is still able to claim a larger share for Scotland, on the basis of needs.

It can be argued that, since the main powers of economic policy (e.g. taxation, general level of industrial incentives, and location of industry) are wielded by non-Scottish bodies, the economic policy-process is essentially outside the Scottish political system. It is true that until 1975 the only direct powers of the Scottish Office in the field related to 'infrastructure' (roads, houses, etc.), and expenditure for these has to be negotiated with the Treasury.

Nevertheless, the 1960s began a new phase in the activities of the Scottish Office, so that economic planning was added to the already long list of its functions. The department has published a plan for the Scottish economy (1966), and has its own economic agencies. It cannot compete with the Treasury or the Departments of Trade, Industry and Energy in its financial, professional or political resources. It works entirely within the framework of British planning, and British thought on regional policy. But it can influence that policy, perhaps more than other departments.

It pioneered the 'growth area' approach to development, in the Toothill Report, and anticipated the functions of the Department of Economic Affairs (1964–70) in the Scottish Development Department and SDG (1962). Its wide range of activities was also reproduced in the Department of the Environment (1970), which covers such services as housing, local government and transport. As noted earlier, it inspired the decentralisation of Trade and Industry's industrial development administration to regional offices in March 1972. In 1975 it gained selective regional assistance and a share in industrial reorganisation from the Department of Industry (Scottish Development Agency).

Judged by results, the contribution of the Scottish Office to the health of the Scottish economy has been only partly successful. While expenditure on relevant identifiable services is in line with needs, regional policies have not been able to overturn the much higher rate of unemployment, a poor record in attracting new industry (at least since 1968), lower incomes, and continuing emigration. A fundamental criticism is that the requirements of growth in the Scottish economy have not been met by British policy. Deflationary policies suitable for the 'over-heated' areas of England were inappropriate for Scotland, where reflation was needed. The selective employment tax hit Scotland badly, and the neglect of the 'growth areas', after a promising start in 1963–4, flew in the face of Scottish Office planning. No attempt was made to introduce differential tax rates for Scotland, although a plethora of tax allowances and grants was introduced.[10]

No doubt things would have been much worse without the forceful advocacy of the Scottish Office. But the posture of the Scots is not a happy one: they know Scottish needs better than the men of Whitehall, but are powerless to act on their own initiative in the major economic decisions. They must seek to convert a naturally suspicious British minister or official to the view that what is good for Scotland is also good for Britain. As it happens, the theory of regional economics and the realities of political life now combine to give them every assistance in this endeavour. In particular, the importance of North Sea oil in the British economy, and the role of the Scottish Office in its development, guarantees power to Scotland, which devolution will render more complete.

(b) Social Services (education, health, social work, and housing)

The social services in Scotland are the responsibility of the Scottish Office (except for the social security cash payments made by the Department of Health and Social Security). The basic principles governing these services are common to the whole of the United Kingdom, and such variations from English practice as there are in Northern Ireland, Scotland and Wales are considered to be adaptations of British policy to the particular needs of these areas.

In fact, these 'adaptations' constitute in many cases a radical departure from a uniform system. The most obvious example is education, where Scotland has had its own traditions in schools and universities for hundreds of years.[11] While the Scottish and

English educational systems have grown closer together in recent years, there remains a strong contrast in the curriculum, the organisation of the schools, and the training, remuneration and careers of teachers. The universities, too, have their distinctive degrees and teaching methods.

The autonomy of the policy-process in Scottish education is based securely on the strength of the Scottish 'education world'.[12] It is this world which determines educational policy, although it is not impervious to outside influences and general social demands. As with economic planning, its main components are academics, pressure groups and government departments.

The Scottish education world is remarkably insulated from that of England. This is due to the demarcation between the educational systems, especially at the school level, which inhibits mobility of the teaching profession. But the division also prevents a continuous discourse at other levels, for example, in the colleges of education and in the civil service.

The account of the policy process in English education in *The Politics of Education* (see n. 12) reveals many contrasts with the corresponding process in Scotland. First, the influence of strong education ministers such as Boyle and Crosland was crucial to the development of the English system. These men gave practically their whole attention to education, and discussed its problems for hours with prominent educationists (see Crosland's accounts of evenings with John Vaizey, Michael Young, Noel Annan, etc., *The Politics of Education*, p. 185). They were strongly influenced by the current of academic work in the field, and sought to realise its conclusions in government policy.

Scotland has no education minister of this kind. The Scottish Secretary must deal with the economy, agriculture, health and welfare (to name but a few of his responsibilities), as well as education. While he may be personally interested in the educational system, he cannot afford to devote too much time to it (neither can his junior ministers, who also have multiple briefs).

This means that the initiative tends to pass to the other parts of the education world (the professionals and the civil servants). But even this sector is unlike that in England. The long series of influential reports on education in England (e.g. the Plowden, Newsom and Crowther Reports) have had less impact in Scotland because they dealt essentially with what were seen as English problems. The Robbins Report on Higher Education (1963), on the other hand, was as important for Scotland as it was for the rest of the U.K.

The Scottish educational world has produced its own Reports, which to some extent parallel those for England and Wales.[13] They are the work of academics, inspectors of schools, and teachers, working in Scotland. If they are not as famous, or as influential, as those produced in England, this is in part because most Scots have not seen the need for a fundamental re-appraisal of their educational system. They believe it to be superior to that of England in terms of coverage of the population (a career open to talents), and content (a broad curriculum and well-proven teaching methods).

In effect, Scottish traditionalism in education is perpetuated by the lack of communication between the Scottish and English education worlds. At ministerial level, the discourse concerns only those aspects of education which raise political implications. Thus, the decision to 'go comprehensive' in England in 1965 (DES Circular 10/65) was automatically followed by a corresponding circular from the Scottish Education Department (Circular 600). In 1970, with the return of a Conservative government, both education departments issued similar circulars allowing local authorities the freedom to reject comprehensivisation (DES Circular 10/70; SED Circular 762). Clearly, it was party politics which drew the countries together in this case. The Labour and Conservative philosophies were shared by the Scottish and English members of the parties, and demanded uniformity of policy.

Another example of concerted action is that of the school-leaving age. It is unthinkable that this should have been raised in England but not in Scotland, although the problems of doing so might be different if the supply of teachers and school buildings were different in the two countries (no clear evidence exists on this). According to the SED's written evidence to the Constitutional Commission (Kilbrandon 2, p. 25), 'Where the Government take major decisions of policy, which may be social as well as educational . . . they apply to Scottish schools as well as to schools in England and Wales'. Such matters include the two mentioned above, and items like school meals and school milk.

On these topics there is probably no conflict between Scottish and English ministers anyway. But over the whole gamut of educational policy outside this narrowly defined 'social' sphere, the Scottish education world rules supreme. According to the then Secretary of the SED, Mr (now Sir) Norman Graham, 'I cannot think offhand of any important matter on which Scotland has been prevented . . . from taking a decision that ministers wanted to take' (Kilbrandon 4, p. 103).

It is easy to produce evidence that Scotland has gone its own way in educational policy in such matters as the curriculum, examinations, age of transfer to secondary education, Roman Catholic schools, the binary system of higher education, and even university degrees. To call these 'educational' decisions as opposed to 'social' decisions, is to make a fine distinction which becomes increasingly difficult to sustain as the links between education and socialisation become daily more clear.

All of the so-called 'educational' decisions about Scottish education are made within the Scottish political system. The legislation governing education in Scotland is Scottish legislation which has been drafted in the SED, with the help of Scottish educational organisations, and debated largely by Scottish M.P.s Its administration is in the hands of the Scottish Office.

Contact between civil servants of the SED and DES rarely concerns substantive matters of policy. It is assumed that each department has its own educational system to administer, and that the one should not get in the other's way. The closest liaison is on the resources of education (e.g. the Buildings and Finance Divisions) and on some 'new' areas of education such as further education where there are British examinations, and where the different traditions of school education in the two countries begin to lose their distinctive characteristics. In fact, most SED trips to London are to the Treasury, or to Parliament, when legislation is being pushed through.

The principal policy-makers in Scottish education today are the permanent officials at the SED (especially the secretary), the inspectors of schools (a more powerful body in Scotland than in England),[14] the local authority directors of education, and the teachers' organisations. Since 1965, the General Teaching Council for Scotland has headed the list of official bodies representing the education world, but the Scottish Certificate of Education Examination Board and the Consultative Committee on the Curriculum are also as important. In the late 1950s and early 1960s, a strong influence was that of the senior Chief Inspector of Schools, John S. Brunton.[15] He dominated the department and much of educational thinking in Scotland; the Brunton Report, *From School to Further Education*, was published in 1963, and was the Scottish counterpart of the Newsom Report, *Half Our Future*, also issued in 1963.

What is lacking in this network is the influence of the layman. The politicians (including ministers) are weak, and the consumers (parents and pupils) are almost totally excluded. The forces for change come indirectly from English and foreign examples, partly through inter-communication, and partly from the need for Scots to get jobs outside Scotland (cf. Kilbrandon 4, p. 104, for a Scottish trade unionist's distaste for separate Scottish qualifications which prevent Scots getting into English universities and colleges). Education is one of the best-defined 'arenas' of Scottish life, and one which most strongly maintains the boundary of the Scottish political system.

.   .   .

A rather less-defined Scottish arena is that of health and welfare. The National Health Service is a British scheme, and the principles of the welfare state (like the so-called social aspects of education) are uniform throughout the country.

Yet here too one discovers marked divergencies in Scotland. The medical profession must deal with Scottish government agencies, especially the Scottish Home and Health Department, and the health boards. The Scottish Secretary appoints these boards (just one aspect of his vast patronage), and administers the Health Service with the assistance of such powerful professionals as the Chief Medical Officer at the Scottish Office (since 1964, Sir J. H. F. Brotherston).[16] Scottish doctors rarely see anything of the Department of Health and Social Security, except when Scottish officials of the BMA are negotiating scales of remuneration and general conditions of service.

The Scottish medical world (like that of education) has its own distinctive history. The teaching of medicine has been an outstanding tradition. Scottish universities and their medical schools co-operate with the health boards in the teaching of medical students, and the teaching hospitals are relatively more numerous than in England. All such hospitals in Scotland come under the health boards, while in England they have their own boards of governors. The position of the teaching hospitals was one of the strongest reasons for a separate administration of the Health Service in Scotland.[17]

Since its establishment in 1948, the National Health Service in Scotland has developed along lines appropriate to the needs of the country. Decisions about charges and remuneration are taken on a British basis, but hospital organisation and general medical practice continue to show differences in Scotland. There are more G.P.s, hospital beds, nurses and hospital medical staff in proportion to population in Scotland than in England and Wales. More is spent *per capita* over all the health and welfare services (Kilbrandon 2, p. 34). Scotland has pioneered some aspects of medical administration, notably training for hospital administrators.[18] The reorganisation of the health service into area health boards has a special form in Scotland. The principal difference between the proposed schemes for Scotland and England is that in the former country a single-tier structure of health boards has been adopted, while in the latter a two-tier system of area and regional boards is established. While the English area boards have boundaries corresponding to the proposed counties and metropolitan districts in the new local government structure, 6 of the 15 boards in Scotland do not correspond to the regional authorities in local government. Moreover, in England the local authorities appoint some of the members of the area boards, but all the members of the Scottish boards are chosen by the Secretary of State for Scotland. There is a common service agency for the whole of Scotland, while the English regional boards have their own agencies.[19] It is worth noting that the Scottish legislation went ahead in 1972, a year before the corresponding English reform.

Social work is another area in which Scotland has pointed the way for England. The Social Work (Scotland) Act 1968 established social work departments in counties, cities and large burghs in Scotland. The new departments brought together services previously exercised in local authority departments such as the children's, welfare, and education departments, and the probation service. One director of social work now takes charge of these services in each authority (since 1975, the regions and islands).

The process of policy-formulation for the Social Work Act involved a subtle interaction of Scottish and English decision-makers.[20] Discontent with the state of local authority social work services had been expressed in reports of official committees in England and Scotland in the 1950s and early 1960s. The first positive move was made by the Home Office over a matter of law reform relating to juvenile courts. In 1960, a report appeared on the subject (*Children and Young Persons*, Cmnd. 1191) which covered England and Wales. The subject was taken up in Scotland with a committee under Lord Kilbrandon,[21] which reported in 1964 (*Children and Young Persons (Scotland) Report*, Cmnd. 2036). Meanwhile, an inter-departmental committee covering all Great Britain reported on the probation service (Cmnd. 1650, 1962).

From being a matter of law reform, the question became one of reforming local authority social services (including probation) to make one social work department. The Scots and English now went separate ways. A Scottish White Paper was issued (*Social Work and the Community*, Cmnd. 3065, 1966) which recommended the setting up of social work departments, and led directly to the introduction of the Social Work (Scotland) Bill in March 1968.

The English, on the other hand, did not begin their enquiry until December 1968 (the Seebohm Committee), and excluded any examination of the probation service. This was because there was much opposition in England to the reform of the juvenile courts and to the merging of the probation service with social work departments.

The Scottish legislation was essentially different from that which was eventually produced in England and Wales. Apart from the omission of the probation service in the English and Welsh social services departments, these departments also suffered in comparison with the Scottish social work departments in their lack of powers. Section 12 of the Social Work (Scotland) Act gave local authorities a duty to provide generally for social welfare, while the English and Welsh Act merely brought together existing statutory functions. One example of the implications of this was that Scottish social work departments could give cash assistance to persons in need, while in England such payments were restricted to needy children.

The drafting of the Bill was a matter for Scottish decision-makers. An account of this process was given to the Constitutional Commission by the Secretary of the Scottish Education Department (N. W. Graham):

> The framing of this was entirely in the hands of the Scottish Office. All the preliminary work, stemming from Lord Kilbrandon's committee, was done in Scotland. There was a working party with local authorities, with which three social work professional advisers were associated. Then there was a White Paper, and then there was the legislation. All this was done in Scotland. Naturally in the ordinary course of business the English departments interested were kept in touch. At a point along this line the Seebohm Committee was set up to look at more or less, but not quite, the same territory, in England and Wales, and the English Departments have known throughout what we were doing, and were very interested in what we were doing. But the decisions which were taken were in the Scottish context, with the Secretary of State of course consulting his colleagues, who were thus aware of the proposed legislation. (Kilbrandon 4, p. 109.)

It was possible to move faster in Scotland than in England towards the reform of social work because the Scottish Office had a more comprehensive range of functions than any department in England. It could therefore deal intra-departmentally with problems which in England had to be negotiated between several ministers. The Scottish Office ministers (particularly Judith Hart, then a Parliamentary Under-Secretary in the department) gave the subject a political impetus which it could not obtain in England. They were able to convince anxious English ministers that an experiment could be made in Scotland which need not be a precedent for England or Wales. It would provide Whitehall with the evidence of a 'pilot project', from which they could learn valuable lessons. Nevertheless, the Home Secretary attacked the Bill in the Cabinet, and William Ross, the Scottish Secretary, had to fight for its survival.

There were other factors in Scotland favouring acceptance of the Bill. The local authorities and pressure groups have a much closer liaison with the Scottish Office than the corresponding English bodies have with the Department of the Environment.[22]

This smoothed the way for a radical change, and reduced the need for prolonged discussions.

One of the virtues of the Scottish political system is that its small size enables most of the policy-formulators to know each other personally. This is especially true of central–local government relations. Negotiations between governments and local authorities can proceed more quickly in Scotland, while in England they can get bogged down as a result of the scale involved and the more entrenched power of local government in the political system. Thus the regionalisation of water supplies took place in Scotland in 1968, years before it happened in England. Another illustration of this difference was found in the negotiations over the Countryside Bills for Scotland and England and Wales (1967). The Scots proposed a strong Bill which encroached on the power of local authorities. In England, the resistance of these authorities was so great that the government threatened to drop both Bills. The Scots insisted on theirs, thereby forcing the English to produce a stronger Bill (Countryside (Scotland) Act 1967, and Countryside Act 1968). Yet even in Scotland the local authorities can show their power, for during the Social Work Bill discussions they insisted that large burghs should have social work departments, although the 1966 White Paper had restricted these to counties and cities. The government gave in on this point.

A policy area where local authorities and central government in Scotland do not have smooth relations is that concerning council-house rents. Scottish local authority housing rents are only 64% the amount on average of those in England. At the same time, council houses make up twice the proportion of the housing stock. In Scotland the average council rent in 1970 was £1·42 per week compared with £2·23 in England and Wales. Houses provided by public authorities represent about half of all houses in Scotland (*The Reform of Housing Finance in Scotland*, Cmnd. 4727, 1971, p. 2). In some local authorities, the proportion of houses rented from the council is over three-quarters of the total housing stock, and the issue of 'council' rent is always a matter of politics. The Labour Party maintains power in many of these councils because it is the party which will guarantee low rents and build a large number of council houses (whose tenants usually then vote Labour).

The central government (i.e. the Scottish Office) has only limited powers to raise the level of rents, desirable as this may be from the point of view of economic allocation of resources and the health of the private sector in housing. Over the years, public enquiries have been held to determine whether certain authorities have fulfilled their statutory duties to review regularly the level of rents, and some authorities have been forced to make increases (e.g. Glasgow, Dundee, Dunbartonshire and Coatbridge).

Both Labour and Conservative governments have been appalled at the low level of rents in Scotland, but for political reasons only the latter has been confident enough to act strongly to remedy the situation. In 1971 the Conservative government proposed in a White Paper (Cmnd. 4727, 1971) that weekly rents should rise by annual steps of 50p. until housing accounts were balanced. It also announced that privately rented accommodation should be brought into a 'fair rents' system, and that tenants of these properties would be eligible for rent rebates. Legislation followed in 1972.

A corresponding White Paper was introduced for England and Wales (*Fair Deal for Housing*, Cmnd. 4728, 1971). But while the general philosophy behind both papers was the same (to move from subsidising houses to subsidising people), in England and Wales it was proposed that 'fair rents' (or market rents) for council houses be established. In Scotland the criterion was the balancing of local authority housing accounts. The difference is explained by the fact that the housing accounts of local authorities are already balanced in England and Wales, while they are heavily subsidised and deeply in debt in Scotland. Thus it is necessary to achieve balanced accounts in Scotland before going on to 'fair rents' (in about five years, according to the White Paper). Even then, the Scottish Secretary would merely 'consider the possibility' of making the transition (Cmnd. 4727, p. 3).

It is clear that the different conditions in Scotland in housing tenure have made it necessary for the government to modify seriously its policy for the two countries (counting England and Wales as one country in this respect). The party philosophy remains the same for both, and the direction of the legislation is similar, but the problems of implementation are very different. They will not be ironed out for a generation at least.

These examples of Scottish policy-making in the social services show that a separate political decision-making network is involved from that which operates in England. This is partly the result of the existence of the Scottish Office, the separate system of local authorities, and the differences between Scots and English Law. The case-studies also bring in a separate 'Establishment' of professionals such as educationists and doctors, who belong to their own Scottish world, one stage removed from the political system. And the case of housing points to the importance of the social structure of Scotland in conditioning policy.

In none of these areas do Scottish decision-makers work in total isolation from those in England. Indeed, we have seen that as regards the Social Work Act, the repercussions for England were appreciated up to Cabinet level, and some argument took place. Yet the outcome was two Acts of Parliament, with separate provisions for Scotland and for England and Wales. The same applies to the Housing Acts. Thus in the social services, the principle of uniformity for the whole of the U.K. must be flexible enough to allow for regional variations between Scottish and English practice.

(c) Law reform

Scotland and England have separate legal systems, and much of the separateness of their political systems stems from this fact. All the while, however, the law is undergoing change, and some of this process has led to a greater correspondence between the Scottish and English systems. There is a greater area of so-called 'British' law today than there was even fifty years ago, because of the development of the welfare state, government regulation of the economy, and the large area of commercial and public law which is common to both countries.

All law in Scotland is technically 'Scottish' law, since it is subject to interpretation by the Scottish Courts (and in civil cases to the House of Lords, sitting, some say, as a Scottish court).[23] But in substance, much law is British in that it lays down the same rights, duties and conditions for citizens throughout Great Britain.

The area of law reform which concerns us here is that area where the special characteristics of Scots Law remain so strong that separate Scottish legislation is required to deal with them. Many Scots lawyers would maintain that far more separate Scottish legislation should be passed, to take account of the separate legal system.[24] And they would be willing to reform that system without reference to English developments.

What has happened is that only certain areas of law and legal administration in Scotland have developed along totally indigenous lines (notably property law, much personal law and the organisation of the courts). Reform proposals here come largely from the 'legal world', with some prompting from Scottish politicians. For example, the system of feudal land tenure was attacked by radicals in the Labour and Liberal Parties over the years. It also stood in the way of Conservative government plans for land use and economic development in the early 1960s. In 1964, a committee under Professor J. M. Halliday of Glasgow University was set up by Conservative Scottish Secretary, Michael Noble, to investigate and report. The result was a series of sweeping proposals for the abolition of feu-duties and of the power of feudal superiors over development.[25]

The subject was so complex that the incoming Labour government was reluctant to tackle it. Considerable drafting problems arose, and legislative time had to be found. Scottish law reforms have often been held up because of the apparent lack of time in the Scottish committees of the House of Commons.[26]

Pressure continued from back-benchers, and a Liberal M.P., James Davidson, introduced his own Bill on the subject. Eventually the government brought forward a Bill in 1969 (the Conveyancing and Feudal Reform (Scotland) Bill) which tackled some of the problems involved (but not the redemption of feu-duties). In the Scottish Standing Committee of the House of Commons, the debates were severely handicapped by the technical nature of the legislation and the almost total absence of lawyer M.P.s from Scottish constituencies. Even the government speakers were at a loss during much of the discussion (at this time the Scottish Law Officers were not in the Commons), though the Conservatives had at least one articulate Scots lawyer, Norman Wylie, Q.C., among their M.P.s (later Lord Advocate, 1970). Total reform followed in the 1970s.

The less political areas of Scots Law, such as the organisation of the sheriff courts and the law of succession, have been reformed by the familiar method of a report by a professional committee of enquiry, and a non-contentious law reform bill.[27] Since 1965, Scotland has had its own Scottish Law Commission,[28] which has issued several reports on the more technical aspects of law reform. Some of these subjects have also been dealt with by the (English and Welsh) Law Commission, and occasionally a joint report is issued by the two Commissions. In such cases, there is a cross-fertilisation of ideas between Scotland and England, and this has also been in evidence during the 1960s in several law reforms (or proposals for reform) which have taken place in England. The subjects include majority verdicts, pre-trial publicity, public prosecutions, and private bargains before house purchase. In all these, Scottish practice has been commended by English reformers. Organisations such as Justice (the British section of the International Commission of Jurists) have been especially aware of Scots Law, despite its traditional neglect in England.[29]

Scots, for their part, have not been immune to English influence. The feudal reform proposals bring Scotland more into line with the freehold tenure of England, and in personal law the example of English reforms has been powerful. The passing of the Divorce Reform Act 1969 (a Private Member's Bill which applies only to England and Wales) opened up a gulf between the two legal systems in that subject, which had previously been narrowing in the direction of Scotland. The Law Commissions had recommended reform throughout Great Britain, and in Scotland the Church of Scotland gave qualified support. Yet Scottish

Private Members' Bills between 1970 and 1975 failed to get the support of enough Scottish M.P.s in the House of Commons to survive the difficulties placed in the path of such non-government Bills.

Several attempts were made to secure legislation. The first, introduced by Donald Dewar under the 'ten-minute rule', on 27 January 1970, received 113 votes to 82 against. But the Scottish M.P.s voted 18 for to 24 against. The government gave no further time for this Bill. In the new Parliament, Robert Hughes introduced a Bill on 22 January 1971, which failed to come to a second reading, since the closure motion was lost by 71 votes to 15 (Scottish M.P.s now 21 for to 11 against).

On 19 February 1971, the Bill was unexpectedly given a second reading 'on the nod', when its opponents were not present. But the committee stage now proved a problem. Since there was a reference in the Bill to maintenance orders in England, it was not given a Speaker's Certificate as an 'exclusively Scottish' Bill. This meant that instead of being referred to the Scottish Standing Committee, it was referred to a normal Standing Committee, and had to take its place in a queue with other Bills. When it reached the Committee in May 1971, it was too late to deal with all the amendments which had been tabled (some by English M.P.s), and the Bill was lost. At the start of 1975, legislation had still not been passed, despite several efforts to have it debated. It would seem that religious pressures play a large part in the attitude of many Scottish M.P.s, especially those who were Roman Catholics[30] and puritanical Kirk members (a similar coalition developed over homosexual law reform, which was not introduced in Scotland; it failed to prevent David Steel's Abortion Bill being passed in 1967, largely because that was a British measure).

Decision-making in law reform therefore involves a different set of actors according to the amount of controversy which is aroused. The most technical questions are settled in the 'legal world' in much the same way as technical matters in education and medicine are left to the relevant professions. Usually this means a committee of enquiry, followed by consultation with government over legislation. Scots lawyers show a high degree of independence from England in this sphere, though some apparently accept assimilation cheerfully. But they complain that the processes of reform are slow, and that M.P.s are ignorant of legal matters.[31]

The M.P.s come into their own, however, when political, religious, or social considerations are involved. Land reform and 'permissive' legislation (including also liquor licensing, Sunday observance and family planning) are traditional battlefields where Scottish M.P.s have strong prejudices. They are often able to veto the extension to Scotland of English Private Members' legislation, and a puritanical (or politically sensitive) Scottish Secretary can delay the application of a government 'permissive' Bill to Scotland. Thus William Ross stopped the application of the National Health Service (Family Planning) Act 1967 to Scotland, ostensibly on economic grounds. This Act allowed local authorities to provide free contraceptives and was opposed by Roman Catholics and some Kirkmen. Public and medical opinion was mobilised, however, and the Health Services and Public Health Act 1968 (sec. 15) extended the 1967 provisions to Scotland.

Opinion in Scotland about such matters is expressed through the channels of representation analysed in the last chapter. Some of these channels go no further than the Scottish political and social systems, and a solution is found in purely Scottish terms. But many bring in communication between Scotland and England, and involve a comparison of the legal developments in the two countries. The influence of TV in publicising English law reforms (often without explaining that they do not apply to Scotland) makes citizens in Scotland restless when it is discovered that such measures are purely English. Conversely, discussion of the flaws in English law nowadays increasingly draws upon the lessons to be learnt from Scottish experience. In this way, a gradual assimilation takes place.

Conclusion

The three policy areas chosen for discussion in this chapter provide illustrations of the varying degrees of autonomy possessed by decision-makers in the Scottish political system.

In economic planning, the major decisions are taken by the British departments such as the Treasury, Trade, Industry and Energy. Yet the policy formulation is influenced by Scottish academics, pressure groups, administrators and ministers (not of course in that order of importance!), and its execution is co-ordinated by the Scottish Office. There are signs that the Scottish political system is increasing its hold over this sector.

Education, health, social work, and housing have strong Scottish traditions, with separate 'worlds' of their own. The British system of government, and the philosophies of the parties, allow Scotland scope to experiment and go its own way, as long as general standards are maintained and the repercussions for England are not too grave. There is perhaps more autonomy in large matters such as the curriculum in the schools, than there is in 'social' or financial details such as school milk, which are politically sensitive and must be seen to be uniform throughout Britain.

Finally, law reform also illustrates the different decision-making processes which operate within the system. At one extreme there is the self-contained world of the Scottish lawyer, with his ability to control the technical aspects of Scottish law reform. At the other, there is the political discourse between M.P.s and the public on divorce, abortion and other 'moral' issues. While each process belongs inside the Scottish political system, in the sense of being primarily a matter of communication among those in Scotland with only incidental references to England, the boundaries break down to some extent through the awareness of English practices, the increasing assimilation of Scottish society to that of England, and the desire in Great Britain to establish 'equal rights' for all citizens.

The philosophies of the political parties are conducive to the principle of legal and social equality in this sense. In Britain, diversity in policy-making between parts of the country is only tolerable if it concerns 'means' rather than 'ends'. The distinction is not easy to draw in many cases, but there is no doubt that the central government can, if it wishes, impose its will to secure uniformity even in minor matters. The strong action taken in 1971 against local authorities in Scotland, England and Wales who sought to provide free milk to over-sevens in schools, when such provision had been made illegal, is an illustration of this.

What holds back an even tighter centralisation of power in Britain is the historic strength of the nations and regions, with their vested professional interests in law, education, medicine, etc., the sentiment of nationalism, and the lingering ideology of local self-rule derived in part from thinkers such as John Stuart Mill (a Scot by paternal parentage).

The policy process in Scotland is based on these foundations of opinions and power, and its autonomy shows few signs of weakening, despite the general movement towards social homogeneity in Britain.

12

The Highland periphery*

The Highlands of Scotland[1] form part of the northern periphery of Europe, an area which extends in an arc from Ireland in the west, through northern Scandinavia, to arctic Russia. The periphery is distinguished from the rest of the continent by its cool climate, its difficult soil, its proximity to the sea, its sparsity of population, its culture and ethnic composition. Distance from cities and from centres of industry and government gives a special character to its societies. They are Europe's most isolated and most individual peoples.[2]

There are 281,200 inhabitants in the seven 'crofting counties' of Scotland. They live in an area of over fourteen million square miles, at a density of nineteen people to the square mile. Although 40% live in towns, the largest of these is Inverness (34,665) and the next in size are Dunoon (9,680) and Thurso (9,122). There are only eight other towns over 4,000. The Highlands contain 5% of the population of Scotland and 47% of its area (16% of the area of Great Britain).

It is an important political region in Scotland, and deserves to be treated separately, since it is so untypical. (Cf. Butler and Pinto-Duschinsky, pp. 356–7 for political regions in electoral terms.) It has for hundreds of years been the object of interest and concern on account of its romantic and tragic history, which has included such events as the Jacobite rebellions of the eighteenth century and the clearances in the eighteenth and nineteenth centuries. The sympathy aroused in the Lowlands of Scotland and even in England on account of these happenings is still very much alive today. It can be seen in the numerous books and articles written about the area, and by such practical political

* The Borders are to some extent a second Scottish periphery. They include the constituencies of Berwick and East Lothian, Roxburgh–Peebles–Selkirk, and Dumfries-shire. Like the Highlands, they have been strongly Liberal, and a Liberal M.P. (David Steel) has sat for Roxburgh since 1965. The area is much closer to population centres than the Highlands, and there is no crofting economy. The Gaelic culture is absent, so that cultural cleavages with the rest of Scotland are much less marked.

measures as the setting-up in 1965 of the Highlands and Islands Development Board. The Board took its place at the end of a series of special government agencies for the Highlands, of which the Crofters Commission (1886–1911; 1955–   ), the Congested Districts Board (1897–1911), and the Advisory Panel on the Highlands and Islands (1947–65) are the other principal examples.

Many of the symbolic aspects of Scottish nationality are derived from Highland, rather than Lowland, culture. Tartans, kilts, clans, bagpipes and country dancing are now built into the Scottish image, although before the nineteenth century Lowland Scots despised the 'barbaric' Highlanders and supported the suppression of the kilt and the clans by the government, after the 1745 Jacobite rebellion.

Sir Walter Scott in his novels converted most people to a romantic view of the Highlands, and George IV was prevailed upon to wear the kilt in Edinburgh in 1822, a precedent for the Royal Family ever since. It can be claimed that the Highlands now occupy in Scottish mythology something of the character of the 'Wild West' in America: an ideal landscape ('land of bens and glens') peopled with rugged individualists.[3] Much of the sympathy for the Highlands is based on the feeling that if its way of life were to perish, Scottish nationality itself would be in danger. This accounts for the adoption of pseudo-Highland ways in the Lowlands, and for the support given for public expenditure to prop up the Highland economy.

The political history of the Highlands shows that for 150 years it has been a distinct region in terms of electoral behaviour. Until 1884, when the franchise in the counties was extended to male householders, the number of voters in Highland constituencies was extremely small. For example, Sutherland had 104 electors in 1832, rising to only 325 in 1880. There were no contested elections in that county until 1885, and in other Highland seats contests were rare. Ross and Cromarty went uncontested from 1837 to 1852, and from 1857 to 1884. Inverness-shire was similarly dormant from 1838 to 1865, and from 1868 to 1880. Some of these seats could be considered to be 'rotten counties', in the gift of a landed patron, or at most a bone of contention between rival landowners. Highland seats controlled by patrons between 1868 and 1885 were Argyllshire (Duke of Argyll), Orkney and Shetland (Earl of Zetland), and Sutherlandshire (Duke of Sutherland). (Hanham 1, pp. 407–8. For the period 1885–1910, see also Henry Pelling, *Social Geography of British Elections 1885–1910*, Macmillan (London, 1967), pp. 37–96.)

The extension of the franchise in 1884 revolutionised Highland politics. The crofters were given the vote, and at one stroke the electorate in some constituencies rose dramatically (e.g. in Sutherland to 3,185; in Ross and Cromarty from 1,720 to 10,265). In the election of 1885, a Highland political party, the Crofters Party, ousted the landlords' nominees from five of the Highland seats. These 'Crofter' M.P.s retained their position as an 'independent Labour party' in Parliament until 1895, when they merged with the Liberals.[4] They gave an early indication of the Highlanders' disregard for the conventions of the British two-party system.

That system has never been strong in the crofting counties, since its principal basis, an identification of each of the principal parties with the interests of a social class, has had little relevance to Highland society. Class divisions do exist in the Highlands, but they are unlike those in the rest of the country (especially in the urban areas). Since only 10% of the employed people are engaged in manufacturing (SCSA, 3, p. 29), and there is little urbanisation, the main divisions tend to be diffused and personalised. Landlord and tenant conflicts produced social and political cleavages in the nineteenth and early twentieth centuries, of which the Crofters' War (1882–8) and the Crofters Party are examples.[4] But the effect of the Crofters Acts, and public ownership of much of the land through the Department of Agriculture and Fisheries for Scotland and the Forestry Commission, has been to diminish greatly such conflicts. Crofters' security of tenure and low rents have transformed Highland politics from latent revolution into peaceful 'pressure' politics. Such politics involve playing one party off against another to secure greater attention for the Highlands.

This strategy is politically both conservative and swift to change, in terms of voting loyalties. Its conservatism is seen in the lingering strength of the Liberal Party, after it had declined in most parts of Britain. This strength was partially maintained during the 1930s and 1940s, and revived in the 1950s and 1960s. Jo Grimond, the leader of the Liberal Party from 1956 to 1967, entered Parliament in 1950 as M.P. for Orkney and Shetland. In 1964, Liberals took four of the six Highland seats. In 1970, although the Liberals generally suffered a setback, Russell Johnston, M.P. for Inverness-shire, was returned with an increased majority, despite a new challenge from the SNP (see table 29).

No party can rely entirely on Highland loyalty, for that is often given to outstanding candidates irrespective of political allegiance, or to candidates who will upset political predictions, and thereby attract publicity. This is the second Highland strategy: the unexpected result.

Table 29 shows the political 'fickleness' of the Highland seats from 1959 to 1970. Although the constituencies are broadly similar in social and economic terms,[5] their political allegiance

Table 29   *Election results in Highland constituencies, 1959–70*

Constituency	Election			
	1959 %	1964 %	1966 %	1970 %
Argyll	C 58·4	C 47·2	C 43·2	C 44·8
	Lab 25·9	Lab 28·9	Lab 30·1	SNP 29·9
	L 15·7	L 23·9	L 26·7	Lab 25·3
Caithness and Sutherland	Ind C 65·4	L 36·1	Lab 39·1	Lab 36·7
	Lab 34·6	Lab 30·3	L 38·9	L 25·4
		C 20·8	C 22·0	C 22·4
		Ind C 12·8		SNP 15·5
Inverness	C 44·3	L 39·8	L 39·4	L 38·4
	L 32·9	C 33·9	C 32·9	C 31·5
	Lab 22·8	Lab 26·3	Lab 27·7	Lab 23·0
				SNP 7·1
Orkney and Shetland	L 64·2	L 62·6	L 59·1	L 47·0
	C 18·5	C 20·0	C 22·3	C 31·9
	Lab 17·3	Lab 17·4	Lab 18·6	Lab 21·1
Ross and Cromarty	NL & C 47·2	L 40·2	L 42·0	C 33·2
	Lab 29·1	NL & C 32·1	Lab 30·4	L 29·1
	L 23·7	Lab 27·7	C 27·6	Lab 26·0
				SNP 11·7
Western Isles	Lab 53·6	Lab 55·1	Lab 61·0	SNP 43·1
	NL & C 46·4	L 30·9	C 20·2	Lab 38·4
		C 14·0	L 18·8	C 18·5

Key
L   Liberal   C   Conservative
Lab   Labour   NL & C National Liberal and
SNP   Scottish National Party   Conservative
                           Ind C   Independent Conservative

varies considerably, as does the progression of each party's support from election to election. In 1970, the M.P.s were two Conservatives, two Liberals, one Labour and one SNP. Some of these seats reveal examples of the 'unexpected change'. Caithness and Sutherland became Independent (Conservative) in 1959 as a result of the resignation of the Conservative whip by the sitting member, Sir David Robertson, and his subsequent re-election at the general election of that year. In 1964 the seat went Liberal, and in 1966 it became Labour (which it remained in 1970). While some of the change in voting behaviour in that constituency is due to the industrial developments round Thurso (Dounreay atomic research station), much seems to be the result of a desire to choose the best candidate, irrespective of his party, and thereby create the maximum political effect (Grimble, in Butler and King, pp. 227–32).

An example of unexpected change is the SNP gain in the Western Isles in 1970, something that even the SNP headquarters did not foresee. Such dramatic switches may, however, indicate that these are 're-aligning' elections, and that stability will follow as a result of the emergence of a new majority party (cf. Grimble, *op. cit.* p. 232). In February 1974, the SNP won 67% of the vote.

In the absence of academic research into Highland electoral politics, any hypotheses about electoral behaviour there have yet to be tested. At this stage, it is worth pointing to certain features of Highland elections, and to the assumed perceptions Highlanders have of elections and parties.

The importance of the candidate is probably greater in the Highlands than in other areas, even in other rural areas (Grimble, *op. cit.* p. 230). A local man, or a man with local connections, is almost essential, and such a person should have a strong personal connection, through kinship or face-to-face contacts, with the electorate. Something of the 'clan' loyalties of bygone years is still present in the Highlands, and votes may go to a Macleod or a Campbell through such ties. This may mean supporting a Conservative laird, or it may mean voting for a Labour schoolteacher.

The localism of the election is further stressed by the absence of interest in great national issues. Such issues are often considered foreign to the Highlands, where the sole demand is for increased aid. To some extent the candidates differ as to what use should be made of such aid, and the activities of the Highland Board have become controversial. But it is usually impossible to put a party label to such differences, especially since the Conservatives now fully accept the powers of the Board and its strategy, which they did not in 1965.

An exception to the absence of national issues in Highland elections was the question of British entry to the E.E.C. in 1970. This was widely discussed, and the prevailing opposition to entry helped to win votes for the SNP, as the only party which sympathised with that view. The E.E.C. was seen as a threat to the fishing industry and to the subsidies given to marginal farmers. It threatened to remove the centre of government even further from the periphery. These feelings were not adequately represented by the main parties nationally (though candidates did voice them locally), and the Highlanders felt no compunction in giving strong support to a fourth party (the SNP) which had previously been largely inactive in the area. But the strength of feeling for nationalism and self-government apparently expressed in such support was not clear. In the E.E.C. Referendum in June 1975, Shetland and the Western Isles were the only regions in Britain to vote 'No'.

The pattern of communications is a crucial factor in Highland elections. Local newspapers and election meetings play a greater part in shaping opinion than they do in the rest of the country. The London (or Glasgow) media are relatively less important, and give a very inadequate coverage of Highland news. Large areas of the Highlands have poor or non-existent TV reception, especially of ITV, and newspapers are often delivered late.

Candidates must cover vast areas during election campaigns, so that they can make appearances in all communities, no matter how small. Failure to cultivate support in this way between elections, as well as during election campaigns, can prove fatal for a candidate or sitting member. (Labour's loss of the Western Isles in 1970 was probably related to this factor.)

The influence of local notables on political behaviour is important, if little understood by political scientists at present. Traditionally, the laird commanded a following from his tenants and employees, but his influence is now on the wane (cf. Grimble, in Butler and King, p. 228). The schoolteachers of the Western Isles were the bulwark of Labour support there, until many revolted in 1970 to join the SNP. Ministers and priests have their say in elections, and in 1970 the 'permissive' legislation of the Labour government was strongly attacked in the Western Isles and in other Highland constituencies. The strictly puritanical Free Church of Scotland is influential in some places, but television and tourism have successfully challenged its power.

The role of the 'political entrepreneur' is essential in peripheral areas.[6] He is the man who links the local community with the centres of government, and so has a foot in both worlds. He has a necessary function in the Highlands, since the Highlander feels isolated and culturally distinct from the major part of the population, especially from government decision-makers.

The western part of the Highlands contains the bulk of the Gaelic-speaking community, rising to over 80% of the population in parts of the Western Isles (they almost all speak English as well) (Thomson and Grimble, p. 178). This linguistic characteristic is accompanied by others of a cultural, ethnic and economic nature. The Gaelic Highlands are dependent on the political entrepreneur, as the man who can move freely between the Celtic and non-Celtic communities, and can communicate the demands of the grass-roots to the government, as well as the government's response to such demands.

The eastern Highlands do not possess the same cultural distinctness, though it should be said that Orkney and Shetland have traditionally been considered by their inhabitants to be outside Scotland altogether, as part of Scandinavia. They have resisted merging with a Highland local authority, for they do not feel 'Highland' (Thomson and Grimble, pp. 268–9). Most easterners find no difficulty in communicating with outsiders, and are not averse to cultural change. They are more inclined than their western neighbours to take the hard, materialist view of life, and to seek means of providing for rapid commercial advancement. Significantly, the Highland Board has promoted most of its industrial development policies in the eastern Highlands, partly because of natural resources, but also because the population there is more responsive to industrialisation.

But the political entrepreneur is needed in the east as well as in the west. Both parts are recognisably Highland, and are far from London and Edinburgh in spirit as well as in geography. Sir David Robertson, M.P. for Caithness and Sutherland from 1950 to 1964, typified the role of entrepreneur, for he sought government recognition for Highland problems, while maintaining a firm base of support against the neglect of the Highlands by the Conservative government. His successors have also been independents in action if not in form. Most Highland M.P.s are constituency men first, and party men afterwards, and even Jo Grimond (Orkney and Shetland) retains most of his electoral support through his Orkney lineage and his constant advocacy of local interests.

Other entrepreneurs are the councillors and (before 1975) district clerks (the latter performing a wide range of social security duties), the schoolteachers, doctors and hoteliers. The landowner is prominent in some areas (e.g. Argyll, Inverness-shire and Ross and Cromarty), though in the Western Isles and Caithness and Sutherland his influence is on the wane (Grimble, in Butler and King, p. 228). An analysis of Highland county councils in January 1967 showed that landowners and farmers accounted for only 84 out of 317 Highland councillors, while there were 132 businessmen and miscellaneous white-collar workers. But there were only 20 crofters and 20 manual workers, and lairds held convenerships in several counties (Magnusson, 'Highland Administration', in Thomson and Grimble, p. 301).

The average age of councillors in the seven counties in 1967 was 57·7 years, with an average length of residence in their respective counties of 43·7 years, and an average term of council service of 11·5 years (Magnusson, op. cit. p. 300). Even more than most rural areas, the Highland councils seem dependent on retired or self-employed persons of advanced years and comfortable financial means.

Party politics is not usual in local government in rural Scotland, least of all in the Highlands. Most councillors are independents, and represent their own constituents before all else. The few towns exercise only a slight influence on the counties, although 10 out of 42 Caithness councillors were technicians, reflecting the presence of the Dounreay atomic research station. The burgh councils were generally run on non-party lines, although Campbeltown (Argyll) was Labour-controlled for several years. The Progressive Party and SNP have won seats in that burgh, and there have been Labour councillors in Lerwick (Shetland), Labour and Communist (Mrs M. P. Skinner, elected in 1968) councillors in Inverness, and Labour and SNP councillors in Fort William (Inverness-shire). For the 1974 elections, see table 23, p. 150.

Attempts to reform Highland local government have met with strong resistance. The Wheatley Report proposal to create one large Highland region from Argyll to Shetland was bitterly attacked, and in 1971 the Conservative government gave large concessions to Highland opinion. Orkney, Shetland and the Western Isles were each made virtually all-purpose authorities, co-operating with other authorities only for some aspects of education and social work, and for police and fire services. The Wheatley Highland region was further reduced in size by extracting most of Argyll and adding it to the Strathclyde region.

Such successes achieved by Highland pressure groups can be related to the precarious politics of the area, and to the desire of governments to win marginal seats there. Other examples have been the postponement of rail closures, first in the early 1960s, when the 'MacPuff' campaign and the protests of the Highlands and Islands Advisory Panel stopped the 'Beeching Axe' falling on Highland lines, and then at the end of 1971, when the Dingwall-Kyle of Lochalsh line was reprieved for two years, at a net cost of about £200,000 per annum (Glasgow Herald, 23 December 1971).

The establishment of the Highlands and Islands Development Board in November 1965 was a sign that political pressures from the area were at last beginning to lead to strong executive action. Not the least of Highland problems has been the chaotic administrative problems endured by the region (Magnusson, 'Highland Administration', in Thomson and Grimble, pp. 243–96; also Farquhar Gillanders, 'The Economic Life of Gaelic Scotland Today', ibid. pp. 95–150). Around fifty government agencies, as well as the local authorities, have a hand in Highland development, a fact that makes the Board's functions a little difficult to isolate (cf. SCSA 3, pp. 18–20, for a list of government and other agencies operating in the Highlands).

The Board was created by Act of Parliament, and vested with executive powers to acquire land, erect buildings, carry on business, give grants and loans, and provide a wide range of advisory and publicity services (SCSA 3, pp. 2–3). As mentioned in the previous chapter, its finance comes from a grant-in-aid on the vote of the Scottish Economic Planning Department, and some projects need the Secretary of State for Scotland's approval, or must be sanctioned by the Treasury. The grants which the Board can give to firms are similar to those given by the government in development areas. The Board can, however, give assistance to 'non-economic' projects which are social or partly social in character, and special assistance to other projects which will eventually become successful economically. Loans are offered at standard government interest rates and periods of repayment (SCSA 3, pp. 16–17, and *Glasgow Herald*, 11 January 1972).

The Highlands must compete with other development areas and with 'special development areas' in the attraction of industry. Since March 1971, the special development areas have included west central Scotland, Tyneside, and south Wales. In these areas additional incentives to incoming industry are offered to those given in development areas, including operational grants for three years, amounting to 30% of wage and salary costs. Although the Highlands cannot offer such bonuses, its position in the attraction of industry has of course been transformed since the advent of North Sea oil. International companies have flooded into the area, with platform sites, supply bases, pipe-line and oil-rig construction camps. The challenge to the traditional way of life has been severe, and campaigns were mounted by certain interests to prevent developments taking place. Other sections of Highland opinion were strongly in favour of oil-related industry, and the Scottish Office had to take the final decisions on planning approval, often after lengthy public inquiries. The Board has been something of a bystander in this area, since its powers do not extend into town and country planning, nor has it played any important part in shaping the oil developments which have taken place largely over its head. Local authorities such as Shetland have made their own deals with the oil companies, and have acquired special powers by Act of Parliament. At the other end of the governmental spectrum, the Department of Energy in London has handled most of the relations with the oil companies, and the Department of Industry the relations with the on-shore companies.

The chief advantage in having the Board is that the region possesses a government agency dedicated to attracting industry to it, and to no other. The Department of Industry gives no priority to the Highlands (SCSA 2, p. 127, Q. 610), and the Scottish Office has often proved sceptical of many Highland developments. The Board has a large team (7 members and 180 staff), and it is the only regional development body with statutory powers to dispense government money on its own authority.

In the six years to November 1971, £9½m. was given by the Board in grant and loan assistance to 1,658 projects (*Glasgow Herald*, 2 November 1971). At the end of that period, the Board was spending about £3m. per annum. This should be compared with the £43m. spent in 1968–9 in the seven counties by the Scottish Office and Forestry Commission (SCSA 3, p. 25), and the considerable sums spent by other government agencies in the area (rail subsidies alone in 1969 came to over £1½m. (SCSA 2, p. 311). By 1974, £20m. had been expended by the Board.

The Board's view of the Highland economy was initially one of bold thinking directed towards the establishment of large industrial development 'growth areas' (three were chosen). One of these areas, the Moray Firth (the others were Lochaber and Wick/Thurso) was given special attention, and a plan to make the area a metropolis with half a million people was suggested by the first chairman, Professor Sir Robert Grieve[7] (*Scotsman*, 22 April 1966). Invergordon was to be developed as a deep-water port, with large aluminium and petro-chemical works. Inverness was to be the administrative centre, with a new university.

Such schemes soon aroused the opposition of Highland traditionalists, such as lairds and Gaels, who feared that the Highland way of life was being threatened. Many on the west coast wondered whether the Board had their interests at heart, and they did not relish emigrating to the east coast to get work, any more than having to go to Glasgow or London. Sniping at the Board became a popular pastime (see even Grimble, in Butler and King, pp. 230–1), and the *Scottish Daily Express* waged a campaign against some of its members. One member resigned in March 1967, on account of the outcry about his personal commercial interest in the establishment of a petro-chemical works by a particular firm at Invergordon. Another went in July of the same year, bitter about the poor support which he said the Scottish Office was giving to the Board (*Scotsman*, 8 July 1967).

With the passage of time, these events can be seen as teething troubles. The Board was an administrative invention, and such animals are not welcome to traditional politicians and civil servants. Its members were chosen from academic, commercial and public life, and they did not always understand the diplomatic subtleties (hypocrisies?) of government.

Nor were they 'political entrepreneurs' of the kind understood in the Highlands. They were neither local men (on the whole) nor government men, and so fell between two stools. They spoke out boldly for their schemes, and so offended the vested interests of the counties, St Andrew's House, and Whitehall. At one point, they were rebuked by the Scottish Office Minister of State for dealing with big developments. These were the government's concern, said St Andrew's House, and the Board's role was to help small industrial concerns, and to deal with land use, forestry, fishing, tourism and agriculture. The Board telegrammed its chairman, Professor Grieve, who was abroad: 'Continue to think big. Staff behind you' (*Glasgow Herald*, 2 September 1967).

Such unsavoury washing of the Board's linen in public brought it new support in the Highlands. It was now seen more clearly as a body fighting the Highland cause against the obstruction and indifference of remote ministers and bureaucrats, and its position in the communications media, especially television, improved. Despite the warning not to meddle with 'big stuff', the Board persisted in its advocacy of the Invergordon developments, and in the siting of a nuclear fast breeder reactor in Dounreay. Grieve and other members of the Board (especially William Scholes) paid visits to the Cabinet in London and persuaded key ministers such as Frank Cousins (Minister of Technology, 1964–6) to sanction the Board's proposals. Cousins was impressed by the argument that the south of England could not support further population expansion, and by the vision of the Highlands as an ideal industrial centre of the future. Such reasoning would have appeared madness just a few years before, and its success was a tribute to the persuasive powers of members of the Board, and to the support which William Ross (the Scottish Secretary) gave the Board in the Cabinet.

The reactor came to Dounreay, and the aluminium works came to Invergordon. These were the great Highland triumphs of the period, though each was beyond the Board's financial powers. The petro-chemical works did not materialise, nor did the Highland university. In the first five years, 5,000 new jobs were created, and assistance given for 209 fishing vessels.[8] Tourism was developed by the building of a chain of hotels in the islands, and by grants to the Cairngorms Winter Sports Development Company. A publicity campaign was undertaken by the Board, and its advertisements became prominent in the media. At last the Highlands were firmly on the map.

But it is difficult to be confident about the future of the Highlands, and perhaps even of the Board. The population of most rural areas continues to decline, and is only offset by the increase in the 'growth areas'. (The preliminary figures from the 1971 Census show a rise in population in the Highlands since 1961 of 6,443, but 5,147 of this was in Inverness burgh alone. Counties declining were Sutherland, Orkney and Shetland.) While many applaud this development, it does nothing to maintain isolated communities in their traditional way of life. Without such communities, the Highlands will become pockets of industrialisation surrounded by emptiness. These industries are sometimes commercially precarious (cf. the current difficulties of the aluminium industry). Even the stupendous impact of oil wells off the coasts of northern Scotland may be an insecure basis for the Highland economy in the long run, despite considerable activity related to the construction and maintenance of oil rigs, platforms and pipelines. Much the same could be said for the fishing industry, which is thriving in the Shetlands and elsewhere (with grants from the Board), but which is subject to periodic depressions.

The Board's future as an agency of government is probably assured, but its character changes with its personnel. In 1970, it was reconstituted under a new chairman, Sir Andrew Gilchrist, a retired diplomat. Four new members were appointed, and two members reappointed. The new Board was rather different from the old. Five of the seven members were over sixty, and the new chairman was unlike Sir Robert Grieve in personal temperament, although both were practically unknown in the Highlands. Most people believed that the bold (wild?) period was over, and that the Board would settle down to seeking solid, if less ambitious, advances (cf. Report of the Board for 1970, Inverness 1971).

Highland politics have changed greatly in the last decade, and will change substantially in the next. Since 1959, the old pattern of party politics has been transformed by the increased strength of the Liberal Party, the Labour Party and the SNP. This has of course weakened the Conservative Party, and emphasised the separateness of the electoral behaviour of the region.

In administration, the Highland Board has been the culmination of years of pressure for a strong body to develop the resources of the Highlands. In part, this campaign has been realised. The reform of local government strengthens its activities by setting up a Highland region, and a new authority for the Western Isles. The position of Argyll will be anomalous, in that it goes to the Strathclyde local government region, but still comes under the Highland Board and Crofters Commission (etc.) as a 'Highland' area. Argyll is maintained financially on the west's purse, but the other Highland authorities are heavily dependent on central grants (at present running to 80% of income in some counties).

Such is the state of dependency in which the periphery is placed, until its new-found wealth is realised for the benefit of its own inhabitants.

Conclusion: Scotland in a comparative context

There are two important questions which have to be asked, and if possible, answered, at the end of this study of the Scottish political system. The first relates to the position of Scotland within the United Kingdom. Is the Scottish political system merely a sub-system of the British political system without independent means of support, and without effective power over the 'allocation of values'? Secondly, how does one relate the study of Scottish politics to that of comparative government as a whole? Such basic problems, which must arise from the material which has been presented, ought to engage the attention of any political scientist who carries forward the study of the Scottish political system.

At this stage, with the limited amount of research which is completed (reflecting the limited interest in the subject), there can only be hypotheses, largely untested. Compared with other political systems, that of Scotland has received very little attention from academic students of politics. In the U.S.A., states such as California require their university students to study the government and politics of the state, and school-children are expected to know something about state institutions. Most European nations have developed their own political studies, including such near neighbours as Ireland.[1]

In Scotland, on the other hand, the universities largely ignore the teaching of Scottish politics, although they have lately encouraged *research* in Scottish voting behaviour, local government and central administration.[2] This is partly because, in a crowded teaching programme, Scotland does not seem to warrant much space. Partly, too, the academic staff find that the subject has a lack of published work, and so naturally steer clear of it.

But it is also curiously because the Scottish students themselves are not anxious to devote time to it. As with the study of recent Scottish history (see ch. 7 on Scottish nationalism), there is traditionally a feeling that what happens in Scotland is unimportant in British terms, and certainly in world terms. Perhaps because of the native strength of Scottish universities (74% of students at Scottish universities in 1967 were Scots, most attending their nearest university, and about half living at home. In 1969–70,

Glasgow University, the most local, was 90% Scottish, and 66% home-based),[3] many students wish to escape from things Scottish in their studies. Those who hope to become academics themselves tend to avoid a specialism in Scottish politics because of the supposed difficulties that this would place in the way of obtaining employment in universities outside Scotland. And they too are generally impressed with the argument that the subject is basically unimportant.

All this seems to add up to a kind of inferiority complex regarding things Scottish, particularly among the bulk of Scots in higher education. They are reluctant to assert their Scottish identity or to spend time on things Scottish unless there is some material advantage in doing so. Where there is such an advantage, as in school-teaching, the law, and the Church, then 'Scottishness' is rampant. But these occupations do not contribute directly to the study of Scottish politics. Often it is non-Scots, who have come to work in Scotland and see most clearly how distinctive the society is, who take up the subject.[4]

This may appear to answer the first question posed at the beginning of the chapter; is the Scottish system an independent one, with power over its own values? To the majority of Scots it is not, and they therefore direct their attention to the British system, which is apparently the only one that counts. If this is the predominant view in Scotland, is it not well justified?

Beliefs about how government operates are, of course, not the same thing as evidence of its operations. Most Scots are totally unaware of how the Scottish Office, local government and the Scottish committees of the House of Commons function, and many are probably totally unaware of the existence of the last (cf. Budge and Urwin, p. 129, and Wheatley 3, pp. 39–45). But then, people throughout Britain are largely ignorant about British politics (Butler and Stokes, pp. 24–7).

Those whose business it is to know about Scottish politics (and here, unfortunately, most political scientists must be excluded), have a very different picture. Carpet-bagging M.P.s who come from England to Scottish seats (they are less numerous today than in the time of Gladstone (Midlothian, 1880–95), Asquith (East Fife, 1886–1918; Paisley, 1920–4), and Churchill (Dundee, 1908–1922)) soon learn how different politics are in Scotland, and ignore such differences at their peril.[5]

Members of British Cabinets are forcibly reminded by Scottish Secretaries that Scotland has its own problems and form of government, and civil servants in Whitehall are similarly educated by St Andrew's House. In Scotland itself, each point in the eternal triangle of St Andrew's House, local authorities and organised groups knows exactly the other's capabilities and limitations.

The evidence of this book demonstrates the existence of a Scottish political system comprising a large number of actors engaged in a wide range of political activities. These activities or functions are partly exercised through the medium of political structures such as the Scottish Office and the organised groups, and partly through the expression of public opinion in the media, or by direct action. Such activities are recognisably Scottish because they take place within a political and social system which history has differentiated at many key points from that of England. Most relevant, of course, are Scottish national consciousness, the religious, educational and legal institutions, and the socio-economic conditions (e.g. in housing), which have led to the setting up of Scottish political institutions. In the Highland periphery, cultural and linguistic characteristics, crofting and separate administrative agencies, make up a sub-system of the Scottish system.

The Scottish system can be defined by the flow of communications. In table 24, ch. 9, a diagram was drawn to show the principal channels of communication in the Scottish system, and between Scotland and London. While the flows could be charted in all directions, there were two basic patterns, that within Scotland towards St Andrew's House, and that from Scotland to the government in London. The former was a Scottish communications system, the latter a British one.

In political terms, these systems are less easy to separate. The Scottish communications network which focusses on the Scottish Office involves the British political system, for the Scottish Office is a department of the British government, with a minister in the British Cabinet. Decisions of that Cabinet are binding on the Scottish Office, and the Scottish communications network must therefore be finally dependent on the vital link between London and Edinburgh.

Conversely, the activity of Scottish M.P.s in Parliament with regard to Scottish legislation and Scottish administration, though geographically in the British system (or London 'activity area') is more sensibly seen as being within the Scottish system in a 'detached portion'. This is because communication here is almost entirely between the Scottish M.P.s, who are primarily involved in the Scottish committees and in Scottish question time. Even on British issues, their main interest is in the Scottish aspects.

One can move from a communication model to a decision-making model. In chapter 11, the policy process was examined to discover who the principal decision-makers were in specified areas of policy. Once more, the question of system and sub-system was involved, for in some areas of policy the Scottish system was dominant, while in others it was dependent. The chief examples of the former were education, social work and law, and of the latter, economic policy and the financial aspects of welfare. The crucial function of allocation of resources was in the British system, with Scottish influence nevertheless asserting itself to a remarkable degree.

Was 'allocation of values' British? If so, the idea of a political system in Easton's terms[6] is not present in Scotland. But we have seen that in the crucial areas of education, religion and law, Scotland stands apart from England, and these institutions represent values. Many were, of course, 'allocated' in the distant past, when Scotland was an independent state, but they have grown autonomously since then within the structure of the British state. This is because Scots have been able to allocate the values within Scotland to their own satisfaction, usually without let or hindrance from London. Clearly a conflict may develop when the party majorities in Scotland and in Britain as a whole are at variance. Even then, the British government must adapt its policies to take account of the demands of the Scottish system.

Scots have shaped the style of Scottish government to their own taste. They created the Scottish Office in the 1880s by their demands, and have added continuously to its functions. The Scottish committees of the House of Commons established a sort of 'parliament within parliament'. In the 1970s, they adopted a local government system significantly different from that of England.

In all these political institutions there is an element of strong, centralised government, based on Edinburgh (not London). The Scottish Office is an 'omnibus' department encompassing functions distributed among several departments in England. This naturally concentrates power in the hands of one minister. Similarly, the regional structure of local government and the tradition of strong central government control over local authorities limits the scope of local self-government. Finally, of course, the Scots have only now demanded unequivocally a parliament for Scotland, although they have flirted with the idea, and with the SNP, for many years. Perhaps the 'civic culture' of Scotland is rather more of a 'subject political culture'[7] than that of England (itself more 'subject' than that of the U.S.A.), since its citizens have delayed in insisting on a democratic institution to underpin the administrative and legal autonomy of the system. But this may be because they have been able to get their way by other means.

There are now only a limited number of policy areas where Scots are determined to act independently of England. Thus the allocation of 'British' values is acceptable to Scotland in many important respects. Despite its divergencies from England noted above, the Scottish political culture is essentially at one with that of England on fundamentals. That this is so can be seen clearly by comparison with the political culture of Northern Ireland where

225

'Governing without Consensus' (Rose 4) is the norm. In Scotland, there is no fundamental challenge to the constitution (despite the SNP), and politics is not dominated by religion, although there are special correlations between religion and voting in Scotland (see ch. 6, pp. 102–5). Religious issues, especially denominational education, have been as important in English politics in the twentieth century as they have been in Scottish.

Some say that a separate parliament in Scotland would undermine the consensus. But this seems to be an exaggerated fear. Political tensions usually manifest themselves independently of the existence of legislatures, and Ulster's problems were obvious long before the Parliament of Stormont was set up in 1920. What is likely to happen under devolution in Scotland is a new confidence that Scots can take decisions for Scotland which in the past have been left to London.

If the political cultures of England and Scotland are similar, and many of the basic values are allocated by the British system of government, does this not reduce the present Scottish political system to the level of a sub-system?

This is obviously a matter of definition and a matter of opinion as to what is sufficiently important to constitute a system. The discipline of political science is not precise enough to distinguish clearly between a sub-system in politics,[8] and all systems are sub-systems of some greater system (e.g. Britain will undoubtedly become a sub-system of the E.E.C. for economic planning). But just as Britain will lose some of her independence as a system ('sovereignty' in old-fashioned language) by entering the European community, she will undoubtedly remain a strong political system in other respects. The analogy with Scotland and the Union of 1707 is not completely satisfactory, but the implications are similar. Scotland and England came under one government with shared values, but each retained its identity and something of its political system. The evidence in this book shows how much has been retained over the past 270 years, and how much has been added.

It hardly needs demonstrating that people in Scotland ought to know about the government of the country they live in. If it is said that they can do so from what has already been written on British government, then it is the purpose of this book to challenge such a view, and to present Scotland as a definable political system with its own characteristics.

This interpretation has implications for the study of British government, and for comparative government. The simplistic view of the British system as a unitary, homogeneous, and stable polity faltered in the late 1960s. First the Welsh and Scottish Nationalists, then the Irish, showed how 'multi-national' the

226

United Kingdom was, and how divergent were many of its regional political cultures. At the time it was not clear whether the British system was being fundamentally challenged in Wales and Scotland, or whether the people in these nations wished for marginal improvements that could be negotiated (by 1970, the latter seemed to be the case yet in 1974 the challenge had re-appeared in Scotland). In Northern Ireland, a fundamental con-stitutional and religious conflict flared up, which upset the British system profoundly. An alternative view, rejected by Richard Rose (Rose 4, p. 73), is that the British system was not upset, since Northern Ireland was not a part of it. British governments, how-ever, consistently act as if Northern Ireland were part of the U.K. As a result of the nationalist movements of the 1960s and early 1970s, the meaning of the British system altered, and England and English nationality came to be seen as something different from British nationality.[9]

Interest in Scotland within the field of comparative politics and government increased in the 1960s, and its potential contribution to the discipline began to be realised. At first, it was the rise of the SNP which attracted scholars throughout the world. Scottish nationalism had long had its place in the literature of nation-alism,[10] and its ups and downs in the 1960s proved as inexplicable as ever. The literature suffered from an analytic confusion, which did not relate the nation-building process in Scotland, Ireland, Wales and England to that of Britain as a whole. Karl Deutsch had attempted an analysis of Scottish nationalism in the early 1950s,[11] but most of his attention was focussed on the Gaelic language. By 1970, most scholars were still unable to explain the meaning and strength of Scottish nationalism, although a con-siderable amount had been written on the subject (ch. 7).

The study of Scottish voting behaviour, which the successes of the SNP largely inspired, led to discoveries about the correlations in Scotland between religion and voting, and about regionalism in the social-class support for the major parties (see ch. 6). The Highlands as a peripheral region in British political behaviour called for attention, especially after the election of an SNP M.P. for the Western Isles in 1970.

The Highlands also offered a potential area of study in the political ecology of peripheries, building on the work of Stein Rokkan of Bergen University in Norway, and others. The political cleavages in these Scandinavian peripheries resemble in some respects those in the Scottish Highlands, and detailed cross-national comparisons could well be made. North Sea oil gives added importance to studies of this kind.

Scotland as a whole, as a periphery of the European 'heart-land', gives scope for comparative work with the other 'smaller

European democracies'. Countries of between five to ten million people, with a high degree of sophistication of political culture, are an alternative model of development to the giant states of western Europe and America.

If it be argued that it is invalid to bring Scotland into such comparisions, since it is not a state, the reply of this book is that it is nevertheless a political system. There are features of state-hood in that system, such as separate laws, administration, church and education. Through these, the system allocates the values which maintain its identity. The establishment of a Scottish Parliament and Government will no doubt inaugurate a new phase in its development, and alter many of its characteristics. Political science can learn from studying such a nation and its political system, and the system itself can be improved on the basis of the knowledge so generated.

Notes

Chapter 1

1. *Whitaker's Almanack 1972*, pp. 610–12.
2. E.g. T. B. Smith, 'The Union of 1707 as fundamental law', *Public Law* XCIX (1957).
3. Lord Cooper in the case *MacCormick and another v. The Lord Advocate*, 30 July 1953. Report in *Scots Law Times*, 17 October 1953, p. 262.
4. K. W. Deutsch, *Nationalism and Social Communication*, M.I.T. Press (Massachusetts, 1953), p. 70.
5. Various surveys in recent years support this statement. Rose quotes three, conducted in 1968, covering Glasgow, Wales and Northern Ireland. In Glasgow and Wales over two-thirds of respondents thought of themselves as Scottish and Welsh respectively, and under 30% as British or English. In Northern Ireland, 43% said they were Irish, 21% Ulster, and 29% British (Rose 3, p. 10).
6. For a detailed account of Scottish social institutions, see J. G. Kellas, *Modern Scotland*, Pall Mall Press (London, 1968).
7. J. M. Bochel and D. J. Denver, 'Religion and Voting: A Critical view and a new analysis', *Political Studies* XVIII (1970), 205–19.
8. Readership figures are from the *National Readership Survey 1973*, Joint Industry Committee for National Readership Surveys, London, 1974.
9. *Annual Report and Accounts of the British Broadcasting Corporation, 1969–70*, HMSO, Cmnd. 4250 (November 1970), p. 127.
10. *Household Food Consumption and Expenditure; 1967*, Report of National Food Survey Committee, 1967, HMSO (London, 1969), pp. 19–23, 39–40.
11. K. W. Deutsch, *National and Social Communication*, p. 71.
12. P. Self and H. J. Storing, *The State and the Farmer*, Allen and Unwin (London, 1962), p. 194. See also R. W. Howarth, 'The Political strength of British agriculture', *Political Studies* XVII (1969), 458–69.
13. See D. I. MacKay and G. A. Mackay, *The Political Economy of North Sea Oil*, Martin Robertson (London, 1975).
14. The concept of 'arenas' in politics is adapted from F. G. Bailey, *Stratagems and Spoils*, Blackwell (Oxford, 1969), p. 153.
15. D. Easton, *The Political System*, Alfred Knopf (New York, 1953), pp. 134–40.

16. D. Easton, *A Systems Analysis of Political Life*, John Wiley (New York, 1965), p. 61. Easton, however, goes out of his way to exclude Scotland as a political system, since it has been 'absorbed into an alien system' (*A Framework for Political Analysis*, Prentice-Hall New Jersey, 1965), p. 83. That this contradiction is unresolved is discussed by Michael Evans in 'Notes on David Easton's model of the political system', *Journal of Commonwealth Political Studies* VIII (1970), 133, n. 69.

17. K. W. Deutsch, *Politics and Government*, Houghton Miflin (Boston, 1970), pp. 126–7.

18. Talcott Parsons *et al.*, *Theories of Society*, Free Press (New York, 1961), 1, 30–79. A general discussion of the concept of the political system is found in Peter Nettl, 'The concept of system in political science', *Political Studies* XIV (1966), 305–88.

Chapter 2

1. On this, see T. B. Smith, 'The Union as fundamental law', *Public Law* XCIV (1957), and *Scotland*, Stevens (London, 1962), p. 52.

2. A. V. Dicey, *Introduction to the Study of the Law of the Constitution*, first published 1885. Tenth edition, London, 1959, especially introduction by E. C. S. Wade, pp. lxiv–lxvi.

3. Reported in *Scots Law Times*, 24 October 1953, p. 262.

4. T. B. Smith, *Scotland*, p. 32.

5. *Scotsman*, 5 May 1967.

6. 'The prosecution process in England and Wales', *Report by Justice* (London, 1970).

7. But see T. B. Smith, *Scotland*, 'Special Aspects of Scottish Constitutional Law', pp. 61–79.

Chapter 3

1. Other boards, such as the Board of Manufactures (1726–1906) and the Fishery Board (1808–1939) were not as closely linked to local government, and the Registrar General for Scotland (1855–) conducts the Census of Scotland as well as supervising local registrars. The Lord Clerk Register (Scottish Record Office) and Lord Lyon King of Arms (heraldry) are medieval survivals.

2. Scottish Secretaries from 1955 to 1970 have had a year's extra stay in office, compared with the ministers in charge of other major departments. R. Rose, 'The making of Cabinet ministers', *British Journal of Political Science* 1, 408.

3. Statement by Michael Noble (Secretary of State for Scotland, 1962–4), *Scotsman*, 19 September 1966.

4. *Scotsman*, 16 November 1966, 10 March 1970, 30 April 1970.

5. John Warden, 'Scotland at Westminster', *Glasgow Herald Trade Review*, January 1972, p. 24.

Chapter 4

1. Defined here as those receiving at least part of their education in Scotland. This is obviously only a rough indication of whether an applicant is Scottish or not, but it is the only available criterion for this purpose given in the Civil Service Commissioners' Reports. A Scottish school is probably a better guide to 'Scottishness' than a Scottish university.
2. *6th Report from the Estimates Committee*, H.C. 308 (1964–5), p. 29.
3. *Ibid.*
4. *P.E.P. Planning* XXVI, No. 444 (12 September 1960), 'Local self-government; the experience of the United Kingdom, the Isle of Man, and the Channel Islands', p. 245. See also the 'Hardman Report', *The Dispersal of Government Work from London*, Cmnd. 5322, 1973, p. 197.

Chapter 5

1. Sir Ivor Jennings, *Party Politics. I: Appeal to the People*, C.U.P. (Cambridge, 1960), p. 37.
2. Only 21 Scottish Labour M.P.s made 4 or more speeches covering at least 10 lines in Hansard in 1969–70. Most of these speeches were on topics relating to Scotland. 15 Conservatives and 4 Liberals also made speeches, making a total of 40 Scottish M.P.s. The Scottish party distribution at this time was Labour 44, Conservative 21, Liberal 4 and SNP 1. In the whole House, 358 were frequent speechmakers in the same period. R. Oakley and P. Rose, *The Political Year 1970*, Pitman (London, 1970), pp. 204–10.
3. Compare the *Memorandum of Evidence of the Law Society of Scotland to the Commission on the Constitution* (Edinburgh, 1970), p. 6, par. 17.
4. J. H. Burns, 'The Scottish Committees of the House of Commons, 1948–59', *Political Studies* VIII (1960), 272–96.
5. Sir Ivor Jennings, *Parliament*, 2nd ed., C.U.P. (Cambridge, 1957), p. 272.
6. See 'The Scottish Penitentiary', in Emrys Hughes, *Parliament and Mumbo-Jumbo*, Hillary (London, 1966).
7. *Standing Committee. Return for Session 1968–69.* H.C. 9 (1969–70).
8. *Parliamentary Debates* H.C., 1st Scottish Standing Committee, 18 January 1972, cols. 7–8, 26–7.
9. The Law Society of Scotland's Evidence to the Commission on the Constitution (p. 11) cites 7 examples of delays in Scots Law reforms. These are:
    1. Mackintosh Report on Succession (1951); legislation, 1964.
    2. McKechnie Report on Diligence (1958); legislation, none.
    3. Guest Report on Licensing Law (1963); legislation, partial 1969.

4. Reid Report on Registration of Title to Land (1963); legislation, none.
5. Hunter Report on Salmon and Trout Fisheries (1965); legislation, none.
6. Halliday Report on Conveyancing (1966); legislation, partial 1970.
7. Grant Report on the Sheriff Court (1967); legislation, none.
10. *Glasgow Herald*, 24 February 1971.
11. Law Society of Scotland's Evidence to the Kilbrandon Commission, p. 5.
12. *Hansard*, 5th Series, vol. 756, cols. 1375–6, 20 December 1967.
13. Some of the most prolific questioners in Parliament are the Scottish M.P.s. In session 1968–9, for example, Mrs Ewing (SNP) asked 516 questions (for oral and written answer). This was the second highest for any M.P. Other notable questioners in Scotland were Bruce-Gardyne (C) 387; Dalyell (Lab) 386; Taylor (C) 335; and Eadie (Lab) 224. These were all in the 'top ten' of the House of Commons. *The Political Companion, No. 1*, October–December 1969 (Glasgow, 1969), pp. 149–67.

Chapter 6

1. A. J. Beattie, *English Party Politics*, Weidenfeld and Nicolson (London, 1970), 2 vols.
2. A. H. Birch, *The British System of Government*, 1st ed., Allen and Unwin (London, 1967).
3. G. Moodie, *The Government of Great Britain*, 1st ed., Crowell (New York, 1961), p. 1n.
4. Cf. H. J. Hanham, *The Scottish Political Tradition*, University of Edinburgh, Inaugural Lecture No. 19 (1964), pp. 17–18.
5. J. G. Kellas, 'The Mid-Lanark By-election (1888) and the Scottish Party (1888–1894)', *Parliamentary Affairs*, XVIII, No. 3 (Summer 1965), 318–29.
6. E.g. Sir Ivor Jennings, *Party Politics*, C.U.P. (Cambridge, 1960–2), 3 vols.; J. Blondel, *Voters, Parties and Leaders*, Penguin Books (London, 1963). S. H. Beer, *Modern British Politics*, Faber (London, 1965); and Butler and Stokes.
7. The description of the Conservative and Labour Parties as class parties is obviously an over-simplification. For the relationship between class and party see Butler and Stokes, chs. 4–5.
8. His argument can only be briefly summarised here. Under (1) he illustrates the territorial and social diversity of Britain (covering 'natural frontiers', ethnic groups, competing forms of centralisation in the four nations, institutional decentralisation, and subjective national identification). The difficulty here is evaluating the pull of these centrifugal forces as compared with those leading to homogeneity. Under (2) he shows the different religious profiles of the nations, but admits that 'religious issues as such rarely become prominent in British politics today' (p. 13). For (3) he says much the same, since the politics of agriculture is a 'matter in which English

and non-English farmers can both press claims'. Under (4) he gives interesting evidence that working-class consciousness and trade union affiliation are stronger in Scotland and Wales than in England. (In Northern Ireland class consciousness is weak, though trade union affiliation is high.) Variations in electoral behaviour between the nations are also examined (Rose 3, pp. 4–19).

9. For this period, see particularly, Henry Pelling, *Social Geography of British Elections, 1885–1910*, Macmillan (London, 1967), ch. 16. J. F. McCaffrey, 'The origins of Liberal Unionism in the West of Scotland', *Scottish Historical Review* L, No. 149 (April 1971), 47–71.

10. J. M. Bochel and D. J. Denver, 'Religion and voting: A critical review and a new analysis', *Political Studies* XVIII, No. 2 (June 1970), 205–19.

11. The principal towns in Scotland with a strong Catholic population are Coatbridge (43% of population R.C.), Port Glasgow (42%), Dumbarton (40%), Rutherglen (38%), Greenock (36%), Airdrie (36%), Glasgow, (30%), Motherwell and Wishaw (27%), Hamilton (26%) and Paisley (22%) (*The Western Catholic Calendar*, John S. Burns (Glasgow, 1970)).

12. Cf. George Scott, *The Roman Catholics*, Hutchinson (London, 1967). Constituencies most affected are (or were) Coatbridge and Airdrie, Motherwell, Glasgow Bridgeton and Glasgow Gorbals.

13. R. T. McKenzie, *British Political Parties*, 2nd ed., Heinemann (London, 1964), p. 488.

14. These are listed in the annual *Reports* of the Labour Party (Scottish Council).

15. D. W. Urwin, 'The development of the Conservative Party organisation in Scotland until 1912', *Scottish Historical Review* XLIV, No 138 (October 1965), 90–111.

16. D. W. Urwin, 'Scottish Conservatism: A party organisation in transition', *Political Studies* XIV, No. 2 (June 1966), 145–62.

17. F. Bealey and H. Pelling, *Labour and Politics, 1900–1906*, Macmillan (London, 1958), pp. 293–7.

18. Labour Party (Scottish Council), *Constitution and Standing Orders*, p. 12.

19. Labour Party (Scottish Council) *Report 1969*, pp. 6–7; *Report, 1970*, p. 8. From 1972, the Labour Party Constitution allowed regional councils (including the Scottish Conference) official freedom to discuss any issue, except international affairs.

20. *Report 1970, loc. cit.*

21. Michael Rush, *The Selection of Parliamentary Candidates*, Nelson (London, 1969), p. 289.

22. *Ibid.* p. 135.

23. Labour Party (Scottish Council), *Constitution and Standing Orders*, p. 11.

24. Scottish Conservative Central Office, *Briefing: Party Finances* (Edinburgh, 1971).

25. *Glasgow Herald*, 28 April 1970.

26. *Glasgow Herald*, 6 January 1971.

27. Labour Party (Scottish Council), *Report 1971*, pp. 14–15, 33.

28. *Ibid. Reports 1968, 1969, 1970.*
29. D. W. Urwin, 'Scottish Conservatism'.
30. *Scotsman,* 30 June 1969.
31. *Ibid.* 28 April 1971.

Chapter 7

1. G. Jahoda, 'The development of children's ideas about country and nationality', *British Journal of Educational Psychology,* XXXIII (February and June 1963), 47–60, 143–53.
2. English nationalism has not yet attracted the attention of political sociologists. English children (and most adults) call their country 'England' rather than 'Britain', but this is partly the well-known confusion regarding the use of England to include Scotland, Wales and even Northern Ireland. See J. Dennis, L. Linberg and D. McCrone, 'Support for nation and government among English children', *British Journal of Political Science* 1 (January 1971), 25–48, and comments by A. H. Birch, *ibid.* (October 1971), 519–20.
3. In Jahoda's survey of Glasgow children's ideas about country and nationality (*op. cit.* p. 149) a picture of Burns was recognised by 88% of children aged 10–11. Jahoda remarks, 'Evidently Burns constitutes one of the most potent Scottish national symbols, as early as childhood.' Other symbols of Scottishness (costumes, landscapes, buildings, songs and emblems) were readily identified as such.
4. The nineteenth-century debate between Anglicisers and nationalists in the Scottish universities is dealt with in G. E. Davie, *The Democratic Intellect,* Edinburgh University Press (Edinburgh, 1961).
5. See J. Highet, *The Scottish Churches,* Skeffington (London, 1960), pp. 153–9, and I. Henderson, *Power without Glory,* Hutchinson (London, 1967).
6. The Law Society of Scotland stated in evidence to the Commission on the Constitution that 'further developments towards the assimilation of the law and legal systems of Scotland and England are inevitable and desirable' (*Memorandum of Evidence,* p. 8). Yet a large number of Scots lawyers have argued to the contrary.
7. Works of relevance quoted in the bibliography are: Budge and Urwin (1966), Hanham 3 (1969), Mackintosh 1 (1968), Rose 3 (1970) and Wolfe (1969). Others are: H. J. Paton, *The Claim of Scotland,* Allen and Unwin (London, 1968); A. Hargrave, *Scotland: The Third Choice,* Fabian Tract 392, March 1969; G. McCrone, *Scotland's Future: The Economics of Nationalism,* Blackwell (Oxford, 1969); O. D. Edwards *et al., Celtic Nationalism,* Barnes and Noble (London, 1968); J. McMillan, *Anatomy of Scotland,* Frewin (London, 1969); N. MacCormick (ed.), *The Scottish Debate,* O.U.P. (London, 1970); J. C. Banks, *Federal Britain? The Case for Regionalism,* Harrap (London, 1971); Duncan Glen (ed.), *Whither Scotland?,* Gollancz (London, 1971); W. Thornhill, *The Case for Regional Reform,* Nelson (London, 1972). Articles include W. P. Grant and R. J. C. Preece, 'Welsh and Scottish Nationalism'.

Parliamentary Affairs xxi, No. 3 (Summer 1968), 255–65, and I. McLean, 'The rise and fall of the Scottish National Party', *Political Studies* xviii, No. 3 (1970), 357–72, and J. E. Schwartz, 'The Scottish National Party: non-violent separatism and theories of violence', *World Politics* (July 1970), 496–517.

8. J. A. Brand, 'These are the Scotnats', *New Statesman*, 17 May 1968.
9. J. E. Schwartz, 'The Scottish National Party'.
10. Mark Abrams, 'The lost Labour voter', *Socialist Commentary*, February 1969, pp. 17–34. The 6 Scottish seats in the survey were Glasgow Gorbals, Glasgow Springburn, Hamilton, Edinburgh East, Leith and Midlothian.
11. *Glasgow Herald*, 11 March 1970.
12. *Ibid.* 13, 16, 18 March 1970.

Chapter 8

1. The Maud Report (Cmnd. 4040) called for indirectly elected provincial councils, but its main proposal was for 58 'all-purpose' authorities throughout most of England. Three conurbations would have a two-tier structure, and London would continue to have a separate system. The government in February 1971 decided to introduce a two-tier structure of 38 counties and 300 districts, which appeared to resemble that proposed by Wheatley. But there were to be six metropolitan areas, and the provincial level was dropped. The English reform remained a much less drastic revision than the Scottish, and was essentially one of amalgamated counties. The Local Government Act 1972 established 39 non-metropolitan counties and 296 county districts, 6 metropolitan counties and 36 metropolitan districts. The London system was retained as were about 10,500 parish councils and meetings.
2. I am indebted to Professor W. J. M. Mackenzie for this insight. He developed it in a paper delivered to the Royal Institute of Public Administration Glasgow and West of Scotland Regional Group Conference in 1970. See published *Report*, Glasgow, 1970.

Chapter 9

1. For a general treatment of pressure groups see S. E. Finer, *Anonymous Empire*, 2nd ed., Pall Mall Press (London, 1966); A. M. Potter, *Organised Groups in British National Politics*, Faber (London, 1961).
2. Interest groups as here defined are organisations formed to defend the (generally economic) interests of their members. Examples are trade unions and employers' associations. Attitude (or promotional) groups draw support from the public generally in pursuit of a cause. Examples are the Lord's Day Observance Society and Oxfam. Cf. Finer, *op. cit.* pp. 3–5.
3. These include the Scottish Council of Social Service, Standing

Council on Youth and Community Service in Scotland, Transport Users Consultative Committee for Scotland, Advisory Council on Education in Scotland, School Broadcasting Council for Scotland, Scottish Hospital Scientific Council (established 1971), and the Scottish Economic Council (downgraded in 1970 from the Scottish Economic Planning Council). See also appendix to this chapter.

4. Cf. J. T. Cox, *Practice and Procedure in the Church of Scotland*, 5th ed., Church of Scotland (Edinburgh, 1964).

5. See Sister Martha Skinnider, 'Catholic Elementary Education in Glasgow, 1818–1918', in T. R. Bone (ed.), *Studies in the History of Scottish Education*, University of London Press (London, 1967). Also Rev. Brother Kenneth, 'The Education (Scotland) Act, 1918, in the making', *Innes Review* xiv, No. 2 (Autumn 1968), 91–128.

6. A survey in Glasgow in 1967 found that 63% of Glasgow Catholics favoured integrating Protestant and Catholic schools, *Glasgow Herald*, 29 April 1967.

7. *Glasgow Herald*, 3 April 1971.

8. R. Thomasson, 'Home rule for teachers', *New Society*, 25 September 1969, pp. 476–7.

9. In 1971, the last major Scottish industrial union, the Scottish Commercial Motormen's Union (21,000), merged with the Transport and General Workers Union. The remaining Scottish unions affiliated to the STUC were the Scottish Union of Bakers and Allied Workers (11,566 members), Scottish Typographical Association (7,050), Scottish Carpet Trade and Factory Workers' Union (6,734), Scottish Colliery Enginemen, Boilermen and Tradesmen's Association (5,600) and 7 other Scottish unions with under 5,000 members. *STUC 74th Annual Report*, 1971. In 1970–1 the Educational Institute of Scotland (30,000), the Scottish Schoolmasters' Association (3,000) and the Scottish Further Education Association (1,050) affiliated to the STUC. (1970 figures; for 1974 figures, see p. 158.)

10. Scottish Trades Union Congress, *Submission to Royal Commission on Trade Unions and Employers' Associations*, Glasgow, 6 May 1966, p. 1. Compare the STUC General Council *Memorandum of Evidence to the Commission on the Constitution*, May 1970, p. 3: 'It may be appropriate to recall that when the Scottish Trades Union Congress was formed in 1897 the circumstances surrounding its formation reflected the uneasiness in Scottish trade union circles about the "remoteness" of London, the inability of the people there, including trade union people, to understand or be interested in the Scottish scene, especially with regard to the unfair interpretation by the Sheriff Courts of the law as it affected workpeople and their dependents.' Wherever Scots Law is involved, there is a strong impetus to establish a separate Scottish organisation.

11. See Scottish Council, *Centralisation*, March 1969. The Council held a conference on that theme in November 1970, in which several speakers bemoaned the lack of Scottish 'decision-making' power. See also Jack McGill, *Scotland's Goals*, Collins (Glasgow and London, 1974).

12. *Glasgow Herald*, 14 October 1970.

13. *Ibid.* 8 May 1971, 18 September 1971.
14. *Ibid.* 29 September 1971.
15. Cf. the English National Society for the Prevention of Cruelty to Children. Other groups of this type in a Scottish form include the National Society for the Prevention of Cruelty to Animals (Eng. RSPCA), the Scottish Temperance Alliance, the Saltire Society (promotes Scottish culture), the National Trust for Scotland, Scottish Band of Hope Union, etc.

Chapter 10

1. *Report of the Committee of Privy Councillors appointed to inquire into 'D' Notice matters, HMSO,* Cmnd. 3309, pp. 180, 206.
2. *Annual Report and Accounts of the British Broadcasting Corporation, 1969–70,* HMSO, Cmnd. 4520, p. 127.
3. *BBC Handbook 1971* (London, 1971), p. 60.

Chapter 11

1. The distinction between a social and political system is not always clear (cf. G. A. Almond and G. B. Powell, *Comparative Politics* (Boston, 1966), p. 20): 'The same individuals who perform roles in the political system perform roles in other social systems such as the economy, the religious community, the family, and voluntary associations.' Since most of these 'social systems' are heavily dependent on the political system it is difficult to draw boundaries round them.
2. Sir Alec Cairncross, Master of St Peter's College, Oxford, since 1969. Born 1911, in Scotland. Educated Hamilton Academy, Glasgow and Cambridge Universities. Professor of Applied Economics, University of Glasgow, 1951–61. Economic Adviser to Board of Trade, 1946–9; to H.M. Government, 1961–4; Head of Government Economic Service, 1964–9; Chancellor, Glasgow University, 1972. Edited *The Scottish Economy,* C.U.P. (Cambridge, 1954), amongst other works.
3. Professor T. Wilson, Professor of Political Economy, University of Glasgow, since 1958. Born 1916, Northern Ireland. Educated Methodist College, Belfast; Universities of Belfast and London; Vice-chairman of Toothill Committee on the Scottish Economy (1961–2). Books include *Planning and Growth,* Macmillan (London, 1964); *Policies for Regional Development,* Oliver and Boyd (Edinburgh, 1964); *Papers on Regional Development* (ed.), Blackwell (Oxford, 1965); contribution to *Economic Development in Northern Ireland* (Belfast, 1965), Cmnd. 479.
4. For example, the works of Gavin McCrone (McCrone 1–3), G. C. Cameron, G. L. Reid, K. J. Allen and M. C. McLennan of Glasgow University. The work of the last two named includes a study of regional planning in the E.E.C. (*Regional Problems and Policies in Italy and France,* Allen and Unwin (London, 1970)), while the first

two have written such works as *Scottish Economic Planning and the Attraction of Industry*, Oliver and Boyd (Edinburgh, 1966).

5. *Report of the Committee on Local Development in Scotland*, Scottish Council (Development and Industry), Edinburgh, 1952.

6. The plans for the Lothians, Falkirk/Grangemouth, Greater Livingston, Central Borders, Tayside and the north-east.

7. *Glasgow Herald*, 13 July 1971.

8. J. H. McGuinness, Assistant Under-Secretary of State, Scottish Office, until 1972. Born 1912, Leeds. Educated St Aloysius College, Glasgow, Glasgow University and Trinity College, Oxford. Ministry of Transport before 1939, Scottish Office since 1946.

9. Named after G. J. Goschen, Chancellor of the Exchequer (1887–92), who introduced the formula in 1888.

10. See *Scottish Economic Bulletin*, No. 1, HMSO (Summer 1971), pp. 2–5.

11. A work comparing the Scottish and English educational systems in G. S. Osborne, *Scottish and English Schools*, Longmans (London, 1966).

12. For the English education world see Edward Boyle and Anthony Crosland in conversation with M. Kogan, *The Politics of Education*, Penguin Books (London, 1971).

13. For example, the Reports of the Scottish Advisory Council on Education. A list of these reports is given in Osborne, *Scottish and English Schools*, p. 345.

14. T. R. Bone, *School inspection in Scotland, 1840–1966*, University of London Press (London, 1968).

15. John S. Brunton, born 1903. Educated Albert Road Academy, Glasgow, and Glasgow University. H.M. Inspector of Schools 1932–51, Assistant Secretary, Scottish Education Department 1951–5. H.M. Senior Chief Inspector of Schools, 1955–6. 'Brunton Report', *From School to Further Education*, Scottish Education Department, Edinburgh, 1963.

16. Sir John H. F. Brotherston, Chief Medical Officer, Scottish Home and Health Department, since 1964. Born 1915, Edinburgh. Educated George Watson's College, Edinburgh, and University of Edinburgh. Professor of Public Health and Social Medicine, University of Edinburgh, 1955–64.

17. *Hansard*, 5th Series, vol. 431, col. 1003, 10 December 1946.

18. L. A. Gunn and R. Mair, 'Staffing the National Health Service', in J. Revans and G. McLachlan, *Challenges for Change: Essays on the Next Decade in the National Health Service*, O.U.P. (London, 1971), pp. 277–8.

19. National Health Service (Scotland) Act 1972; National Health Reorganisation Act 1973.

20. I am indebted to Robert Mair of Glasgow University for permission to draw upon his unpublished case study of the Social Work (Scotland) Act.

21. Lord Kilbrandon, Scottish Law Lord since 1959 and Life Peer, 1971 (Charles J. D. Shaw). Born 1906, Ayrshire. Educated Charterhouse, Balliol College, Oxford, and Edinburgh University. Scottish Bar, 1932; Sheriff, 1954–9. Chairman of Scottish Law

Commission, 1965–71, and member of (Crowther) Commission on the Constitution, 1969; Chairman of Commission on the Constitution, March 1972.

22. Up to 1970, the Ministry of Housing and Local Government was the relevant department in England. For this aspect of central-local relations, and further discussion of the formulation of the policy relating to social work in Scotland, see Kilbrandon 4, pp. 109–10, also p. 37.

23. But see T. B. Smith, *British Justice: The Scottish Contribution*, Stevens (London, 1961), p. 84.

24. Law Society of Scotland, *Memorandum of Evidence to the Commission on the Constitution* (Edinburgh, 1971), p. 5.

25. *Conveyancing Legislation and Practice*, Cmnd. 3118, 1966.

26. Law Society, *loc. cit.*

27. *Sheriff Courts: Report of the Grant Committee*, Cmnd. 3248, 1967, followed by Sheriff Courts (Scotland) Bill 1971. *Law of Succession: Report of the Mackintosh Committee*, Cmd. 8144, 1950, followed by Succession (Scotland) Act 1964.

28. In 1971 the members were Lord Hunter (chairman), Ewen Stewart, Q.C., Professors Anton, Halliday and Smith. Lord Kilbrandon was chairman from 1965 to 1971.

29. Justice, *The Prosecution Process in England and Wales* (London, 1970), pp. 9–12.

30. But there were only four of these in the Parliament elected in 1970. House of Commons Debates. *Hansard*, 5th Series, vol. 809, 1970–1, col, 1507, 22 January 1971.

31. Law Society, *op. cit.* p. 4.

Chapter 12

1. The counties of Argyll, Inverness, Ross and Cromarty, Caithness, Sutherland, Orkney and Zetland (Shetland). These are also known as the seven 'crofting counties', from their inclusion in the Crofters Acts. There are, however, only about 60,000 people out of the total of 281,000 living in crofts (Thomson and Grimble, p. 276). The parliamentary constituencies are Argyll, Inverness, Ross and Cromarty, Western Isles, Caithness and Sutherland, and Orkney and Shetland.

2. Political studies of the European periphery are contained in Basil Chubb, *The Government and Politics of Ireland*, O.U.P. (London, 1970), Henry Valen, *Regional Contrasts in Norwegian Politics*, Chr. Michelson Inst. (Bergen, 1964); Stein Rokkan, 'The mobilisation of the periphery', in *Citizen, Elections, Parties*, Universitets Forlaget (Oslo, 1970), pp. 181–225; and articles in *Scandinavian Political Studies* (1966–   ).

3. For further discussion, see R. D. Lobban, 'Highlanders in the Lowlands', *Scottish International*, September 1971.

4. J. G. Kellas, 'The Crofters' War, 1882–1888', *History Today*, April 1962; 'Highland migration to Glasgow and the origin of the Scottish Labour movement', *Bulletin of the Society for the Study of*

Labour History, No. 12 (Spring 1966), 9–12. D. W. Crowley, 'The Crofters Party, 1885–1895', *Scottish Historical Review*, XXXV (1956), 110–26. H. J. Hanham, 'The Problem of Highland Discontent, 1880–85'. *Trans. R. Hist. Soc. 5th series* XIX (1969), 21–65.

5. The sample Census of 1966 records the percentage of males engaged in agriculture in the constituencies as Argyll, 24.9; Caithness and Sutherland, 27.4; Inverness, 16.4; Ross and Cromarty, 25.7; Western Isles, 11.4; Orkney and Shetland, 36.3 (*Census 1966*, U.K. General and Pariamentary Tables, Table 4, HMSO, 1969). The low figure for the Western Isles is distorted by the number of crofters who are employed in tweed manufacture or public works, and who are recorded as non-agricultural.

6. Frederik Barth (ed.), *The Role of the Entrepreneur in Social Change in Northern Norway*, Norwegian University Press (Bergen/Oslo, 1963).

7. Professor Sir Robert Grieve, born 1910. Educated North Kelvinside School, Glasgow, and Royal College of Science and Technology, Glasgow (now Strathclyde University). Civil engineer with Glasgow Corporation and Renfrew County, subsequently Chief Planning Assistant, 1927–39; Regional Planning Officer, Department of Health for Scotland, 1946–60, Chief Planner, Scottish Office, 1960–4; Professor of Town and Regional Planning, Glasgow University, 1964–74. Seconded to Highland Board, 1965–70. Recreations: mountaineering, ski-ing and canoeing.

8. *Highlands and Islands Development Board, Fifth Report 1970*, Inverness 1971, pp. 16, 36.

Chapter 13

1. A notable work about Irish politics is Basil Chubb, *The Government and Politics of Ireland*, O.U.P. (London, 1970).

2. The Universities of Strathclyde, Aberdeen, Dundee and Edinburgh are most active in voting behaviour and local government. Glasgow is most active in central administration.

3. Scottish Education Department, *Student Numbers in Higher Education in Scotland*, HMSO, Edinburgh 1970, p. 12; University of Glasgow, *Report of University Court, 1969–70*, Glasgow, n.d., pp. 57–8.

4. Non-Scots who have written on Scottish politics include Hanham, Rose, Urwin (Budge and Urwin), Coupland, Grimble (Thomson and Grimble), and Cornford (ed. Wolfe). These are referred to in the bibliography.

5. E.g. Winston Churchill in 1922. W. M. Walker, 'Dundee's disenchantment with Churchill', *Scottish Historical Review* XLIX (1970), 85–108.

6. David Easton, *The Political System* (New York, 1953), pp. 134–40.

7. A 'subject political culture' is one in which the citizens have no great urge to participate in government themselves (Almond and Verba, *The Civic Culture*, p. 17). It is difficult to apply this idea to

Scotland, since it depends on whether the appropriate centre of government is London or Edinburgh. Scots participate in the British Parliament but do not have a parliament in Scotland. While they seek greater devolution, it is not usually a political priority for them.

8. Cf. K. W. Deutsch, *Politics and Government*, pp. 126–7, where all levels of politics from the individual to the U.N. are described as 'systems'.

9. Julius Gould, 'A sociological portrait: nationality and ethnicity', *New Society*, 30 December 1971, p. 1282. 'Unlike America, Britain does not give any structural supremacy to White Anglo-Saxon Protestantism, but outsiders, even British "nationals", can feel and can be made to feel, selectively excluded. It is often a tacit major premise, but at times it can become almost whimsically articulate. During the revivals of Welsh and Scots nationalism in the late 1960s, Englishmen were heard to say, half-seriously, that they, too, should strive for automony via regional devolution.'

10. E.g. Hans Kohn, *The Idea of Nationalism*, Macmillan (New York, 1944).

11. K. W. Deutsch, *National and Social Communication*.

Bibliography

Balfour, Royal Commission on Scottish Affairs, 1952–4 (Balfour Commission), *Report*, HMSO, Cmd. 9212, 1954.

Budge, I. and Urwin, D. W., *Scottish Political Behaviour*, Longmans (London, 1966).

Butler, D. and King, A., *The British General Election of 1966*, Macmillan (London, 1966).

Butler, D. and Pinto-Duschinsky, M., *The British General Election of 1970*, Macmillan (London, 1971).

Butler, D. and Stokes, D., *Political Change in Britain*, Macmillan (London, 1969).

Coupland, Sir Reginald, *Welsh and Scottish Nationalism*, Collins (London, 1954).

Fulton, Committee on the Civil Service (1966–8) (Fulton Committee)
  1. *Report*, Cmnd. 3638, 1968.
  2. *Surveys and Investigations*, vol. 3(1), 1969.

Gilmour, Committee on Scottish Administration (Gilmour Committee), *Report*, HMSO, Cmd. 5563, 1937.

Hanham, H. J.
  1. *Elections and Party Management: Politics in the Time of Disraeli and Gladstone*, Longmans (London, 1959).
  2. 'The Creation of the Scottish Office, 1881–7', *Juridical Review* (1965), 205–44.
  3. *Scottish Nationalism*, Faber (London, 1969).

Kilbrandon, Commission on the Constitution (1969–73) (known as the Crowther Commission until March 1972, when on Lord Crowther's death Lord Kilbrandon became Chairman).
  1. *Written Evidence 1* (The Welsh Office) (1969).
  2. *Written Evidence 2* (The Scottish Office, The Lord Advocate's Department and the Crown Office) (1969).
  3. *Minutes of Evidence I* Wales (September and November 1969).
  4. *Minutes of Evidence II* Scotland (September and November 1969).
  5. Vol. I, *Report*, HMSO, Cmnd. 5460, 1973.
  6. Vol. II, *Memorandum of Dissent*, HMSO, Cmnd. 5460–I, 1973.
  7. Research Paper 7, *Devolution and Other Aspects of Government: An Attitudes Survey* (1973).

Mackintosh, J. P.
  1. *The Devolution of Power*, Penguin (London, 1968).
  2. 'The Royal Commission on Local Government in Scotland, 1966–1969', *Public Administration*, Spring 1970, pp. 49–56

McCrone, Gavin

1. *Scotland's Economic Progress, 1951–60*, University of Glasgow Social and Economic Studies No. 4, Allen and Unwin (London, 1965).
2. *Scotland's Future: The Economics of Nationalism*, Blackwell (Oxford, 1969).
3. *Regional Policy in Britain*, Allen and Unwin (London, 1969).

Milne, Sir David, *The Scottish Office*, Allen and Unwin (London, 1957).

Rose, Richard

1. *Politics in England*, Faber (London, 1965).
2. *Class and Party Divisions: Britain as a Test Case*, Survey Research Centre, University of Strathclyde, Occasional Paper No. 1 (Glasgow, 1969); also *Sociology* II, No. 2 (May 1968).
3. *The United Kingdom as a Multi-national State*, Survey Research Centre, University of Strathclyde, Occasional Paper No. 6 (Glasgow, 1970).
4. *Governing without Consensus*, Faber (London, 1971).

SCSA (House of Commons Select Committee on Scottish Affairs, 1969–70)

1. *Report*, H.C. 267 (1969–70).
2. *Minutes of Evidence*, vol. I, H.C. 397 (1968–9).
3. *Minutes of Evidence*, vol. II, H.C. 267–1 (1969–70).

Thomson, Derick C. and Grimble, Ian (eds.), *The Future of the Highlands*, Routledge and Kegan Paul (London, 1968).

Toothill, Committee of Inquiry into the Scottish Economy (Toothill Committee), *Report*, Scottish Council (Development and Industry), (Edinburgh, 1961).

Wheatley, Royal Commission on Local Government in Scotland, 1966–9 (Wheatley Commission), HMSO, Edinburgh, 1969

1. *Report*, Cmnd. 4150.
2. *Appendices*, Cmnd. 4150.
3. *Community Survey: Scotland*, Research Studies 2.

Wolfe, J. N. (ed.), *Government and Nationalism in Scotland*, Edinburgh University Press (Edinburgh, 1969).

Index

Stenhouse, Hugh, 57
STV, 7, 171, 177–9, 182–3

television, 7, 38, 106, 171, **177–83**, 208
Thatcher, Margaret, 51, 95
Thomson, George, 39
Thomson, Lord, 175
Thorpe, Jeremy, 96
Toothill Report (1961), 56, 180, 193, 195
trade unions, 13, 18, 134, **161–3**, 166, 168–9, 236
Trades Union Congress, 112, 162–3
transport, 46–7, 53–5, 190, 217
Trevelyan, Sir George, 39

unemployment, 12, 122
Union of 1707, *see* Act of Union
United States of America, 4, 20, 44, 185, 222
universities, 2, 6, 41, 43, **50–2**, 67–8, 80, 92, 120, 159–60, 196–7, 222–3
University Grants Committee, 6, 35, 50–2, 159

Upper Clyde Shipbuilders, 38, 47, 57, 61, 88, 121, 175, 177, 191

veto polls, 8
voting behaviour, **91–142** *passim*, 211–15, 227; *see also* elections

Wales, 1, 4, 8–10, 12–13, 24, 27, 37, 41, 57–9, 91–2, 94, 102–3, 114, 196, 227
water, 203
Welsh Grand Committee, 1
Welsh Office, 1, 27, 47, 58, 68
Westminster Confession of Faith (1647), 20
Wheatley, Lord, 22–3; *see also* Royal Commission on Local Government in Scotland
White Fish Authority, 12, 166
Wilson, Sir Charles, 138
Wilson, Harold, 39–40, 95, 156, 175–6
Wilson, Professor Thomas, 187, 237
Wolfe, William, 124
Wylie, Norman, 206

Younger, Sir William McEwan, 138

250